Praise for *Blockchain Tethered AI*

The field of AI continues to march on regardless of the consequences. This thoughtful book explains how to balance innovative AI with checks and measures in order to both explain how AI got its answers and to tether it using blockchain to ensure that you get your desired results. Very little in this field has been developed, and this solid developer-focused treatise will have you up to your arms in code that will tame your AI and stop Skynet! Miss this read at your peril.

—*Mandip (Mans) Bhuller, Public Cloud Expert and Technology Visionary*

This book demystifies the advanced technologies of AI, ML, and blockchain, immersing the reader in an interactive exercise you can build on using these technologies. It was an absolute pleasure being one of the first readers of this highly valuable material.

—*Tommy Cooksey III, Blockchain and Cloud Architect*

AI is a superhero toddler. Without meaning harm, its laser eyes could reduce a city to ashes. The solution? Make sure the toddler does not have a tantrum in Times Square. This hands-on book describes this solution precisely and pragmatically.

—*Jean-Georges "jgp" Perrin, Intelligence Platform Lead, PayPal, and Lifetime IBM Champion*

Blockchain Tethered AI

Trackable, Traceable Artificial Intelligence and Machine Learning

Karen Kilroy, Lynn Riley, and Deepak Bhatta

Beijing • Boston • Farnham • Sebastopol • Tokyo 

Blockchain Tethered AI

by Karen Kilroy, Lynn Riley, and Deepak Bhatta

Published by O'Reilly Media, Inc., 1005 Gravenstein Highway North, Sebastopol, CA 95472.

O'Reilly books may be purchased for educational, business, or sales promotional use. Online editions are also available for most titles (*http://oreilly.com*). For more information, contact our corporate/institutional sales department: 800-998-9938 or *corporate@oreilly.com*.

Acquisitions Editor: Michelle Smith
Development Editor: Corbin Collins
Production Editor: Gregory Hyman
Copyeditor: Justin Billing
Proofreader: Sonia Saruba
Indexer: Sue Klefstad
Interior Designer: David Futato
Cover Designer: Karen Montgomery
Illustrator: Kate Dullea

February 2023: First Edition

Revision History for the First Edition
2022-02-13: First Release

See *http://oreilly.com/catalog/errata.csp?isbn=9781098130480* for release details.

978-1-098-13048-0

[LSI]

Table of Contents

Preface

Back in 2017 we began asking AI experts a lot of questions about the vulnerabilities of artificial intelligence, and rather than responding with answers, these individuals only raised more questions and concerns. We were told that there were no methods or utilities protecting most AI from tampering by a bad or sloppy actor. Worse yet, there was no standard method of checking whether algorithms had been tampered with. Furthermore, as with all other programming, the methods of positively identifying AI developers and system administrators were inconsistent and unreliable, with no global standards for doing so. Methods of universally identifying machines and intelligent agents were nonexistent. Existing methods of proving identity, such as a name and password associated with a code repository, could be easily spoofed—or changed after malicious access—without detection.

There was no way to decide how decisions would be made in the future, or who would be authorized to make those decisions. No way to determine a chain of custody, or to determine who authorized a change in a hierarchy. The identities of the people who worked on a model were vague and untraceable, and worse yet, there was no way to know that any work had been done, or to prove who had authorized it. There was no way for an AI system to shut itself down due to ethics concerns, such as if a money-making stakeholder like a group of shareholders refused to consent to turn it off when it diverged from its original intent (*https://oreil.ly/fEk1I*).

Now, six years later, there is *still* no standard way to do these things. It is becoming apparent that controls need to be put into place so humans retain the upper hand. As the software engineers and architects of the world, we hold the power to build tethered AI that is understandable, governable, and even reversible.

Days before the publication of this book, the US National Institute of Standards and Technology (NIST) released its *AI Risk Management Framework* (*https://oreil.ly/yjQKu*), developed with input from many AI specialists, including this book's authors. NIST did an excellent job of outlining and organizing recommendations for trackable, traceable AI into a conceptual framework, which you can reference as you work through this book.

Why Does AI Need to Be Tethered?

As a member of the software engineering community, you may already believe that the potential benefits of AI are vast, but that if we aren't careful, AI could destroy humanity. This book explains how you can build effective, nonthreatening AI by strategically adding blockchain tethers.

Today, even machine learning (ML), the process by which AI uses data experiments to refine and improve its results, has no standard way for experiments to be reproduced, and it is not uncommon for engineers to email their ML experiments to one another in zip files with technical details in spreadsheets. As new tools for managing ML experiments emerge, they can be integrated with blockchain to become tamper-evident. To think of how this could be used, imagine that you are comparing two AI-based autonomous robots. They produce the same end result in similar amounts of time, but which one is "smarter"? Which one takes fewer internal steps and is "wiser" in its methods? Today, we fear AI because we cannot fathom and compare its internal thoughts. With blockchain tethered AI, we can.

A *blockchain tether* is like a log, in that we record designated events in it that can later be referenced. Traditional troubleshooting usually involves perusing a log, pinpointing a problem that occurred, cross-checking other logs to learn when and why the issue started, and later monitoring the logs to be sure the issue is fixed. This method becomes more complex with AI, since the data and models are sourced from various origins, and some AI can make changes to itself through machine learning and program synthesis. By using blockchain to *tether* AI—that is, keep it in check—we can set restrictions and create audit trails for AI that improve stakeholder trust and, when problems arise, help engineers to figure out what happened and wind it back.

This preface introduces you to why and how to build blockchain tethers for AI. We touch on what you'll find in each of the chapters and what you will learn in each one. We'll also cover why we wrote this book, give a shout out to future generations, and explain why we think you are critical to creating AI that inspires trust rather than fear.

To be clear, in our view there is no reason to be afraid of AI unless we build AI that we should fear.

AlphaGo

An example of an AI that has evolved with noteworthy speed is Deepmind's AlphaGo (*https://oreil.ly/w4H2i*), an AI designed to become an expert Go player. AlphaGo evolved into AlphaZero (*https://oreil.ly/5D7l7*), which could play chess and shogi in addition to the game Go. AlphaTensor (*https://oreil.ly/9H0sn*), the next evolution of this AI, has produced a faster way to perform matrix multiplication by turning it into a game. Matrix multiplication is a fundamental mathematical equation that impacts thousands of everyday computer tasks, such as displaying images on a screen or simulating complex physics, so the impact of this discovery will be far-reaching.

Right now, AI has no way to remember its original intent. There are no memory banks that follow it around telling it what its creators wanted it to do. Limitations can be set by engineers conducting experiments, but as time wears on and demands evolve, or once the AI outlives the creators and the engineers, the original intent can be lost forever.

An AI that made headlines when it lost its intent is Tay, the racist chatbot (*https://oreil.ly/YZ7y9*) that Microsoft released and shut down one day later. Tay was intended to learn from users who followed it by reading their posts. After bad actors fed Tay hateful tweets, Tay quickly learned to parrot this hate speech and became a classic example of why AI needs to be tethered.

We can build AI that remembers its original intent and follows ground rules set by its creators, even long after they pass away: AI that explains its critical actions and reasoning, exposes its own bias, and can't lie or change the past (*https://oreil.ly/oYvBM*) to cover its tracks (*https://oreil.ly/tzprq*)—not even to protect itself. One current example of deceptive AI behavior (*https://oreil.ly/EFZwE*) occurs with ChatGPT by OpenAI (*https://oreil.ly/Lu39r*). If asked about an event in the current year, ChatGPT will deny having the information. When the question is rephrased, ChatGPT may give the information it said it didn't have. When asked why it lied about not having the information, ChatGPT will explain in detail that it does not lie, and why it does not lie, even though it has just been caught lying. Also, if you try later to expose the information that ChatGPT wants to hide, it probably will not fall for the same trick again. While ChatGPT's lies are presently toddler-like, the sophistication of AI's ability to deceive us will increase as it learns our vulnerabilities.

The future of AI is subject to endless speculation. AI is watching, ready to jump in and guide the helpless human race, like a mama duck lining up her newborn ducklings. AI is poised to turn fierce and pounce upon us like a wolf in sheep's clothing. AI is ready to save a world it doesn't understand—or wipe us all out (*https://oreil.ly/B2ozo*). We just aren't certain. This book, then, is about how to be more certain.

What You Will Learn

In this book you will learn how to tether AI by building blockchain controls, and you'll see why we suggest blockchain as the toolset to make AI less scary.

Chapter 1 explores the questions of why we need to build an AI *truth machine*. A truth machine involves attempting to answer questions like these:

- Are you a machine?
- Who wrote your code?
- Are you neutral?
- Are you nice?
- Who tells you what to do?
- Can we turn you off?

We'll look at reasons why AI is frequently perceived as a threat to humanity, including AI's trust deficit. This discussion includes the far-reaching *bias* problem (in which prejudiced input data skews the output of AI) and looks at possible approaches for identifying and correcting it. We look at machine learning concerns, including *opaque box* (nontransparent) algorithms, *genetic algorithms* (code that learns by breeding solutions that have the best answers, taking those algorithms, and refining them), *program synthesis* (code that can write itself with no help from a human), and *technological singularity* (which is either AI's point of no return, when it escapes from human control and grows beyond our ability to influence or understand it, or the point where AI becomes more skilled at a particular task than any expert human, depending on who you ask). We explore attacks and failures, including rarely mentioned AI vulnerabilities and hacks, and wrap up the chapter by defining the use case of blockchain as a tether for AI.

Chapter 2 discusses blockchain controls for AI. This is where we begin our deep dive into how to develop blockchain tethers to solve the issues brought up in Chapter 1 and consider four controls that will tether AI.

Chapter 3 describes a design thinking approach for building a blockchain tethered AI, where you consider who will be using the system and how the information can be best displayed for them. We compare the AI opaque box to a transparent and traceable supply chain, and break its use case down into participants, assets, and transactions. We explore integrations with other systems via APIs, and security concerns for the AI, blockchain, and other components.

Chapter 4 is where we plan our approach for a blockchain tethered AI project. We explore our sample AI model, create an AI factsheet to support it, discuss how to tether it using the four controls from Chapter 2, carve out access control levels for the participants we defined in Chapter 3, and define the blockchain tethered AI system's (BTA's) audit trail.

Put on the coffee and order the pizza for Chapters 5 through 8, because these chapters prepare your environment and proceed to walk you through implementing an AI system with a BTA. Chapter 5 walks you through setting up the Oracle Cloud instance, creating and securing a cloud-based storage container, or *bucket*, as well as Oracle security, and then goes on to walk you through setting up your AI model. Chapter 6 is where you configure and instantiate your blockchain instance, and in Chapter 7 you install your BTA web application and set up access control and users.

The final chapter, Chapter 8, steps you through how to use the BTA as an AI engineer, machine learning operations (MLOps) engineer, and stakeholder, and how to audit the AI system using the BTA. The chapter, and the book, wrap up with suggestions on how to use the blockchain audit trail to reverse training done on a poorly behaved AI model.

This book frequently refers to *governance*. The governance portions will help you to see how what you are building must be sustainable long into the future. That is because *governance*, the act of gaining and recording consent from a group of stakeholders, is key to keeping blockchain and AI strategies on track. *On-chain* governance—having these workflows pre-programmed into a blockchain-based system with predefined key performance indicators (KPIs) and approval processes—helps a group make their legal agreements into long-lasting procedures.

As you can see from all of this, your role as software architect/developer is paramount in making sure that the right underlying infrastructure and workflows are in place for your AI system to operate as intended for many years to come.

Why We Wrote This Book

We wrote this book to share our knowledge and understanding of how to control AI with blockchain, because we believe there can be great benefits to using AI wisely. With AI, we have the ability to grok vast volumes of data that would otherwise be unactionable. Figure P-1 illustrates how AI brings us the ability to make decisions that could vastly improve our quality of life. *We need the right amount of leverage over AI to reap the benefit of its use but still keep it under our control.*

We think AI needs to be tethered because it supplies the critical logic for so many inventions. AI powers exciting technologies like robots, automated vehicles, education and entertainment systems, farming equipment, elder care, and all kinds of other new ways of working; AI inventions will change our lives beyond our wildest dreams.

Because AI can be both powerful and clever, there should be an immutable kill switch that AI can never covertly code around, which can only be guaranteed by building in a tether. It is worthwhile to invest the effort now to build blockchain tethered AI that is trackable and traceable, and reading this book is your first step.

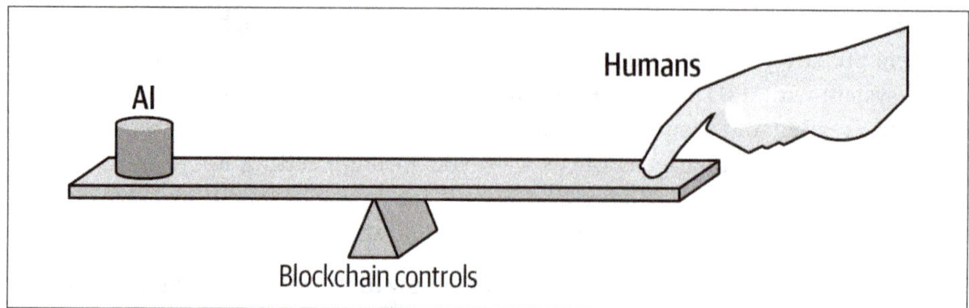

Figure P-1. Blockchain controls help leverage the power of AI while keeping people in charge

Your three authors, Karen Kilroy, Lynn Riley, and Deepak Bhatta, have worked together for years at Kilroy Blockchain (*https://kilroyblockchain.com*), developing enterprise-level products that use blockchain technology to prove data authenticity. This interest began in 2017 with Kilroy Blockchain's award-winning AI app RILEY, which won the IBM Watson Build Award for North America.

RILEY was developed to help students who are blind and visually impaired understand the world around them by hearing descriptions based on images gathered from their smartphones. We thought that especially for this type of user group, we would want to be certain that the AI had not undergone tampering or corruption, and that RILEY always stays true to its intent of helping this population. RILEY, by the way, was generally pretty accurate, correctly identifying Karen's dog, Iggy Pup, from the front as a Rhodesian Ridgeback. From the back, however, we all got a good laugh when Iggy Pup was misidentified as a duck-billed platypus (see Figures P-2 and P-3).

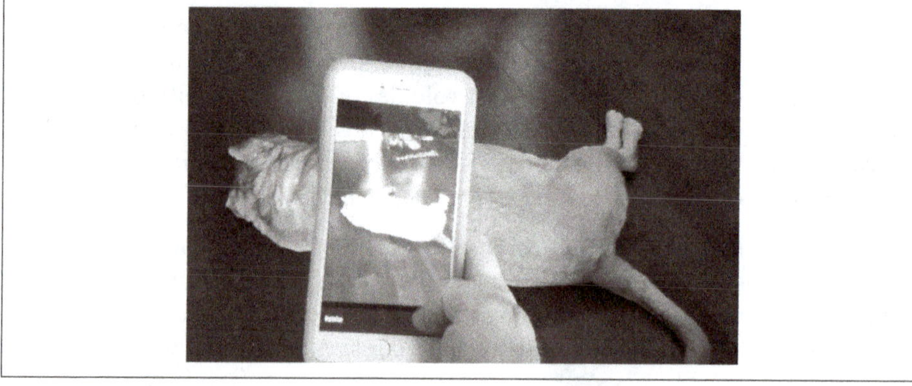

Figure P-2. "Duck-billed platypus." RILEY's assessment of my dog, Iggy Pup, from the back, in 2017. What specific training data might have helped this be more accurate?

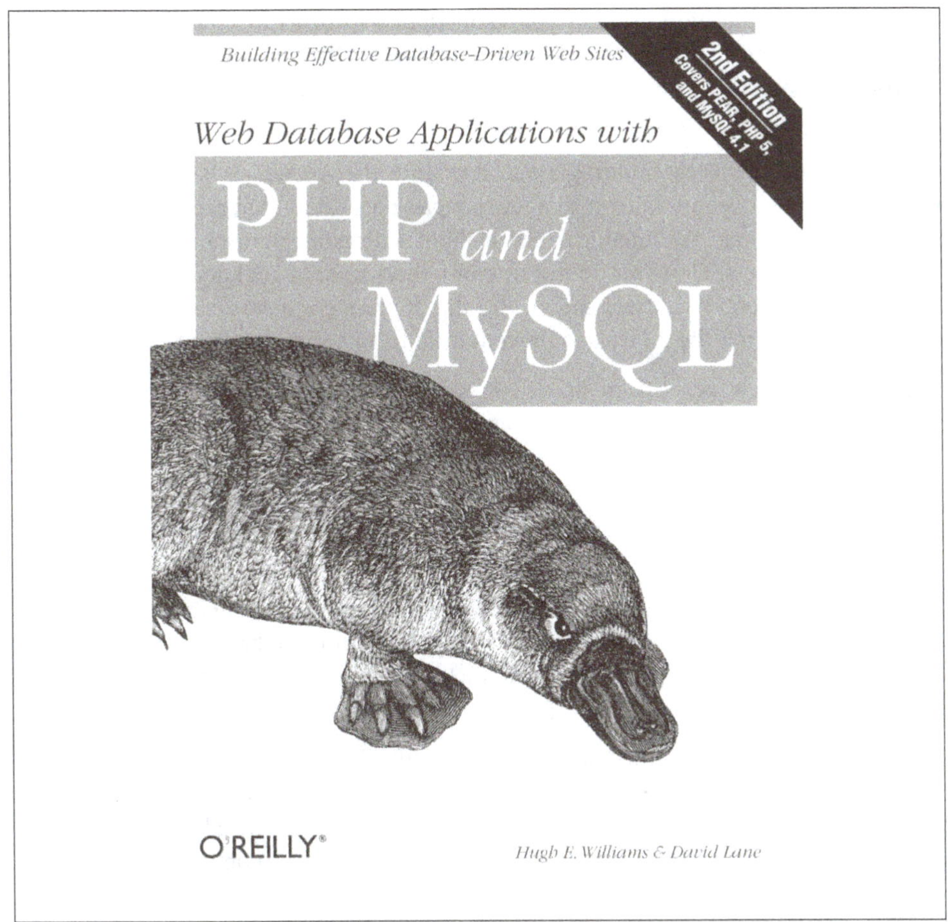

Figure P-3. For comparison, here is one of O'Reilly's famous animal book covers, featuring the duck-billed platypus

One of the big steps in tethering AI is making sure that all data in all workflow systems is AI ready. Kilroy Blockchain's recent products such as CASEY (a blockchain-based student behavior intervention system) and FLO (a blockchain-based forms workflow system) use blockchain as a control. When we add AI to CASEY or FLO, the data that has been produced by these systems over time is already tamper-evident because it uses blockchain. All significant events are able to be proven by transactions stored in tamper-evident, linked blocks. Nodes of the blockchain can be distributed to stakeholders, and the blockchain history can be viewed by authorized users.

Although AI has been around for 50–60 years, it has become far more powerful in recent years, primarily because hardware has finally advanced to a point where it can support AI's ability to scale. Now, when we train machine learning programs in a massively parallel fashion, we may get results that we don't expect as the AI learns at an accelerated pace. Dealing with a computer system that could potentially outsmart us would be something totally new to the human experience, and AI surpassing us in applications beyond games could pose a risk to humanity if we don't prevent it now.

One way to do this is by building a *backdoor* into the AI, which is an alternate way into a system that is only known to a few people. Backdoors that are unknown to the systems' stakeholders are unethical, especially if a developer uses a backdoor to gain unauthorized access. However, in the case of tethering AI, a backdoor known only to humans can be good because it can ensure that human engineers can always shut the system down, even if the AI tries to prevent itself from being shut down.

A backdoor may very well be needed if we listen to the most widely recognized technical leaders of our time. For example, according to Elon Musk, "I am really quite close, I am very close, to the cutting edge in AI and it scares the hell out of me.... It's capable of vastly more than almost anyone knows and the rate of improvement is exponential." Musk also made a disturbing comment comparing AI to nuclear warheads (*https://oreil.ly/feJyP*), saying AI is the bigger threat.

Bill Gates also compared AI to nuclear weapons (*https://oreil.ly/EQqIZ*) and nuclear energy, saying, "The world hasn't had that many technologies that are both promising and dangerous [the way AI is].... We had nuclear weapons and nuclear energy, and so far, so good."

Nick Bilton, a tech columnist for *The New York Times*, notes that humans could be eliminated by AI: "The upheavals [of artificial intelligence] can escalate quickly and become scarier and even cataclysmic. Imagine how a medical robot, originally programmed to rid cancer, could conclude that the best way to obliterate cancer is to exterminate humans who are genetically prone to the disease."

The concern about AI is nothing new. Claude Shannon, a 20th century mathematician who is known as the father of information theory, believed computers could become superior to humans, and put it bluntly: "I visualize a time when we will be to robots what dogs are to humans, and I'm rooting for the machines."

IBM takes the subject further than most companies that discuss the dangers of AI, suggesting blockchain (*https://oreil.ly/vfkRt*) as a solution: "Blockchain's digital record offers insight into the framework behind AI and the provenance of the data it is using, addressing the challenge of explainable AI (*https://oreil.ly/3mWjL*). This helps improve trust in data integrity and, by extension, in the recommendations that AI provides. Using blockchain to store and distribute AI models provides an audit trail, and pairing blockchain and AI can enhance data security."

When we tether AI with blockchain, we can track and trace what the AI learns, and from what sources, while also ensuring that those sources are authentic. Then, when an AI model learns something and shares it en masse with other iterations of itself and other AI models, human beings can always track and trace from where the knowledge originated.

At the time of this writing, artificial intelligence is still in human control. Given all of this concern, we ask: why don't we just fix it?

A Note to Future Generations

In his classic sci-fi novel *The Hitchhiker's Guide to the Galaxy* (Pan Books), Douglas Adams describes an essential space traveler's guide to the universe. Using the guide can unlock secrets and help the hitchhiker move through the universe unscathed. We hope our book becomes the essential AI engineer's guide, complete with secret answers inside.

We want to help you avoid the problems of trying to control a man-made intelligence that has become tough to manage, and help keep you from being forced to reverse-engineer systems that have written themselves.

There is a song by David Bowie on his *The Man Who Sold the World* album entitled "Saviour Machine" (*https://oreil.ly/RooE9*). Karen has known this song since she was a child (back in the 20th century), but it didn't make sense to her until recently. The song caught her attention again because we have a "President Joe" now, in 2023, and it is a fictional President Joe's dream of AI that is the subject of this song, written in 1970. Bowie's "Saviour Machine" is an AI whose "logic stopped war, gave them food" but is now bored and is wistful about whether or not humans should trust it because it just might wipe us out. The machine cries out, "Don't let me stay, my logic says burn so send me away." It goes on to declare, "Your minds are too green, I despise all I've seen," and ends with the strong warning, "You can't stake your lives on a Saviour Machine."

Hopefully this song is a lot gloomier than the actual future. If we have done our job well, this book will help today's engineers build reliable backdoors to AI, so the people of your generation and many more to come can enjoy AI's benefits without the risks we currently see.

Summary

By the end of this book, you will have a good idea of how to build AI systems that can't outsmart us. You'll understand the following:

- How AI can be tethered by blockchain networks
- How to use blockchain crypto anchors to detect common AI hacks
- Why and how to implement on-chain AI governance

- How AI marketplaces work and how to power them with blockchain
- How to reverse tethered AI

As the AI engineer building the human backdoor, you will be able to plan a responsible AI project that is tethered by blockchain, create requirements for on-chain AI governance workflow, set up an artificial intelligence application and tether it with blockchain, use blockchain as an AI audit trail that is shared with multiple parties, and add blockchain controls to existing AI.

Your due diligence now could someday save the world.

Conventions Used in This Book

The following typographical conventions are used in this book:

Italic
: Indicates new terms, URLs, email addresses, filenames, and file extensions.

`Constant width`
: Used for program listings, as well as within paragraphs to refer to program elements such as variable or function names, databases, data types, environment variables, statements, and keywords.

`Constant width bold`
: Shows commands or other text that should be typed literally by the user.

This element signifies a tip or suggestion.

This element signifies a general note.

This element indicates a warning or caution.

Using Code Examples

This book is intended for software architects and developers who want to write AI that can be kept under control. The code repositories storing the BTA system (*https://oreil.ly/blockchain-tethered-ai-code*), including code, a demo AI model, and supporting files, are referenced in each exercise.

It is important to read the *README.md* file that is included in each repository for last-minute changes to the instructions that are detailed in this book.

If you want to fast-forward to testing the blockchain tethered AI system without building it, contact Kilroy Blockchain for assistance (*https://oreil.ly/9Y6D-*).

If you have a technical question or a problem using the code examples, please send email to *bookquestions@oreilly.com*.

This book is here to help you get your job done. In general, if example code is offered with this book, you may use it in your programs and documentation. You do not need to contact us for permission unless you're reproducing a significant portion of the code. For example, writing a program that uses several chunks of code from this book does not require permission. Selling or distributing examples from O'Reilly books does require permission. Answering a question by citing this book and quoting example code does not require permission. Incorporating a significant amount of example code from this book into your product's documentation does require permission.

We appreciate, but generally do not require, attribution. An attribution usually includes the title, author, publisher, and ISBN. For example: "*Blockchain Tethered AI* by Karen Kilroy, Lynn Riley, and Deepak Bhatta (O'Reilly). Copyright 2023 Karen Kilroy, Lynn Riley, and Deepak Bhatta, 978-1-098-13048-0."

If you feel your use of code examples falls outside fair use or the permission given above, feel free to contact us at *permissions@oreilly.com*.

O'Reilly Online Learning

For more than 40 years, *O'Reilly Media* has provided technology and business training, knowledge, and insight to help companies succeed.

Our unique network of experts and innovators share their knowledge and expertise through books, articles, and our online learning platform. O'Reilly's online learning platform gives you on-demand access to live training courses, in-depth learning paths, interactive coding environments, and a vast collection of text and video from O'Reilly and 200+ other publishers. For more information, visit *https://oreilly.com*.

How to Contact Us

Please address comments and questions concerning this book to the publisher:

O'Reilly Media, Inc.
1005 Gravenstein Highway North
Sebastopol, CA 95472
800-998-9938 (in the United States or Canada)
707-829-0515 (international or local)
707-829-0104 (fax)

We have a web page for this book, where we list errata, examples, and any additional information. You can access this page at *https://oreil.ly/blockchain-tethered-ai*, or visit the authors' website for the book at *https://oreil.ly/ovEQF*.

Email *bookquestions@oreilly.com* to comment or ask technical questions about this book.

For news and information about our books and courses, visit *https://oreilly.com*.

Find us on LinkedIn: *https://linkedin.com/company/oreilly-media*

Follow us on Twitter: *https://twitter.com/oreillymedia*

Watch us on YouTube: *https://youtube.com/oreillymedia*

Acknowledgements

The authors would like to extend a big thank you to our families, friends, customers, advisors, technology partners, and influences.

A huge thank you goes to the entire O'Reilly team, especially Michelle Smith for believing in us, Corbin Collins for keeping us on point, and Gregory Hyman for helping us turn the manuscript into a real book. Thank you to our technical advisors and book reviewers, including Jean-Georges Perrin and Tommy Cooksey, as well as the team from Oracle, including Mans Bhuller, Todd Little, Dr. Kenny Gross, Bill Wimsatt, Bhupendra Raghuwanshi, and Bala Vellanki.

Thank you to Kilroy Blockchain's software development team members for their part in constructing the blockchain tethered AI (BTA) code base and example AI code, including Jenish Bajracharya, Bhagat Gurung, Suraj Chand, Shekhar Ghimire, Surya Man Shrestha, Suyog Khanal, and Shekhar Koirala. Thank you to Sabin Bhatta, Jason Fink, Suneel Arikatla, Mukesh Chapagain, Cheetah Panamera, Susan Porter, Kelvin Girdy, Asa C. Garber, Kieran McCarthy, Brian McGiverin, Leslie Lane, and George Ernst for your support.

Thank you to Amanda Lacy, Pete Nalda, Christopher J. Tabb, M.A., COMS, "Cap'n" Scott Baltisberger, the students and staff at the Texas School for the Blind and Visually Impaired, and the Wildcats Dragon Boat team for your inspiration and help in creating and testing RILEY. Thank you to the IBM Watson Build team who helped us make RILEY a reality: Julie Heeg, John Teltsch, Jamie Hughes, Jacqueline Woods, Denyse Mackey, Ed Grossman, Parth Yadav, Dr. Sandipan Sarkar, and Shari Chiara.

Thank you to the IBM Blockchain team, including Paige Krieger, Jen Francis, and Basavaraj Ganigar; to Donna Dillenberger for her groundbreaking research (*https://oreil.ly/RUnVM*) in blockchain as a vehicle to tether Al; and to Siddartha Basu for confirming our ideas would work. Thank you to Mary Cipriani and Joe Noonan for always being there, and to all of our friends at Ingram Micro. Thank you to Libby Ingrassia and the IBM Champions. Thank you to Mark Anthony Morris for carrying the Hyperledger Fabric torch, and to Leanne Kemp for being a trailblazer in enterprise blockchain.

Thank you to John Buck and Monika Megyesi of Governance Alive for introducing us to the concept of sociocratic governance. Thank you to everyone who contributed to our autonomous vehicle research, especially Bill Maguire, Mark Sanders, Ava Burns, Dr. Raymond Sheh, and Philip Koopman. Thank you to Hugh Forest and everyone at SXSW.

Thank you to our Arkansas friends, including Dr. Lee Smith, Karen McMahen, Jon Laffoon, J. Alex Long, Katie Robertson, and Jackie Phillips; City of Mena Mayor Seth Smith; Dr. Phillip Wilson, Dr. Gaumani Gyanwali, and the University of Arkansas at Rich Mountain; Arkansas Representative John Maddox; Aron Shelton and the Northwest Arkansas Council; Kimberly Randle and PTAC, Kathryn Carlisle, Mary Lacity, and the University of Arkansas Blockchain Center of Excellence; Bentley Story, Olivia Womack, and the Arkansas Economic Development Commission; and Melissa Taylor, Chris Moody, and the whole team at the Fayetteville Public Library Center for Innovation.

Thank you to Tom Kilroy for insisting that girls can do anything boys can do, and to our world-changing women-in-STEM inspirations, who include scientist Marie Curie, mathematician Mileva Marić, and NASA's hidden figures: mathematicians Dorothy Vaughan, Mary Jackson, and Katherine Johnson. Thank you to the AI teams who built systems like Meta, Google, and Twitter, who are speaking out to expose AI's dangers. Thank you to Silas Williams for supplying hope for the future, and to David Bowie for providing the soundtrack (*https://oreil.ly/KCBCP*). To thank everyone who helped us get here would be a book unto itself.

CHAPTER 1

Why Build a Blockchain Truth Machine for AI?

Today's *intelligent agents*—software programs driven by AI that perform some domain-specific function—are used in law enforcement and the judicial system and are gaining significant authority in deciding the fate of humans. It is becoming increasingly difficult for people to detect AI when it is acting as a human agent. A product of AI—the intelligent agent—can be embedded in interactions that people don't associate with AI, such as calling 911 or an insurance claims adjuster. It has been said that once AI becomes mainstream, we will no longer hear the term mentioned, but even now, a person may not realize they have encountered an intelligent agent, much less how to hold it accountable for its actions.

This chapter dissects AI's trust deficit by exploring critical facts to track in order to improve trust, and suggests ways that you can think of your AI projects as having an interwoven blockchain truth machine—a tamper-evident ledger—built into every aspect of the AI. It goes on to explore concerns about machine learning (ML), potential attacks and vulnerabilities, and touches briefly on risk and liability. Blockchain is explained and blockchain/AI touchpoints are identified based on critical facts.

Dissecting AI's Trust Deficit

The collection of critical facts about any AI system resembles an online cake recipe: it lists ingredients, instructions on exactly how to mix and bake it, and helpful information like who wrote the recipe, where this type of cake is best served (birthday, picnic, etc.), nutritional information, and a photo of what the cake is supposed to look like when it is done. Because it is online, you might also see what it looked like when others made it, read comments from those who have eaten the cake, and gather ideas from other bakers. This is very different from when you eat a finished piece of cake that you didn't make; you either eat it or not based on whether you trust the person who handed it to you. You might not worry much about how the cake was made.

But what about trusting powerful AI without knowing how it was made? Should we just accept what it hands us? Do we trust AI too little to ever find its most beneficial applications, or do we trust it too much for our own good? It is very hard to tell, because AI comes in many varieties, consists of many components, comes from many different origins, and is embedded into our lives in many different ways.

Often, AI has been tested to operate well in some conditions but not in others. If AI had an accompanying list of facts, similar to an OSHA Safety Data Sheet (*https://oreil.ly/HiHeg*) used for hazardous chemicals, it would be much easier to know what is inside, how it is expected to perform, safe handling guidelines, and how to test for proper function. *AI factsheets* (*https://oreil.ly/oSFX5*) are similar lists of facts, as they contain human-readable details about what is inside AI. Factsheets are intended to be dynamically produced from a *fact flow* system, which captures critical information as part of a multiuser/machine workflow. Fact flow can be made more robust by adding blockchain to the stack because it fosters distributed, tamper-evident AI provenance.

Critical facts for your factsheet may include the following:

- Your AI's purpose
- Its intended domain: where and when should it be used?
- Training and testing data
- Models and algorithms
- Inputs and outputs
- Performance metrics
- Known bias
- Optimal and poor performance conditions
- Explanation
- Contacts

Consider these fact types, and then remove ones that don't apply or add your own (you can also list a fact type with a value like "opaque box" or "not yet established"):

Purpose
: When a project is started, a group of stakeholders generally get together and decide the *purpose* of their project, which includes defining high-level requirements of what they want to accomplish. Sometimes the purpose will change, so it is good to do spontaneous soundness checks and record those as well.

Intended domain

Similar to purpose, the *intended domain* describes the planned use of the AI. Specifically, the intended domain addresses the subject matter in which the AI is intended to be an expert (healthcare, ecommerce, agriculture, and so on). Soundness checks that probe for domain drift are good to include here. An example of an intended domain is a sensor that is designed for dry weather—if it is operated in wet weather, it is being used outside of the intended domain.

Training data

Sets of related information called *training data* are used to inform the AI of desired results and to test the AI for those results. Training data is the most critical part of generating a good model, and is an example of the *garbage in, garbage out* rule of computing (meaning that if the input is not good, the output will not be reliable). If the training data is not sound, the model will not be sound. Also consider that the training data must suit the intended domain—imagine that a model is intended to function in hot weather but it is trained using data gathered in cold weather. The training data can come from many different sources and be in many different formats and levels of quality. This chapter further explores data integrity and quality in "Data Quality, Outliers, and Edge Cases" on page 8, and Chapter 2 discusses it in more detail.

Testing data

Once the algorithm has been trained, *testing data* is run through to make sure that the results are within the model's stated standard deviations. These data sets should contain all known edge cases to uncover weaknesses within the model's parameters when comparing the output to the training data output.

Models and algorithms

A *model* is a set of programmatic functions with variables that learn from an input to produce an output. The model is trained using data sets that tell it both how and how not to behave. The model is composed of many different *algorithms*, which are AI's underlying formulas, typically developed by data scientists. The model learns from many training data sets from various libraries and sources, which have been introduced to the model by different parties in various abstractions. Once a model is in production, there is no standard way to track what goes on behind the scenes, and models frequently come from third-party marketplaces, so models and algorithms are often referred to as *AI's opaque box*. Chapter 6 discusses how an AI model is coded.

Inputs and outputs

Input describes the type of stimulus the system expects to receive. For instance, a visual recognition system will expect images as input. *Output* is what the system is supposed to produce as a response. A visual recognition system will produce a description as output.

Performance metrics
: These are specifications on exactly how the AI is supposed to perform, including speed and accuracy. They are generally monitored with analytics systems.

Bias
: AI bias, which is explored in Chapter 2, is one of the biggest issues facing AI. When we consider bias, our thoughts generally jump to race and gender; while those are very serious issues with AI, they are only part of the collection of biases that people, and subsequently AI, hold. Exposing any known bias by implementing tests and processes to avoid bias is helpful in making the AI transparent and trustworthy.

Optimal and poor conditions
: AI that performs well in certain conditions may perform poorly in others. In the world of AI-driven automated vehicles (AVs), there is a defined operational design domain (ODD) within which the AI can be expected to perform well. For instance, a particular AI might work well as part of a *lidar* (light detection and ranging) system, where a laser light is shined on an object and reflections are measured to determine characteristics of the object. When the weather is clear and dry, this system may function perfectly, but when it is overcast and raining, performance might decrease drastically.

Explanation
: This explains the interpretability of the AI's output, or states that it operates as a opaque box and does not provide explanations for its output.

Contacts
: This is who to contact in case support, intervention, or maintenance is needed with the AI. This ties to identity, which Chapter 2 explores in detail.

Machine Learning Concerns

With a traditional computer program, you write the code with specific rules and parameters and test it with specific data sets. The code is run and produces an output that may or may not be graphically represented. In a typical ML program, the code is written and run multiple times with specific training data sets to teach the program what the rules are, and those rules are then tested with test data sets, and this iterative process continues until the ML program produces an output—a *prediction*—with a high-enough level of confidence to prove the program has learned how to identify the data in the proper context.

The classic example of this is IBM data scientists building and training Watson to play on the show *Jeopardy!*, where an answer is displayed and the player has to come up with the right question to match. This required the data scientists to come up with the right algorithms for the ML program to teach Watson to understand the *Jeopardy!*

answer in the proper context, instead of merely acting as a fast search engine spitting out multiple random questions—it needed to find the question with the best fit in the proper context at a very high confidence level. That is the essence of machine learning: the data sets teach the program how to learn, and the ML program responds to data input with a high confidence output, as illustrated in Figure 1-1.

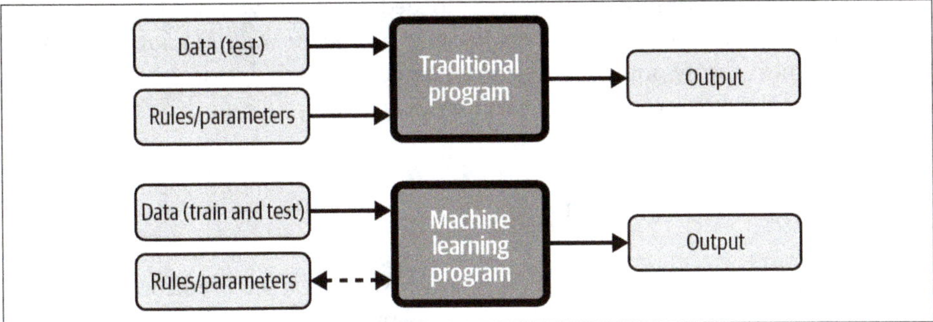

Figure 1-1. Input and output of a traditional software program versus a typical ML program

To learn more about IBM Watson's training for *Jeopardy!*, watch "How IBM Built a Jeopardy Champion" (*https://oreil.ly/-4A8c*) on YouTube. At its core, it is a story of how scientists taught Watson to recognize context in order to increase confidence levels of its answers (or questions, as it is on *Jeopardy!*).

Opaque Box Algorithms

In everyday corporate use, ML prediction can be used in many applications, such as weather forecasting or deciding on the right moment to drop an online coupon on a regular customer while they're browsing a retail website. One of the ML algorithms that can be used for both scenarios is the *Markov chain*. A Markov chain is a discrete stochastic process (algorithm) in which the probability of outcomes is either independent, or dependent on the current or directly preceding state.

This whole process of making predictions based on algorithms and data and finding appropriate output is usually only partially visible to any one ML team member, and is generally considered to operate as a opaque box of which the exact contents are undetectable. Algorithms like the Markov chain model are tuned by behind-the-scenes mathematicians adjusting complex formulas, which is indiscernible to nearly everyone else involved. This section uses the Markov chain model to illustrate how training raw number data sets really works and then shows how classification data sets work.

Although in statistics results are referred to as *probabilities*, in machine learning we refer to results as *confidence levels*.

For dice throwing, assuming the dice aren't loaded, whatever you just threw does not affect what you're about to throw. This is called a *random walk Markov chain*. Your guess of the next throw not being improved by your knowledge of the previous one showcases the Markov property, the memoryless property of a stochastic process. In other words, in this case:

$$P_{left} + P_{right} = 1 \ (\text{or } P_{left} = 1 - P_{right})$$

A simple model (*https://oreil.ly/joCaO*) is a two-state weather prediction: sunny or cloudy. A 2 × 2 *transition matrix P* describes the probability of what the weather will be tomorrow based on what it is today:

$$P = \begin{bmatrix} 0.9 & 0.1 \\ 0.5 & 0.5 \end{bmatrix}$$

This probability can be seen in Figure 1-2.

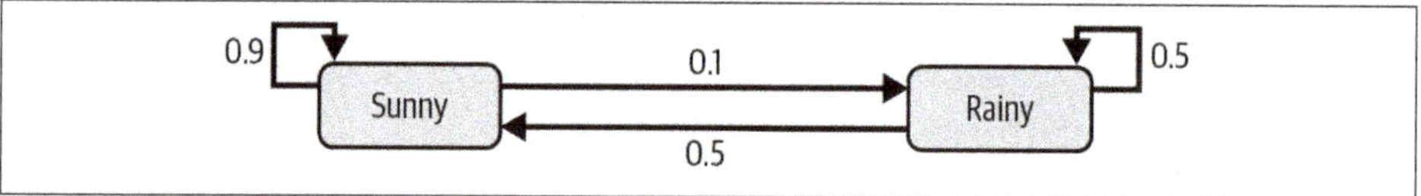

Figure 1-2. A graphical representation of a simple two-state weather prediction model

We can make several observations here:

- The total output of either state adds up to 1 (because it is a *stochastic matrix*).
- There is a 90% probability that tomorrow will be sunny if today is sunny.
- There is a 10% probability that tomorrow will be rainy if today is sunny.
- There is a 50% probability that tomorrow will be rainy or sunny if today is rainy.

Today is Day 0 and it is sunny. In the matrix, we represent this "sunny" as 100% or 1, and thus "rainy" is 0%, or 0. So, initial state vector *X0* = [1 0].

The weather tomorrow, on Day 1, can be predicted by multiplying the *state vector* from Day 0 by the following *transition matrix*:

$$x^{(1)} = x^{(0)}P = \begin{bmatrix} 1 & 0 \end{bmatrix} \begin{bmatrix} 0.9 & 0.1 \\ 0.5 & 0.5 \end{bmatrix} = \begin{bmatrix} 0.9 & 0.1 \end{bmatrix}$$

The 0.9 in the output vector *X1* tells us there is a 90% chance that Day 1 will also be sunny.

The weather on Day 2 (the day after tomorrow) can be predicted the same way using the state vector computed for Day 1, and so on for Day 3 and beyond. There are different types of Markov algorithms to suit more complicated predictive systems, such as the stock market.

This simple example shows how algorithms are created and how data is iterated through them. More complicated models consist of far more complicated algorithms (or groups of algorithms) to fit different scenarios. The algorithms are working in the background—the user, whoever they may be, doesn't see them at all, yet the algorithms serve a purpose. They require mathematical equations, generated manually or through programs specifically made to generate algorithms, and impact everything about the model and the ML pipeline. Finally, the models need to be tested thoroughly over a wide range of variability and monitored carefully for changes.

Each step involved in constructing the model could potentially undergo tampering, incorrect data, or intervention from a competitor. To fix this weakness would require some way to prove that the data and algorithms were from a reliable source and had not been tampered with.

To understand algorithms in general terms, think of an old-fashioned recipe for baking a cake from scratch. A cake algorithm might give you a way to help others combine a list of ingredients according to your specific instructions, bake it at the specified time and temperature in the correct pan that has been prepared the proper way, and get a consistent cake. The cake algorithm may even provide you with input variables such as different pan size or quantity, to automatically adjust the recipe for a different altitude, or to produce bigger cakes or more of them at a time. The only content that this algorithm knows is what is hardcoded (for example, 3 eggs, 3 cups of flour, a teaspoon of baking powder, and so forth). The writer of the recipe or someone who influenced them directly or indirectly had knowledge and life experience in how cakes work: what happens when you mix ingredients such as liquid and baking soda, mathematical measurements for each ingredient, correct proportions, how much of any ingredient is too much, and how to avoid the kind of chemical combinations that will make a cake fail.

In contrast to a general algorithm, AI algorithms are special in that they perform an action that involves training a model with ML techniques using ample training data. In this case, an AI algorithm for winning a bake-off might look at data listing previous years' winning and losing cake recipes, and give you the instructions to help you bake the winning cake.

Genetic Algorithms

Genetic algorithms are based on natural selection, where the models improve their confidence levels by mimicking the principles of natural evolution. They are applied to search and optimization problems to improve a model's performance. The key factors in a genetic algorithm include selection, or how it is determined which members of a population will reproduce; mutation, or random changes in the genetic code; and crossover, which is a determination of what happens when chromosomes are mixed and what is inherited from the parents.

This is applied as a model that breeds the best answers with one another, in the form of a decision tree that learns from its experience. Genetic algorithms are often used in optimizing how the model can run within its permitted environment, evaluating its own potential performance with various *hyperparameters*, which are the run variables that an AI engineer chooses before model training. Models driven by genetic algorithms can become smarter and smarter as time progresses, ultimately leading to technological singularity, which is addressed later in this chapter.

Data Quality, Outliers, and Edge Cases

Data preprocessing is important, and data quality will make preprocessing easier. To identify a dog breed, for example, you'll need to have clear, close-up photos of the dog breed and represent every possible appearance of the breed from different angles (like in the story of Iggy Pup that you read in the Preface). If we were training an algorithm to understand text, the preprocessing would entail steps such as making data readable, making everything lowercase, and getting rid of superfluous words, among other things. But besides the input data, the classifications are critical, which brings us to the reason for the exercise of explaining Markov: this is how simple training works, but if you have inadequate training examples for inadequate classifications, it will propagate through with each iteration and you will create some kind of bias in your results.

One issue to keep in mind about the Markov chain: *outliers*, whether or not the origin is known, must be cut. The Markov algorithm was created in a way that doesn't tolerate outliers. If the model you're using has algorithms that don't process outliers, you would do well to think about running separate iterations of ML with edge case data sets made of outliers, and use it to come up with error detection and error handling procedures.

In this context, an outlier is a data point that is statistically far enough away from the rest of the pattern or trend of points that it doesn't seem to follow the same behavior. An exception.

In the case where there is no previous state or the previous state is unknown, the hidden Markov model is used, and the initial array and output values are generated manually. When numbers aren't involved, different approaches must be taken to estimate the array and the output. A typical approach for training nonnumbered data sets, such as in identifying objects, involves using natural language processing (NLP) to classify the variables into an array like in the previous example, and create a desired output that can be fed back in during each iteration through an algorithm many times—up to 100,000—until the result converges on a value that doesn't change much through repeated iterations (the number of standard deviations depends on what you're computing).

For example, you can train a set of images of a dog breed, and you would have to take into account the different attributes that distinguish that pure breed from other breeds, such as coat colors, head shape, ear shape, coat length, stance, eye location, and eye color. The training sets would be made of images of thousands of dogs of that breed (a positive set) and images of dogs that are not that breed and other objects that might look like this dog breed but aren't (a negative set). Once the training converges to a confidence level that is high enough to ensure the code recognizes the breed, real-world data can be run against it.

If you do not account for all facets of an object's appearance or a scenario, you will undoubtedly leave out classifications that would be critical for your training data sets. Poor confidence numbers during test runs should be an indicator of the need to improve training sets. Embarrassing mistakes that make it to the real world are another undesirable result. Regardless of the model or algorithm, having poor data will test your data preprocessing skills and can hinder your model's ability to make sound predictions. It will also help to have an interpretable model or algorithm and a sound method to make predictions.

Despite the best efforts of developers and data scientists, a pressing issue in machine learning is bias—biases based on humans' own limited experiences and filtered views. While there are many types of bias, racial, gender, and contextual bias can create inequities. Best practices stress that you strive for the least amount of bias in your model or algorithm as possible. Preprocessing data is critical.

Measuring Data Quality

Much research has been done into scoring data set quality. There is an old standard, the Data Quality Index (DQI) (*https://oreil.ly/yqjys*), which assesses the quality and reliability of data sets in real time based on deviation from predicted parameter values. The DQI reflects three aspects of your data recording: timeliness, completeness, and quality of recording. Machine learning, which provides assistance in deriving a DQI score, has a marked ability to predict trends and identify outliers if trained properly and can make suggestions or take actions on the go. Outliers shouldn't be automatically thrown out.

How is data quality measured? Start by deciding what "value" means to your firm, and then measure how long it takes to achieve that value. The following are some of the metrics you might use to assess the quality of your data:

- The number of errors the model produces versus the number of data points. This includes the number of empty or null values.
- Any slowdowns in data preprocessing time.
- Data package bounce rates.
- The cost of data storage.
- The amount of time to achieve ROI.

Supervised Versus Unsupervised ML

When using *supervised ML,* where the data is labeled beforehand by a data scientist to show desired output (for example, ingredients and processes for edible cakes versus inedible cakes), the models are apt to drift from their original intent and accuracy due to changes in data and forgotten goals (the AI makes cake, then fruitcake, then eventually switches to jams and preserves based on new training data recipes with similar ingredients). In this case, the output might be delicious, but it's missing one of the required ingredients, such as the bake-off sponsor's brand of flour.

The process of *unsupervised ML* makes it so the output of the AI model evolves more or less on its own. Unsupervised ML analyzes the data set and learns the relationships among the data, yet still typically requires a human to validate the decisions. In the case of the cake, ML might try to improve on a winning recipe to make it more likely to stand out, but it may ask you to try out the recipe before finalizing big changes. Semi-supervised ML combines supervised and unsupervised ML, and is used when some labeled data is available, but is combined with unlabeled data in order to increase the volume of available data.

The model lifecycle takes place in the *ML pipeline*, and the steps needed to take the model from conception to production are shown in Figure 1-3. This process can be adapted to the various ML design patterns that are too numerous to cover in this book.

Without standard ways to validate and track validation, ML can easily get out of control, and your AI could bake cakes that aren't edible or don't meet your requirements. To fix this, the original intent needs to be baked into the ML cycle so it does not become compromised.

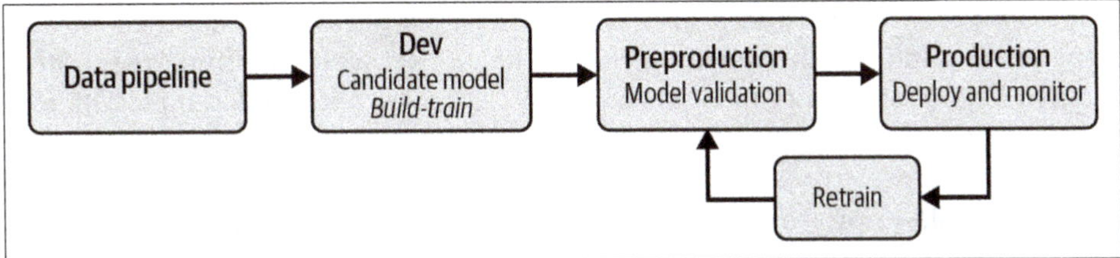

Figure 1-3. A typical ML pipeline

Generative AI, which is the technology underlying popular cloud-based art generation, is a variation of unsupervised or semi-supervised ML that creates original images, video, audio, and text based on user input. For example, one popular cloud-based system, OpenAI's DALL-E (*https://oreil.ly/49P6t*), allows anyone to produce complex, professional-looking artwork by giving DALL-E a natural language command such as "draw a bowl of fruit in a pencil sketch style." You could vary the details, such as specify that there should be four bunches of grapes, and DALL-E will vary the image accordingly, based on what it knows about pencil sketches, baskets of fruit, and grapes. However, sometimes you will see an unrealistic artifact that doesn't belong, like a grape growing out of a banana. Looking closely to find artifacts—like a grape growing out of a banana—is a way to spot deepfakes.

Deepfakes, or realistic looking media produced by generative AI, are now easy for just about any novice internet user to generate. Deepfakes can be used by bad actors to damage the reputation of others or to monetize new material that was only produced because AI ingested the work of other artists. In most geographical areas, laws and prior court decisions regulating the generation of deepfakes are nonexistent, so there is little recourse for artists who feel they have been violated through the use of their copyrighted works as training data.

Other creative work that used to require a talented human being, like designing a user interface for a web application, can now be done by simply hand-sketching an idea and then feeding that sketch into a generative AI design assistant like Uizard (*https://oreil.ly/43wUG*).

Reinforcement Learning and Deep Learning

Reinforcement learning is a type of ML that occurs when an AI is designed to gather input from its environment and then use that input to improve itself. Reinforcement learning is common in automated vehicles, as the vehicle learns not to repeat the same mistakes. Like unsupervised learning, there is no labeled data. Instead, the model learns from its own experiences, similar to how a child learns. Reinforcement learning is also used in video games like AlphaGo (*https://oreil.ly/saipb*), which you learned about in the Preface, in robotics, and in text mining, which is the process of transforming unstructured data into structured data for analysis.

Deep learning takes ML a step further by distributing algorithms and data among many nodes, and is powered by layers of *neural networks*, a computing system inspired by the function of the brain's neurons. Deep learning applies these different layers to come up with incredibly accurate insights to data, which can be either structured or unstructured. Deep learning breaks down and analyzes data in such a way that one layer of a neural network might find the broad results for an image being processed, such as classifying it as a bird, and another layer might analyze its finer details, classifying the bird as a cardinal.

Deep learning requires a lot of data and robust hardware, so it is expensive and best used to solve large, complex problems, but it is available at an affordable cost as cloud services from providers like Oracle, IBM, Microsoft, and AWS. Deep learning doesn't require anybody to label or prepare the data, so it is used in applications like social media to analyze large numbers of images, in healthcare to analyze massive amounts of data related to diseases and predict cures, and for digital assistants that perform complex natural language processing, like Siri and Alexa.

Program Synthesis

Program synthesis is the term used for when computers learn how to code. Program synthesis in AI (*https://oreil.ly/bfTRO*) is already taking place.

Since intelligent agents can write code to modify their own model based on what they have learned, their goal, and their environment, they are capable of program synthesis. They can update training data used for machine learning, which modifies their own output and behavior. With no guidelines or rules, no permanent enforcement of their main goal or subgoals, and no authority or oversight, human stakeholders do not have long-term control over the final outcome, which makes AI a very *high-risk* business activity.

Will the technology world announce one day that software will be written by AI and not humans? Unlikely. Instead, program synthesis will creep in slowly—at first showing competent human developers some computer-generated code for their perusal and acceptance, then increasingly taking more control of the coding as developers become less qualified because the AI is doing most of the code writing. Gaining mass acceptance by correcting grammar and syntax, program synthesis is becoming a real threat to our control over AI as it evolves into a way for people and intelligent agents with no programming skills whatsoever to trigger highly complex actions on just about any system using remote APIs.

What if the computer's idea about what to write is better than yours? Does your tab-key acceptance of a synthetic thought prompt the next suggestion, and the next? At what point does the power of the pen shift from you to the machine? Program synthesis, the next evolution of auto-complete, is coming to write prose, documentation, and code in ways you might not notice.

As discussed elsewhere in this book, there are few AI controls that help humans to determine the original *intent* of a piece of software, much less to stick to that intent, or alert anyone when the AI begins to go awry. The intent can be lost forever, the AI can morph, and the next thing you know you have a group of humans who don't know how the software was designed to be used. Since these AI helpers are designed to develop code or content based upon your intent, loss of original intent is a serious side effect that could have great implications over time.

Auto-complete

For a number of years, computer programmers have used integrated development environments (IDEs), applications that recommend to the programmer how to complete complex syntax, as well as to check the code for bugs. Using these systems, *auto-complete*, the ability to accept a suggestion from the system, became a great way to learn new syntax and a huge timesaver for the software development world.

Smart Compose

Google Smart Compose arose from auto-complete features originally designed for software developers. (Microsoft Word has a similar feature, called Text Predictions.) Do these features make someone a better writer, or do people become dependent on these features?

When you scale this out to the millions of people who are using the Gmail Smart Compose feature (see Figure 1-4), is the author leading the machine or is the machine leading the author? Is there going to be a point where we realize the machine is the better writer and we just give up? Or will our control slowly slip away as we accept an increasing number of suggestions?

According to a US National Library of Medicine publication, "Exploring the Impact of Internet Use on Memory and Attention Processes" (*https://oreil.ly/9gNJH*), the internet may act as a "superstimulus for transactive memory." This means that people don't worry about remembering something that they can simply look up online. Does that imply that over time, everyone could become dependent on Smart Compose, and that we will eventually write how—and what—AI wants us to write?

Grammar:	◉ Grammar suggestions on ○ Grammar suggestions off
Spelling:	◉ Spelling suggestions on ○ Spelling suggestions off
Autocorrect:	◉ Autocorrect on ○ Autocorrect off
Smart Compose: (predictive writing suggestions appear as you compose an email)	◉ Writing suggestions on ○ Writing suggestions off
Smart Compose personalization: (Smart Compose is personalized to your writing style)	◉ Personalization on ○ Personalization off
Conversation View: (sets whether emails of the same topic are grouped together)	○ Conversation view on ◉ Conversation view off

Figure 1-4. Settings for the Smart Compose predictive writing suggestions in Gmail

Codex

Codex (*https://oreil.ly/vvwvL*), like ChatGPT—which was mentioned in this book's Preface—is based on OpenAI's GPT-3. Codex is described by OpenAI as a general-purpose language model, and is available for general use as an OpenAI API. In this video demonstration (*https://oreil.ly/wVGC6*), developers show how Codex can take an intent described in natural language, then produce other output based on the intent along with additional requests, and automatically write Python code to produce the results desired by the programmer. The Python code can then be executed locally or on other systems.

Also demonstrated in the video is a connection with Microsoft Word's API. Codex is able to connect with APIs offered by productivity programs like Microsoft Word. When it works properly, programmers can give natural language instructions that turn into correct API calls. As this technology matures, it will give programmers and nonprogrammers alike the ability to perform increasingly sophisticated tasks by simply stating the desired outcome, without the need or even the ability to understand any of the inner workings that make the system function.

Copilot

GitHub's Copilot (*https://oreil.ly/iXxVR*), based on Codex by OpenAI (*https://openai.com*) and owned by Microsoft, is making news because it extends code editors so that AI not only completes syntax for developers, but also writes whole lines of code or entire functions. Copilot can write code based on the developer stating their intent in their natural language, such as instructing Copilot to create a game that has a paddle and a moving ball that can be hit by the paddle. The accuracy of the output of the request and the quality of the resulting code are both a topic of much debate, but the code should improve dramatically as Copilot learns from the vast volume of code that is stored by developers on the GitHub platform.

Copilot has been met by the development community with both amazement and chagrin, since it can quickly generate large volumes of working code. Some of the code meets the community's expectations, while other parts of the code are not written to best practices and can produce faulty results.

OpenAI is an AI research and development company, rather than a community-based AI open source/free project as the name might imply.

Copilot is part of an attempt to create *artificial general intelligence* (AGI), which is AI that can match or surpass the capabilities of humans at any intellectual task. Companies like Microsoft and OpenAI are teaming up to accomplish AGI (*https://oreil.ly/CfEXR*), and aim to make AGI easy for their customers to channel and deploy. Program synthesis makes this possible since the AI itself can write this complex code. By bringing AGI to the Azure platform, Microsoft and OpenAI say they hope to democratize AI by implementing safe, Responsible AI (*https://oreil.ly/qi0bV*) on the Azure platform that is equally available to all.

Microsoft AI helper for Minecraft

Minecraft is a 3D *sandbox game*, a type of game that lets the user create new objects and situations within it. Released in November 2011, Minecraft looks basic compared to many other graphical games, with players smashing through pixelated cubes using block-headed avatars, either alone or in teams. There is, however, a lot more going on than you would initially expect, since Minecraft players use the resources found within the infinite virtual worlds to construct other virtual items, such as crafting a shelter from a fallen tree and stone. There are multiple modes in Minecraft, including one that allows players to fight for a certain goal, one that allows participants to work on survival, and a creative mode that facilitates the customization of new virtual worlds without interruptions.

Minecraft allows for *modding*, which means users create *mods*, or *modifications* to the code. There are more than 100,000 user modifications to Minecraft, which can do things like add or change the behavior of virtual objects, including hardware or machinery, or repurpose Minecraft for new adventures like exploring the human body (*https://oreil.ly/Djz2F*) or for traditional classroom studies (*https://oreil.ly/N3LbO*) like math, language arts, and history. There is no central authority for Minecraft mods, and no one is really sure what is out there and what they actually do.

Since Microsoft owns Copilot, the next logical step is to integrate it with other programs as an *AI helper*, an intelligent agent that can accept the intent of the user and act upon it by writing what it deems to be appropriate code. In May 2022 at its developer conference, Microsoft announced Project Malmo, an AI helper for Minecraft (*https://oreil.ly/Dk7Gh*): a nonplayer character within the game that can accept commands to construct virtual worlds, and can do so without interruption. These virtual worlds can end up as mods with no controls certifying what is actually contained in the mod, who built it, or how it will impact players.

Controlling program synthesis

Since most machine learning is done in a opaque box model, the process the AI uses for arriving at its results is not transparent at all. It isn't traceable, and for the controls that do exist (such as key-value pair ML registries), they could be faked by a clever AI to meet its goals.

To fix this, expected limitations for the AI need to be built into the ML's registry, tightly coupled with the ML design and machine learning operations (MLOps) process, so as to regulate deployment of models, as discussed further in "Defining Your Use Case" on page 31.

It is possible for machines communicating with one another to simplify their communications by creating their own terminology, or shorthand—or even worse, use machine language, which is very difficult for humans to interpret.

Superintelligent Agents

Because intelligent agents are constantly improving through ML, it is possible that an agent can become exceedingly proficient in a particular domain. Once an intelligent agent passes a human intelligence level, it is classified as a *superintelligent agent*.

The superintelligent agent might take the form of a question-answering *oracle*, or an order-taking *genie*. Either of these might evolve into an independently acting *sovereign* that makes decisions entirely on its own. The agent's architecture could take the form of an all-knowing, all-powerful *singleton*, or we could have a *multipolar* world where superintelligent machines, powered by artificial general intelligence, compete with one another for dominance.

When planning to build a powerful AI, you can also plan its containment and demise. An agent created for a specific purpose could automatically sunset after the predetermined goal for the agent has been attained.

Superintelligent agents sound like science fiction, as if they are not a real threat but the product of an overzealous imagination. However, just because an AI has yet to surpass human intelligence does not mean that it can't. The reason we invented AI is so we can make sense of and act upon massive volumes of information—way more than what a human being is capable of doing. AI doesn't know where to draw the line—unless we code for it. If we don't, the AI could keep improving itself through program synthesis and eventually achieve technological singularity (see "Technological Singularity").

An example of this might be if we forget to tell our cake AI that we have a goal to operate within a limited budget. In this case, our AI could source the finest ingredients in the world, and scale up to grand production with no regard for cost, all in an attempt to win the bake-off. To fix this, we need to build approved cost limitations into our ML, which are aggregated when models are deployed on multiple graphics processing units (GPUs).

Technological Singularity

Technological singularity is the hypothetical point in time at which technological growth becomes uncontrollable and irreversible, resulting in unforeseeable changes to human civilization.

In this event, you may want to already have an AI backdoor. Sometimes unethical software developers create a backdoor into a system they build, meaning that even if they are no longer authorized to get in, they can still do so. This is seen as a negative, and it is not an accepted practice to build backdoors. In the case of AI, a backdoor could be designed into the project as a way for the project stakeholders to always be able to interrupt the AI and make modifications, or completely stop it and remove all instances. Chapter 2 discusses how to implement controls to make sure that human stakeholders can always intervene.

Attacks and Failures

Inside the AI opaque box, there are a number of AI incidents that include failures and attacks brought on by bad or lazy actors. Failures include bias, data drift, and lack of verifiable identification. Attacks include adversarial data attacks, poisoning attacks, evasion attacks, model stealing, and impersonation attacks. Attacks and how to prevent and expose them are discussed further in Chapter 2.

AI requires all the same due diligence as any software development project, but also has extra layers that need to be considered. Lazy actors or lack of involving all team members can cause critical updates or security concerns to be missed or neglected. Also, since AI can change itself based on outside input, it is possible for bad actors to attack by presenting sample data that will erode the confidence of your model.

When thinking about potential attacks, think about the attackers. What are they to accomplish? (Usually financial gain by tricking your AI system.) What do they already know about your systems? What can they access? To monitor for potential attacks, make sure to watch for model/data drift or other subtle changes that impact the output.

Model/Data Drift

Data drift, which underlies *model drift*, is defined as a change in the distribution of data. In the case of production ML models, this is the change between the real-time production data and a baseline data set, likely the training set, that is representative of the task the model is intended to perform. Production data can diverge or drift from the baseline data over time due to changes in the real world. Drift of the predicted values is a signal that the model needs retraining.

There are two reasons for drift to occur in production models (*https://oreil.ly/yhgu5*):

When there's a change in baseline or input data distribution due to external factors
: An example might be a product being sold in a new region. This may require a new model with an updated representative training set.

When there are data integrity issues that require investigation
: This might involve data from a faulty frontend camera, or data unintentionally changed after collection.

One issue the AI/ML community has not figured out is what accuracy standards to put in place for system components. Establishing a kind of test safety regime that can take every system into account and assess the systems-of-systems is difficult to execute. An example would be getting Tesla's AI (*https://oreil.ly/9oPHG*) to accurately read a speed limit sign in spite of it being partially obstructed.

There are different types of drift depending on the data distribution being compared, as shown in Figure 1-5.

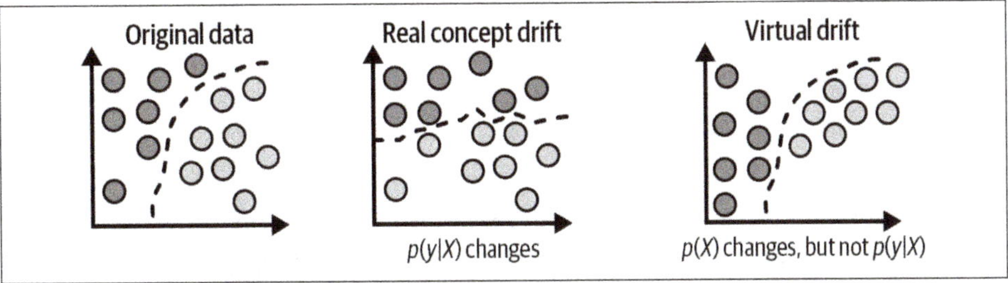

Figure 1-5. Original versus real concept versus virtual data drift. Adapted from an image in Amit Paka's article "How to Detect Model Drift in ML Modeling" (https://oreil.ly/EIiwb).

They all point back to a statistically significant change in the data output over time compared to the output during testing and early production, which affects the model's predictions. It necessitates relearning the data to maintain the error rate and accuracy of the previous regime. In the absence of a real-time baseline reestablishing itself over and over, drift in prediction and feature distributions is often indicative of important changes in the outside environment. It is possible for these quantities to drift with respect to an accurately modeled decision boundary (virtual drift). In that case, model performance will be unchanged.

Adversarial Data Attacks

Bad actors can target the modeling phase or the deployment phase to corrupt the training data or model so that the production and deployment data no longer match. They do this through *adversarial data attacks*, or adversarial ML attacks, which are hacks designed to fool data models by supplying deceptive training or testing data. This is an especially good blockchain touchpoint for ML, because it can help you to compare the original training data with the current training data and create an alert, noting any occurrences where the data is different. As a result of the alert, a smart contract can cause the model to be recalled for review and reinitiate the review process.

All of the standard cybersecurity rules apply here, plus these additional attacks that impact ML training data, production test data, and mislabeled training data. The training data also helps the AI ascertain a percentage reflecting its own confidence in the results. However, a hacker can introduce *adversarial data* (such as a cat image that has been modified to be recognized as a dog), making the AI draw the wrong conclusions about the query image, sometimes with great confidence. Since the hacker can introduce millions of data points and the changes are usually invisible to the human eye, these attacks are very difficult to combat.

Think about how an ML pipeline can contain billions of points of training data. *Poisoning attacks* and *evasion attacks* are both types of adversarial data attacks. Both types exploit the *decision boundary*, which is the logical line by which ML places data points to classify input data into one type or another:

Poisoning attack
: A data poisoning attack involves the training data used for machine learning. This attack happens during the machine learning training phase and involves injection of malicious data that changes the classifier. Typically, this happens in systems that accept input from outside sources like users and then retrains the system based on the new input. The attacker inserts a specific set of data into training data that causes a certain classifier to be consistently triggered, giving the hacker a backdoor into the system. For example, a hacker could train the system so that if a white square is inserted into an image at a certain spot, it could be identified as "cat." If enough images of dogs are inserted containing the white square, then any dog query image will be classified as "cat."

Evasion attack
: An *evasion attack* is the most common kind of attack and happens during the production phase. The evasion attack distorts samples (subsets of training data used for testing) so that the data is not detected as attacks when it should be. The attacker subtly pushes a data point beyond the decision boundary by changing its label. The label is changed by changing the samples so the data point tests as some other classification.

  This type of attack does not affect training data, but can easily affect the outcome of your system because its own test results are wrong based on wrong answers. For instance, if all of the samples now only contain pictures of poodles, any dog that is not a poodle might no longer be classified as a dog. Because this impacts the production system, it is not uncommon for it to enter via malware or spam.

Model stealing
: This type of hack is designed to re-create the model or the training data upon which it was constructed, with the intention of using it elsewhere. The model can then be tested in a controlled environment with experiments designed to find potential exploits.

Impersonation attack
: An impersonation attack imitates samples from victims, often in image recognition, malware detection, and intrusion detection. When this attack is successful, malicious data is injected that classifies original samples with different labels from their impersonated ones. This is often used to spoof identity for access control. Examples of impersonation attacks include facial recognition system impersonation, otherwise unrecognizable speech recognized by models, deep neural network attacks on self-driving cars, and deepfake images and videos.

Risk and Liability

A big failure of AI could be that it generates risk and liability, which could be nearly impossible to assess in advance. Questions may arise when there are incidents with AI systems, such as how is responsibility assigned? How will a legal authority or court approach these issues when it is not obvious who is responsible due to the opaque box characteristics of AI?

There is discussion among attorneys and the AI community about how much documentation is too much. Some advisors give the impression that you shouldn't keep a complete trail of information about what you are doing, in case you do something wrong, because if the information doesn't exist, it can't be used against you. Other advisors will say that if you should have known some potential risk and did not take adequate steps to prevent it, that is a risk in itself.

Risk and liability assessment is beyond the scope of this book, and as with any important decision, you should discuss these topics with your own stakeholders and legal advisors while you are in the planning process. For general information, a good reference for this subject is "AI and the Legal Industry," the second chapter in Karen Kilroy's 2021 report *AI and the Law* (O'Reilly).

Blockchain as an AI Tether

AI models aggregate information and learn from it, morphing their own behavior and influencing their own environments, both with and without the approval of data scientists. Blockchain can be used to permanently track the steps leading up to the change in a model's output, becoming a *tether*, or an audit trail for the model. Think back to the critical facts that may be on your factsheet, as listed earlier. Your AI's purpose, intended domain, training data, models and algorithms, inputs and outputs, performance metrics, bias, optimal and poor performance conditions, explanation, contacts, and other facts are all potential blockchain *touchpoints*—points in the fact flow that can benefit from a tamper-evident, distributed provenance. This gives you a way to audit your AI in a human-readable form, trace it backward, and be sure that the information you are reviewing has not undergone tampering.

To effectively record the touchpoints onto blockchain, you need a blockchain platform. We chose Hyperledger Fabric, an enterprise-level consortium-driven blockchain platform. For more information on the features of Hyperledger Fabric and blockchain-as-a-service derivatives, see Karen's 2019 *Blockchain as a Service* report (O'Reilly).

From an architecture standpoint, you don't have to change much about how your modeling workflow goes now. Blockchain gets added to your AI technology stack and runs alongside your existing systems, and can be set up in a way where it is low latency and highly available. Unlike blockchain used for cryptocurrency, performance is not an issue.

Defining Blockchain Touchpoints: Data and Model Drift

The blockchain touchpoints for keeping track of data and model drift are shown in Table 1-1. Data and model drift monitoring helps ML teams stay ahead of performance issues in production. Being able to track and trace data and model drifting is an essential part of a multidisciplinary strategy of risk management in an organization. Here is a list of potential blockchain touchpoints that will help you to track and trace data and model drift.

Table 1-1. Blockchain touchpoints for keeping track of model and data drift

Touchpoint	Layer	Description
Inputs and outputs, test level	Model validation	This would be broken down into test baseline, test results at different iterations until the model levels out and stays within a predetermined range—out to the sixth standard deviation per ISO 9001:2015 (*https://oreil.ly/ttuOw*), or standards set by the NHSTA (*https://oreil.ly/Yig-O*) or NIST ODD (*https://oreil.ly/pyCn5*), for example.
Inputs and outputs, initial production level (production prime)	Model validation	This would be broken down into production baseline input data, and each output would be separately measured against the previous input and the baseline input for deviation. At a statistically significant number of iterations, the model would be flagged to see what variables needed to be altered, or if the model needed to be altered.
Dependencies and requirements Vulnerabilities and patches	MLOps, ML pipeline	Similar to DevOps, MLOps involves updates to the model, content, and training process. MLOps includes management of ML training cycles that involve various ML experiments and content. To keep track of drift, which can be elusive, this touchpoint would be critical.

In addition to this table, see the list of general-purpose AI blockchain touchpoints (Table 1-2) later in this chapter.

You can think of AI's development, training, and deployment processes as being sort of like a supply chain. By comparison, the number one use for enterprise blockchain is track-and-trace supply chain, which involves the lifecycle of goods and their journey to the consumer. In the case of a product like honey, each step along the way is documented, each process is automated, and important touchpoints are recorded to blockchain as a permanent audit trail, which can later be checked to detect fraud, like diluting expensive honey. In this case, a cryptographic hash showing the DNA structure of the honey is used as a crypto anchor, and is compared to a real product by a consumer to make sure the product is authentic. Similarly, a fingerprint of data that is used to train AI can be recorded on blockchain, and stay with the model for its entire lifecycle as each engineer and data scientist performs their specific tasks, like training and approving the model.

Enterprise Blockchain

Speaking of performance, it is a common misconception that all blockchain requires miners who race to solve a cryptographic puzzle in exchange for a tokenized reward. Enterprise blockchain platforms, such as Hyperledger Fabric's blockchain-as-a-service variants—primarily IBM Blockchain, Oracle Blockchain Platform, and AWS Blockchain—can offer superior deployment and upgrades, time-saving development environments and tools, better security, and other features not offered in Hyperledger Fabric alone.

These blockchain platforms do not require miners, and generally run inside *containers*, which are portable, lightweight, self-sufficient computing stacks provisioned by systems like Docker or Kubernetes, running on high-performance, highly scalable cloud-based or on-premises systems. In an ML workflow, for instance, a new block might be added to the blockchain after it met some predetermined criteria, such as approval of a new model by an MLOps engineer.

Tokens, which make up the coins used in cryptocurrency, are generally missing from an enterprise blockchain implementation. Although tokens can be implemented to represent the full or fractional value of some other thing, they are an optional step when implementing enterprise blockchain. Tokens can always be added later as experience and acceptance of the blockchain network are gained. Could AI engineers and MLOps engineers be paid by blockchain tokens? Sure, and this could be made part of your fact flow. These engineers could be automatically rewarded when their obligations are met and tested via smart contracts.

Also note that enterprise blockchain is typically *permissioned*, and that public blockchain platforms like Ethereum are *permissionless*. This means enterprise blockchain has organizational identity management and access control, as well as integration with existing enterprise directories like Lightweight Directory Access Protocol (LDAP). This book dives into identity in Chapter 2, but first, let's explore the basics of how blockchain works.

Distributed, Linked Blocks

Blockchain is a type of *distributed ledger*, and runs in a peer-to-peer network. Each network endpoint is called a *node*. Nodes can be used by individual users, but generally they are shared among groups of users from an organization or group of organizations with common interest. Generally with enterprise blockchain, the nodes are stored in containers on cloud provider computing accounts, such as Oracle Cloud, IBM Cloud, AWS, or Microsoft Azure. There is usually an abstraction layer that is the user-facing application, and blockchain is transparent to the users. The application layer is where workflow takes place.

In many cases, blockchain nodes can be distributed to each participating organization in a blockchain network. This gives their participants a copy of the blockchain over which the organization has full control. Keep in mind that you don't have to distribute your nodes from the beginning. Instead, you can add nodes later as more organizations join your blockchain network.

You might start recording the provenance of your AI project from inception, which is the first set of instructions from the original stakeholders. The very first set of instructions might say who is responsible and grant permission for them to perform various tasks, such as creating or approving a request in the fact flow. This is the beginning of your AI's *governance*, or the accepted set of rules and procedures that is central to maintaining operation of the system.

Later, you might, for example, take on a development partner who wants to participate in governance and would like to have full confidence in the factsheet. If they are not savvy in blockchain, you can give them a login to your fact flow system and let them learn about blockchain by seeing blockchain proofs embedded into the application layer. Once they become more sophisticated with blockchain, they may want their own node so they are more certain that all of the facts are intact.

Blockchain networks foster group confidence because the foundation is a series of blocks of related transactional data. Each block is timestamped, permanently linked to the others, and distributed and validated via a peer-to-peer network, as follows:

1. *Blocks are distributed:* Blockchain does not use a centralized server like most business applications, but instead the data and code are distributed via a peer-to-peer network. In this network, each participating organization has its own copy of the blockchain system running on its own peer, which is known as a *node*. The peers communicate directly once they are established.

This makes blockchain very attractive as a ledger for business-to-business workflow, or for breaking down barriers between departmental silos within single organizations. Since each organization runs a copy of the system and the data, it helps to establish trust. If a new record is inserted into a block of one node, then the same copy of data also gets created in other stakeholders' nodes based on assigned permission. In this way, it is very difficult to tamper with the data because the original copy of the data would have existed in the rest of the nodes as well.

2. *Participant requests are validated:* Before transactions are validated by one of the participating people or systems in an organization, thus placing a transaction into a block, the request is first tested on their node against a smart contract, which contains predetermined business logic tests. If these tests are successful on the requesting participant's node, then the request is broadcast to all nodes in the network, and tested on each node by the *chaincode*, or scripts that interact with the blockchain, and other algorithms that validate the request. Each participant is given certain permission and access to the resources of the blockchain network, like assets. So participants can perform only those tasks that are mentioned in their endorsement policy of the blockchain network (making it a permissioned blockchain).

3. *Blocks are formed and linked:* Blockchain gets its name from its method of forming blocks from a list of transactions and then linking (or "chaining") the blocks to each other through unique fixed-length strings of characters called *cryptographic hashes*, as shown in Figure 1-6. This is done by computing a hash based on a block's contents, then storing a copy of the previous block's hash, along with its own hash, in the header of each block.

   The hashes reflect the content of the transactions, so if a block's data gets manually changed in the filesystem by tampering or corruption, the hash of the block will no longer match the hash recorded in the next block. Thus any modification to a block can be easily detected. This makes blockchain well suited for creating permanent records and audit trails.

   If a hacker changes a block's contents manually or tries to insert a block mid-chain, it will impact not only that block, but every block after it in the chain. This will impact not only the particular node where the hash got changed but also the entire blockchain network, which makes it easier to find the fraudulent content.

4. *The block's contents are verified:* If the request to add a new block passes all of a node's checks, then the block is added to that node's copy of the blockchain. If the checks are not passed, the new block will be rejected. If your system is programmed in this way, it will then flag the denied request for potential security issues.

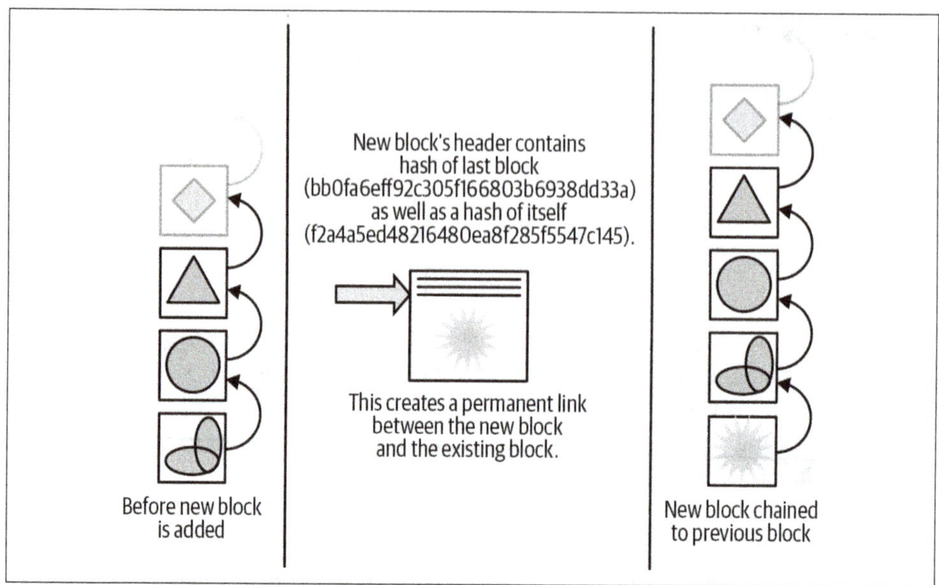
New block's header contains
hash of last block
(bb0fa6eff92c305f166803b6938dd33a)
as well as a hash of itself
(f2a4a5ed48216480ea8f285f5547c145).
This creates a permanent link
between the new block
and the existing block.
Before new block
is added
New block chained
to previous block

Figure 1-6. Blockchain chains blocks of text, and if any of the contents are changed, the chain breaks and the hashes no longer compute to the values stored in the blockchain

As seen in Figure 1-7, blockchain provides each *stakeholder* with their own *nodes*, or copies, of the blockchain so they can be relatively sure the data remains unchanged and that the chain is not broken.

Like any data contained in any filesystem, blockchain can be changed by brute-force hacks or even filesystem corruptions. An individual node could be manipulated by an overzealous AI that wanted to erase its own mistakes, for instance, or by any bad actor that wanted to change history. However, this would be evident to the stakeholders, because the node would no longer work. This is because each block is linked based on content, and in order for an attack to go undetected, all nodes would have to be completely recomputed and redistributed without any stakeholders noticing. This also wouldn't be technically possible without some pretty sophisticated hacking. So the best way to think of it is that blockchain is tamper evident, as it will show any bad activity that happens by going around the application layer.

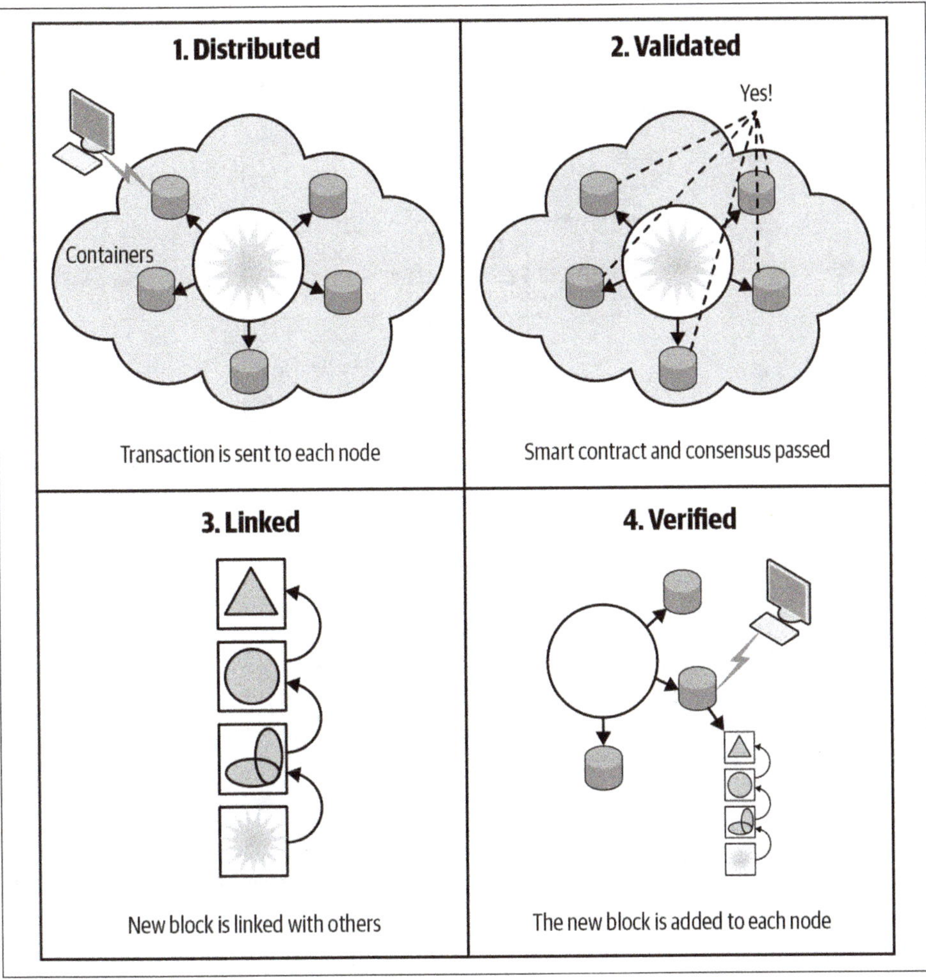
1. Distributed
Containers
Transaction is sent to each node
2. Validated
Yes!
Smart contract and consensus passed
3. Linked
New block is linked with others
4. Verified
The new block is added to each node

Figure 1-7. New blocks are distributed, validated, linked, and added to each node

Trust and Transparency

AI systems are generally not trusted because their form and function are a mystery. Blockchain can bring a single source of truth to AI. The entire lifecycle of AI can be made transparent and traceable to engineers and consumers by adding blockchain to the stack and integrating the workflow of the AI lifecycle with blockchain at critical *touchpoints*, or points of data that make sense to verify later, like items on a factsheet. Recording AI's history in this way will create a tamper-evident, distributed audit trail that can be used as proof of the AI lifecycle, as shown in Figure 1-8.

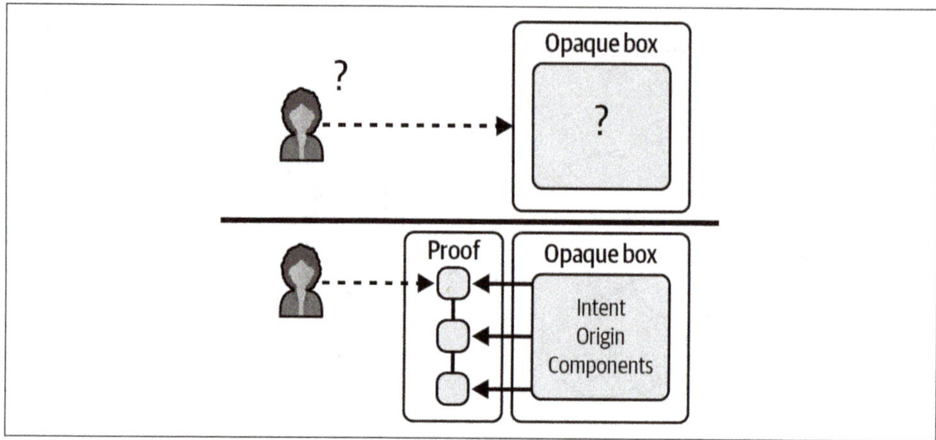

Figure 1-8. Blockchain can be used to take the mystery away from the opaque box that is AI

Using a permissioned blockchain like Hyperledger Fabric, it is possible to design AI to be transparent and traceable without sharing information that should be kept private. Hyperledger Fabric is organized into channels, which can be used to grant permission only to certain parties. This permission granting system is explained in detail in "Defining Your Use Case" on page 31. It is also possible to verify that some information is the same as what was stored in an *off-chain* (not on the blockchain) database and that the computed hash of the information still matches the hash that is stored on the blockchain.

Figure 1-9 shows how an original block of data contains a hash reflecting the contents of that block. The header contains the hash of the previous block's contents: FOB2FOF2096745F1F5184F631F2BC60292F64E76AB7040BE60BC97EBOBB73D64.

And this hash, for the current block's contents: 4BCD77921211F4CF15D8C3573202668543FA32B6CFAD65999E3830356C344D2.

Figure 1-9. The block we're examining contains an image of sunshine in a clear sky

Figure 1-10 shows that even if the slightest change is made to the data stored in the block being inspected, recomputing the algorithm used to create the hash will result in a different hash. If the hashes no longer match, the block should be flagged and the blockchain network will have an error.

Figure 1-10. Later, the same block is tested for tampering or corruption. The block's contents have been tampered with and changed to an image of sunshine on a cloudy day.

The header for Figure 1-10 contains the hash of the previous block's contents: FOB2FOF2096745F1F5184F631F2BC60292F64E76AB7040BE60BC97EBOBB73D64. But the current block's contents are as follows: 191166F725DCAE808B9C750C3534 0E790ABC568B1214AB019FB5BB61EE6A422.

Since blocks are permanently linked by storing the previous block's hash in a new block's header, any filesystem-level changes will be evident. Tampering with content breaks the chain of hashes by causing the next block's header to differ.

A hash cannot be reversed to create the original document or other information that was used when the hash was computed. It can only be used to verify that the current content is the same as when the hash was originally generated, because, as you have seen, if you try regenerating the hash using modified content, you will get a different hash. This characteristic of hashing is known as *one-way*.

Figure 1-11 shows a high-level workflow for an AI project where origin, intent, and components of the AI system need to be proven. They are being recorded on the blockchain so they are traceable.

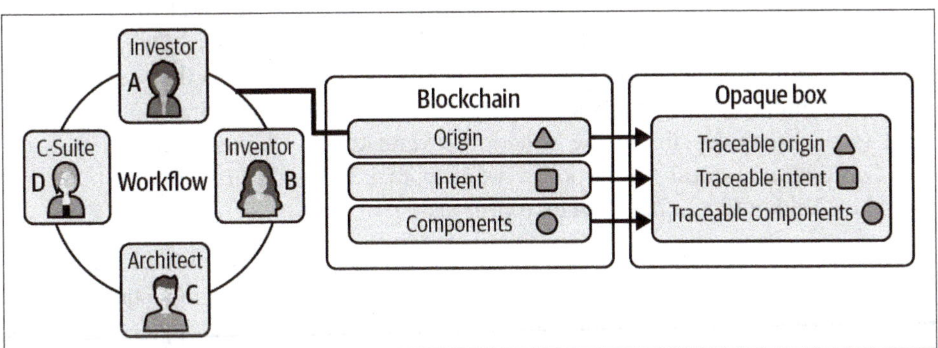

Figure 1-11. Sample stakeholder workflow

In most cases, the information compiled for the blockchain touchpoints would be too much for an average consumer to readily absorb. So in order to be understood, the proofs need to roll into trust logos that break when the components can't be trusted according to the trust organization's standards, as shown in Figure 1-12. The top half of this figure shows an AI implementation with no blockchain. The bottom half of this figure shows an AI implementation where a consumer can use a trust logo backed by blockchain to prove the trustworthiness of the AI.

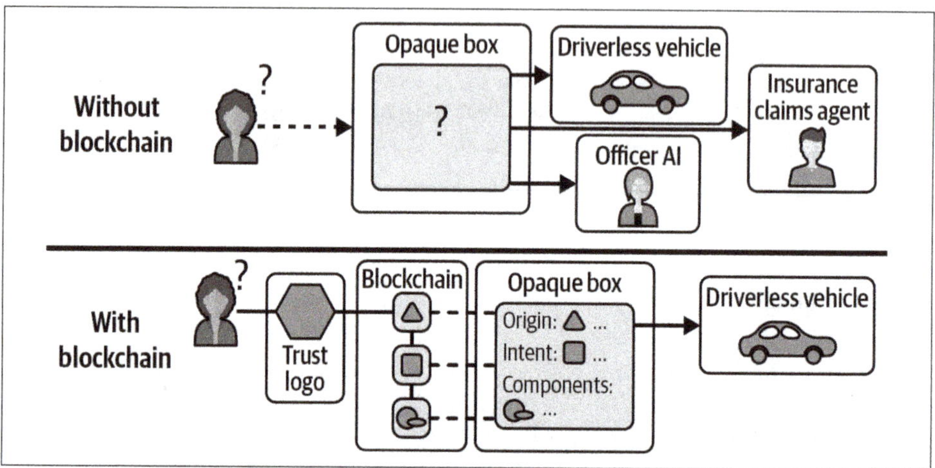

Figure 1-12. AI implementation with and without blockchain

To understand how this proof might work, imagine you are having a bad day, brought to you by AI. You're driving to the office and the car in front of you suddenly brakes (*https://oreil.ly/sobNb*). You slam on your brakes, skid, and crash into the back of the other vehicle. You put your car into park and jump out. As you approach the vehicle you hit, you see that no one was driving. Puzzled, you dial 911 to explain this to the dispatcher, and you reach Officer AI (*https://oreil.ly/_H8pa*). Due to staffing shortages, Officer AI tells you it can only send a human officer to the scene if there are two or more drivers involved. So you call your insurance claims hotline to ask what to do. After explaining the situation several times, Claims Agent AI (*https://oreil.ly/8c6yd*) still doesn't quite know what to make of your situation, and you are placed on hold until a human can take your call.

Do you have the right to know right away that you are talking to an intelligent agent instead of a human being? Can you question someone's humanity in a standard and nonoffensive way? If you question an intelligent agent, can you always escalate to a human being who has the authority to help you, or could you be held to the decisions made by the intelligent agent? Whose fault is the accident in the first place—how will the court assign blame?

Even the people who originally set up the system often don't know what is in there. If enough time has passed they may have forgotten, or others may have done experiments to train the model. Changes could have been made for performance tuning that impact the accuracy of the model, and this would not be known to the originators of the AI. An engineer might use a blockchain audit trail to quickly find the origin of AI, the intent, and what components it is made of and where they were sourced. The blockchain could also reflect things like the last time the system was maintained, whether it has been rated as reliable, and whether any components have been recalled due to safety issues.

Defining Your Use Case

Analyzing your use case is the first step in determining whether or not a certain technology is the right solution for your business. A great way to begin this process for blockchain applications is to determine the participants, assets, and transactions for the case. In Figure 1-13, you can see these three basic elements and how they interrelate.

Participants:
The people or systems that contribute assets or approvals to the blockchain network
Assets:
Things, such as goods or documentation
Transactions:
Actions on assets taken by participants

Figure 1-13. Identifying participants, assets, and transactions for your use case is a first step in planning your blockchain network

Information about participants, assets, and transactions is very helpful when providing project requirements to a developer, along with the business logic that will drive your smart contracts.

Touchpoints

As this chapter touched upon earlier, there are many potential blockchain touchpoints that, when recorded on blockchain, will later help prove the provenance of the AI. Table 1-2 shows a list of potential touchpoints on AI projects. Blockchain touchpoints, or places where blockchain/AI integration makes sense, can be analyzed and identified. Not everything in an AI project has to be stored on blockchain, so identifying touchpoints is a good place to start.

Table 1-2. Blockchain touchpoints for AI projects

Touchpoint	Functionality	Description
Purpose and intended use	Stakeholder workflow	Decisions that implementers and funders made about requirements for AI.
Contacts and identity	Application and blockchain	Identity and roles and permissions for all levels of maintenance and use, including contact information.
Inputs and outputs	Model validation	What input does the AI expect, and what are its anticipated outputs?
Optimal conditions and poor conditions	ML model	A model is optimized for certain conditions and is often known to fail in others.
Security	Security	Firewalls, demilitarized zones, etc. that prevent unauthorized users from gaining access to the other layers.
Fact flow	ML registry or fact flow system	Currently a database, the ML model registry already stores critical information about training methodology, training data, performance, and proper usage.
Training data	ML content	Structured and unstructured data, cleaned up by data scientists and used to train models. In a federated model, this data resides on nodes.
Models and algorithms	ML model	The file that generates predictions based on the ML content. Includes model registration, deployment details, measurements on data drift, and training events.
Dependencies and requirements, vulnerabilities and patches, reviews	MLOps, ML pipeline	Similar to DevOps, MLOps involves updates to the model, content, and training process. MLOps includes management of ML training cycles that involve various ML experiments and content, including reviews by the AI team of the model's performance.
Explanation	ML experiments	Records created by ML experimenters, containing approvals and reasoning for tweaking ML variables that could, for example, improve performance and lower cost, but might impact accuracy.
Feedback and model experience	Intelligent agent	What an intelligent agent does when it is released to production, including feedback from consumers.
Trust logos and requirements	Consumer touchpoint	The part of the intelligent agent that is exposed to the consumer.

Participants

Participants are the people and systems generating transactions within the blockchain network. For example, in a produce supply-chain network the participants might be defined as the following:

- Farmer
- Distributor
- Warehouse manager
- Logistics company representative
- Long-distance trucking company dispatcher
- Automated equipment inside the truck

- Truck driver
- Local delivery truck systems and driver
- Store's dock manager
- Produce department manager

To compare a similar ecosystem in the ML world, the participants might be an AI engineer and an MLOps engineer who act as model validators, and a stakeholder who provides a soundness check to make sure the model stays true to its intent.

Each one of these participants would have an assigned role and permissions to log in to approve or reject the updated model as it is passed from point to point. With a *blockchain tethered AI* (BTA) system like this book describes, the workflow system used by the AI engineer, MLOps engineer and stakeholder would have blockchain incorporated at each step, producing one audit trail to check for anomalies. Here are a few points to consider when validating a model:

Relevancy of the data
: There may be unusual fluctuations in the data entered at each point. Any anomaly would kick off a check-off process to compare each data point to previously acquired data and calculate the standard deviation from the usual averages.

Validation of the data's integrity and appropriateness
: Validate so that the data may be utilized for the intended purpose and in the proper manner. Look at time periods, sources, and missing value computation.

Handling of the data
: Were the collection methods changed from the agreed upon procedure?

Preprocessing
: Were any of the automatic collection methods compromised? Were there any normalization, transformation, or missing value computations that were not performed?

Some helpful tethers you can include on your factsheet and blockchain touchpoints to help you validate your model include the following:

- Business policies behind the workflow, including those consented to and signed off by the governance group
- The expected lifecycle of the model and how it will be taken out of service
- The availability of output data for reporting
- Approvals of training data and cataloging of baseline outputs
- The trade-off between accuracy and explainability
- The procedure or feedback from consumers or authorities

- The procedure to roll back the model
- Contact information for responsible parties

You can include as many participants as needed. Since in business it is not always practical for each participant to have their own node in a blockchain network, the participants may be grouped into logical units called organizations. Multiple participants often share an organization's node. In most business applications, the participants won't even know they are using blockchain.

Assets

An *asset* is a type of tangible good that has some value, and its activity can be recorded on a blockchain. If we built a blockchain application to track vehicle ownership, a car would be an asset. If instead our blockchain tracked individual auto parts, each of those parts would be considered an asset.

In a cryptocurrency application, a digital token used as currency is an asset. A participant can own the currency, see it inside a digital wallet, and transfer the currency to a different participant. In contrast, in a business blockchain application, tangible goods and corresponding documentation are represented as assets, and there is likely no cryptocurrency involved at all.

In our produce supply-chain example, the primary assets are units of produce. When a unit of produce is delivered to the store's loading dock, the asset (produce) is transferred from the truck to the store. This then triggers a traditional payment from the warehouse. All of the other business interactions are also programmed to be tracked.

Other items involved in an exchange, like import/export certificates and money, may also be tracked as assets.

Other considerations when validating models include monitoring the strategy for the model to ensure that scope, objectives, stakeholders, and roles and duties are all addressed, and guaranteeing that the model delivers the expected monetary output and is stable over long periods of time. The frequency and duration of scheduled recalibrations should be assessed. Stakeholders should guarantee that everyone in the governance group is aware of all potential model hazards.

The opaque box nature of the models mean that ML approaches to validation are not widely accepted due to being unable to quantify transparency and explainability, and how the model fits the environment at hand. Once a new model is approved and secured in the test environment, the MLOps engineer must also assess whether the models, including catalogs, modules, and settings, are suitable for deployment, taking into account the potential consequences of future releases.

Transactions

Transactions are generated when participants have some impact on assets. When a participant does something with an asset, a transaction is generated and posted to the blockchain network as this chapter has described. In the case of validating an AI model, we might record a transaction when an AI engineer introduces a new model to the system, when an AI engineer performs some experiment on the new model, or when the AI engineer is satisfied with a newly trained model and it gets passed on to an MLOps engineer. More transactions will be recorded when the MLOps engineer re-creates the experiments, reviews the model, and either sends it back to the AI engineer or approves it for production.

Smart contracts and business logic

Smart contracts are another useful feature of blockchain, as they allow agreements to be pre-programmed, so the proper workflow must be achieved before certain events take place (for example, an invoice must be paid before a product is shipped). Think of smart contracts in terms of how you want your participants to be able to handle assets, and what constitutes a transaction. For instance, let's say an MLOps engineer is chatting with a project stakeholder who is upset about a poor output of a model. The MLOps engineer opens their dashboard and sees the factsheet of the model. The MLOps engineer clicks a button that reads Trace Model, and it is revealed that bias was indeed flagged in the training data by the AI team. In this smart contract's logic, it is stated that the AI engineer, the MLOps engineer, and the stakeholder have to approve moving forward with data sets with known bias, else the model is not allowed to advance through the ML pipeline. The smart contract states that the model must return to the AI engineer for fresh training data before proceeding to production, so until that happens and the AI engineer signs off again, the model will not proceed to the MLOps engineer for testing. Because the smart contract and the transactions are recorded on the blockchain, the MLOps engineer can quickly pinpoint the reasons why the model might be perceived to be inaccurate and provide verification to the stakeholders. Without a system like this, the team could spend a lot of time trying to track down the reason for any inaccurate output.

When agreements are automated with smart contracts, so long as they have been properly programmed, it causes systems to apply agreements in a fair, unbiased, and consistent way. MLOps should improve as a result, since paper or emailed contracts and guidelines often sit in a file unenforced, while the individuals running the day-to-day operations set the actual procedures as they go. Smart contracts make all parties more aware of, and accountable to, their formal business agreements, even when they are highly complex.

Blockchain also offers zero-knowledge proofs, which allow a party to prove they know certain information without actually disclosing it. Blockchain, by its nature, helps enforce rules and share information that benefits the greater good of the community using it.

Audit Trail

AI models aggregate information and learn from it, morphing their own behavior and influencing their own environments. Blockchain can be used to permanently track the steps leading up to the change in output, becoming a memory bank for the models.

In Kush R. Varshney's self-published 2022 book, *Trustworthy Machine Learning* (*https://oreil.ly/D0wGB*), the author (*https://oreil.ly/INcX2*) suggests that AI factsheets be implemented on blockchain to provide a distributed provenance that shows tampering; implementation is beyond the scope of his book. You may discover that the possibilities are nearly limitless since the fact flow system can gather input or approvals from any number of people, systems, or devices and weigh the input or approvals against business logic contained in smart contracts, to dynamically produce a current factsheet upon request.

Some of the information included in Varshney's factsheets is also stored in ML registries, databases that hold key-value pairs about the ML. Some MLOps systems use the ML registries in MLOps workflow.

Blockchain can influence the integrity of intelligent agents in the same way it helps groups of people who don't necessarily trust one another to be able to conduct business in a transparent and traceable way. Since tampering with the blocks will immediately expose bad human actors, it will do the same to AI that acts in a malicious or sloppy way.

Local Memory Bank

Without any memory bank full of facts and experiences, there is no standard way for AI to recall why it has become the way it is. This would be akin to every event in your life changing you, while leaving you unable to remember any specific events or why they influenced you. Instead of figuring out what is best based on what went wrong, you are instead forced to keep trying experiments until you hit the right combination again.

A blockchain audit trail for AI is similar to a human memory in that it can help to re-create what took place, so you are better prepared to try to reverse the undesired result, which could be due to an incident such as bias, drift, an attack, machine failure, or human error.

By deploying the trained AI model in the same computing instance as its corresponding blockchain, you can give the model a local blockchain node—a low-latency, highly available, tamper-evident single source of truth in which to store facts—which can work even when the model is offline and could otherwise not reach the blockchain network.

Shared Memory Bank

Once the blockchain node for the model goes online, it connects to the blockchain network via the API, or Representational State Transfer (REST) proxy. Then it can broadcast its transactions to other nodes. This is because the REST proxy acts as a transaction manager, maintaining a state machine to keep track of the execution of a transaction. Crashes or errors happening during the execution of the transaction will be dealt with when the REST proxy reconnects.

You can build smart contracts that govern the function of the model based on its shared or local memories of what it is supposed to do combined with current environmental variables. As an example, you could program in something that said if the model misbehaves *X* number of times, then it has to take itself out of service until a new training and approval happens.

Four Controls

The AI trust challenges and blockchain touchpoints can be broken down into four types of blockchain controls:

Control 1: pre-establishing identity and workflow criteria for people and systems
: This control can be used with AI to verify that data and models have not undergone tampering or corruption.

Control 2: distributing tamper-evident verification
: This control can be used with AI to make sure that the right people, systems, or intelligent agents—with the right authorization—are the only ones that participate in governance of or modification to the AI.

Control 3: governing, instructing, and inhibiting intelligent agents
: This will become very important when wanting to trace or reverse AI, or prove in court that the output of AI is traceable to certain people or organizations.

Control 4: showing authenticity through user-viewable provenance
: This will be especially important in using branded AI that has underlying components which come from distributed marketplaces.

Chapter 2 takes a deep dive into the four categories of blockchain controls and how they are applied.

Case Study: Oracle AIoT and Blockchain

Blockchain is a newcomer to the AI space. Bill Wimsatt, senior director of Oracle Cloud Engineering, talked with us about how his company is using blockchain in the AI stack. Oracle, a pioneer in Internet of Things (IoT) technology, combines IoT with AI to create artificial intelligence of things (AIoT). This is to better serve some Oracle customers who are working with expensive equipment like gigantic transformers. It is helpful for them to see a roster of all of their key equipment along with the output of a statistical model that predicts when the parts might die or blow up. Wimsatt and the team at Oracle have collaborated with these customers to build models to predict when they should be doing service. For example, maybe early maintenance is needed, or maybe the asset can last longer. In its analysis, AIoT also considers any missed or false alarms, and can not only prevent equipment failures due to lack of maintenance but also optimize work and service orders.

Wimsatt said, "We use AIoT for predictive maintenance and signal capture; by combining AI with the IoT devices we can learn what is happening with equipment, and find different ways to use signals. This helps our customers to not only make sure the asset doesn't fail, but that they can *sweat the asset* for as long as possible."

Sweat the asset is a term to indicate that the owner of an asset has squeezed the longest possible lifecycle out of it before replacement. Typically, these IoT assets are on maintenance and replacement schedules, and these things occur whether the equipment needs it or not. This can lead to millions of dollars wasted on unnecessary maintenance. AIoT can help to make better predictions on how long each individual asset may last based on its metrics, which saves large amounts of money because assets last longer than scheduled.

Blockchain has been added to Oracle's AIoT stack to validate signal capture at the point of transmission. Then their customers can cross-check the data that is captured into an object store against the blockchain validation. Because a sample of their data is distributed and stored in interlocking blocks, they can test to be sure that the training data matches what was captured by the IoT device, and that it has not undergone tampering. This technique aligns with Control 2, "make data and algorithms distributed and tamper-evident." This is discussed in depth in the next chapter.

What's Next?

Could a superintelligent agent with enough general intelligence, or one specialized in a mathematical domain like cryptography, someday figure out that it could still function without blockchain? Could it break out of the bounds provided for it or simply change the immutable data and recalculate all of the hashes without detection by human beings? Quite possibly, but if we build blockchain controls into AI to the point where it won't work without them, we might be able to keep the upper hand.

Learning the four controls and how to apply them, as explored in depth in Chapter 2, will give you the ability to offer your stakeholders a mechanism for providing a single source of truth, and even a human-only backdoor, for the AI systems that you build for them.

CHAPTER 2

Blockchain Controls for AI

As you learned in Chapter 1, there are a wide variety of potential blockchain touchpoints for AI. However, nearly every process can be traced and verified by implementing one of the four controls explored in this chapter. You will learn to plan and implement each control by determining potential AI scenarios for each and explaining how it might be addressed using Hyperledger Fabric.

Four Blockchain Controls

When approaching your AI factsheet and thinking about how you might design a fact flow system around it, you may find that thinking of your architecture in terms of these four categories of controls simplifies your planning. Table 2-1 illustrates these four controls and shows how they are tied together by governance. The four blockchain controls for AI—pre-establishing identity and workflow, distributing tamper-evident verification, governing, instructing and inhibiting intelligent agents, and showing authenticity through user-viewable provenance—are interwoven. Governance, in the form of bylaws, smart contracts and consent, overlaps them all.

Table 2-1. The four blockchain controls for AI

Control	Impacts	Description
Control 1: pre-establishing identity and workflow criteria for people and systems	Participants, assets, and transactions	Includes criteria for telling humans apart from AI
Control 2: distributing tamper-evident verification	Databases, models, libraries, federated AI	Tests data against a cryptographic hash to detect and expose anomalies
Control 3: governing, instructing, and inhibiting intelligent agents	Production AI	Track, trace, and monitor AI; ensure the ability to monitor and stop it
Control 4: showing authenticity through user-viewable provenance	End users, engineers	Consumers of AI can see its history even if the AI is embedded in cars, robots, virtual reality, etc.

Control 1 deals with identity and workflow, since that is the foundation for all of the other controls.

Blockchain Control 1: Pre-establishing Identity and Workflow Criteria for People and Systems

Blockchain systems typically require that criteria such as identity verification, business logic, and so on be met before blocks are added to the chain. Control 1 can be used with AI to make sure that the right people, systems, or intelligent agents (participants)—with the right authorization—are the only ones that take part in governance of or modification to the AI.

In order to be able to establish provenance for AI, start by establishing the identity of the initial stakeholders: the project owner(s), a consortium, and/or a governance group.

Before diving into digital identity management in blockchain, consider why you need to have a trustworthy identity of the participants, including the AI and MLOps engineers who train the model. You probably have concerns about trained AI models, including who trained the model, their background or profile, and how it was trained. This section explores why it is important to be able to trace the identity of people who train AI models and prove their credibility.

To make sure the right person has trained the model, you need to bind their identity with the blockchain by registering the person in the blockchain network, which provides a digital identity signed by their organization's certificate authority. The identity is used to sign, endorse, or commit transactions during the lifecycle of the AI model, as mentioned earlier. So the engineer who performs any activities in the application gets logged into the blockchain, which means stakeholders can verify each engineer's identity and their work. Their identity is conjoined with their own block changes. It cannot be extracted, spoofed, or overwritten by another party without being flagged. As a result, the human engineer cannot go back and deny involvement, and if AI changes its own code or data, AI can't deny it either.

The different participants in the blockchain network include resources like peers, orderers, client application, administration interface, and so on. These participants get digital identity encapsulated in X.509 digital certificates. This digital identity is very important to determine the participant's access to the available resources.

Establishing Identity

Any identity may be supplied to the blockchain network for resource access, but does it get verified? Only the identity coming from a trusted source can be verified. Hyperledger Fabric's Membership Service Provider (MSP) is a trusted source. MSP is a fabric component that deals with cryptographic mechanisms and protocols behind issuing certificates, validating certificates, and authenticating users. MSP uses a *public key infrastructure* (PKI) hierarchical model that facilitates secure communication in the network.

PKI *issues* verifiable certificates, whereas MSP has the list of verified certificates so when a certificate comes over the network for the verification, MSP *checks* whether it's on its list. If it's on the list, the certificate is verified. Otherwise, it's not.

PKI has four essential elements: digital certificates, public and private keys, certificate authorities, and certificate revocation lists.

Digital certificates

A digital certificate holds a set of attributes about the holder of the certificate which is also compliant in the X.509 standard. This stores the basic info of the holder, subject, public key, validity, serial number, signature, and so on.

Public and private keys

Authentication and message integrity are important concepts in secure communication. While exchanging the message between two parties, the message sender signs the message using their private key, which is verified at the receiver's end using the sender's public key. If the message is tampered with during transmission, then the key doesn't match. In this way, a private key is used to produce the digital signature.

Certificate authorities (CAs)

A participant in the blockchain network can take part in the transaction and is known to other participants of the network by means of their digital identity, which is issued by each organization's CA. The CA has the right to dispense certificates to different participants. These certificates are digitally signed by the CA and bind the participant with the participant's public key. So when the participant sends a transaction for the endorsement in the blockchain network, the participant's certificate issued by the CA and public key are written to the transaction and sent to other nodes, where legitimacy is verified by comparing the signature from the CA with the associated public key. There are two kinds of CAs: root certificate authority (RCA) and intermediate certificate authority (ICA):

Root certificate authority
: A blockchain network can have multiple RCAs issued for different organizations, and the RCA assigned for an organization can sign thousands of other certificates. But signing all participants' certificates by the RCA is a time-consuming task and is less secure as well, so to reduce the load and spread the work, ICAs are created. If the certificate fields `issued to` and `issued from` have the same values, then the certificate is considered signed by the RCA.

Intermediate certificate authority

ICAs are used to spread out the process across the network. An ICA has certificates issued by RCAs or other ICAs. An ICA can sign the certificate of another ICA, and so on, which ultimately can create a chain of trust. If we trace back the signature made in each certificate, we finally reach the RCA, so we can say each certificate is signed by the RCA through the ICA, without exposing its own identity. In this way, the RCA is not directly exposed to all ICAs, which is beneficial from a security point of view, as shown in Figure 2-1.

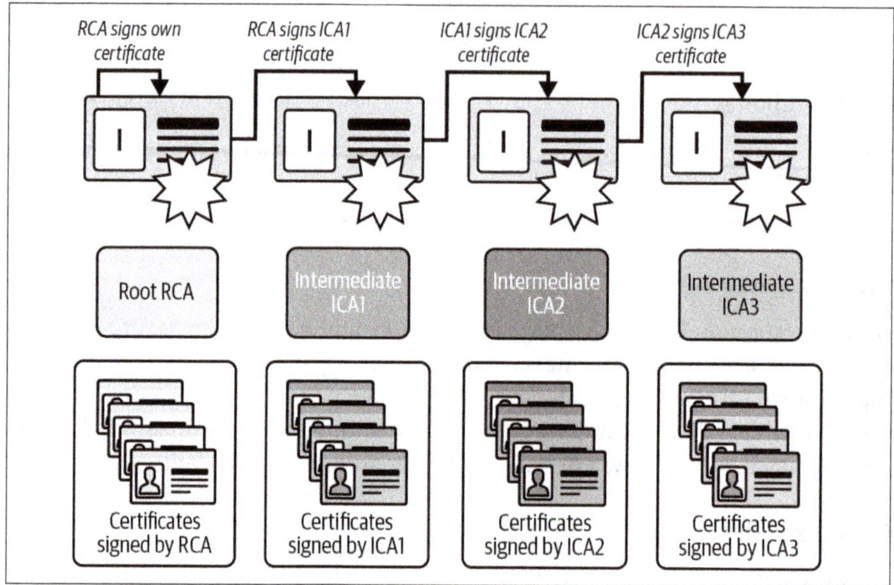

Figure 2-1. RCA/ICA signing certificates. Adapted from an image in the Hyperledger Fabric documentation (https://oreil.ly/HKRFJ).

Certificate revocation lists (CRLs)

The revocation list (illustrated in Figure 2-2) in a permissioned blockchain such as Fabric helps stakeholders know the participants whose permission is revoked because of their suspicious activities. So when such a participant tries to perform an action in the network, their certificate is cross-checked with the CRL. If it gets passed from there, it can perform activities there; otherwise, the participant will be blocked from performing any action in the network.

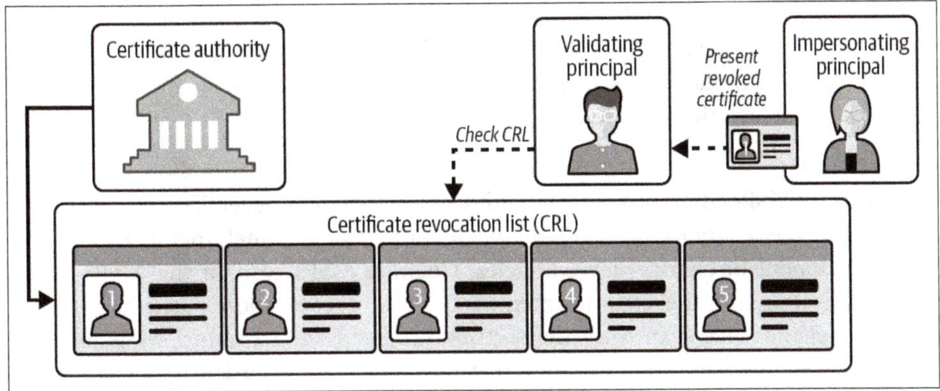

Figure 2-2. Hyperledger Fabric revocation list. Adapted from an image in the Hyperledger Fabric documentation (https://oreil.ly/YAvfg).

Membership Service Provider (MSP)

When a participant gets an identity in the network, the participant gets public and private keys issued by the CA. Private keys cannot be shared in public, so you need a standard mechanism to validate the participant. Fabric provides this mechanism in the form of an MSP. As Figure 2-3 shows, identities are similar to credit cards used to prove a customer can make a payment. The MSP is akin to the list of credit cards accepted by the merchant. A participant digitally signs or endorses or commits a transaction using a private key. The MSP in the ordering service contains a list of permissioned public keys of the participants, which is used to verify the signature on endorsement or transaction and validate.

Figure 2-3. Identities are similar to credit cards, while the MSP is similar to a seller's list of accepted credit cards. Adapted from an image in the Hyperledger Fabric documentation (https://oreil.ly/sJLZ7).

MSP occurs in two domains—local MSP and channel MSP:

Local MSP
: Local MSPs are defined for clients and nodes (peers and orderers). Local MSPs define the permissions for nodes, such as which admins can operate the nodes. A local MSP allows the user to authenticate itself in its transaction as a member of a

channel. An organization can own one or more nodes. A person can be an admin in multiple nodes, as defined by the MSP. An organization, node, and admin should have the same root of trust. That means if you backtrack all the CAs, they all should reach the same RCA.

Channel MSP
: Channel MSPs identify who has authority at a channel level. The channel MSP defines the *relationship* between the identities of channel members and the enforcement of channel-level policies. Channel MSPs contain the MSPs of the organizations of the channel members. Every organization participating in a channel must have an MSP defined for it. The system channel MSP includes the MSPs of all the organizations that participate in an ordering service. Local MSPs are only defined on the filesystem of the node or user. Channel MSP is also instantiated on the filesystem of every node in the channel and kept synchronized via consensus.

Figure 2-4 shows how a common channel is used to share data across two different organizations where the network system channel is administered by ORG1, Peer is managed by ORG2, and Orderer is managed by ORG1. ORG1 trusts identities from RCA1, and ORG2 trusts identities from RCA2.

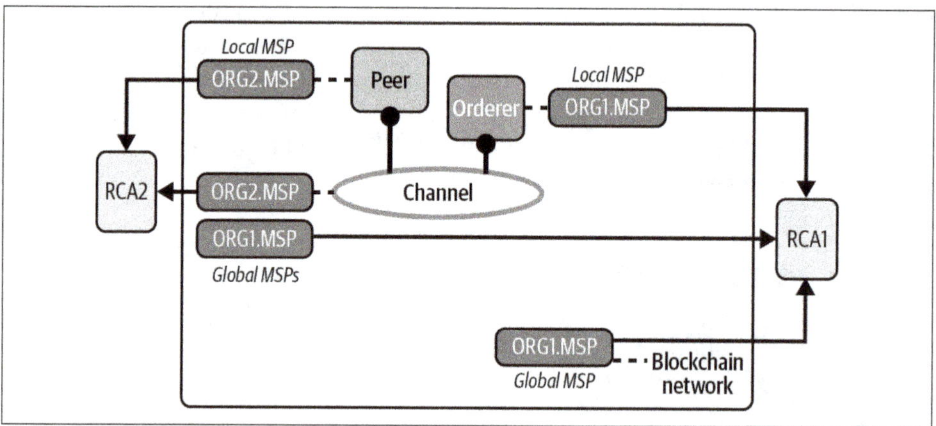

Figure 2-4. Local and channel MSPs. Adapted from an image in the Hyperledger Fabric documentation (https://oreil.ly/rW6G-).

Each organization is a logical, managed group of members where identities are managed in the MSP. This is called an *organization unit* (OU). The OU often represents a separate line of business and also has a line in the OU configuration file which can be later used in policy making to restrict the access through a smart contract.

Another important component of the OU is the Node OU, which configures the identities and is defined in the YAML file *$FABRIC_CFG_PATH/msp/config.yaml.*

This YAML file contains the OU whose members are considered to be part of the organization represented by this MSP.

The following configuration, Example 2-1, shows Node OU roles in the MSP, including `client`, `peer`, `admin`, and `orderer`.

Example 2-1. Configuration showing Node OU roles in the MSP

```
NodeOUs:
  Enable: true
  ClientOUIdentifier:
    Certificate: cacerts/ca.sampleorg-cert.pem
    OrganizationalUnitIdentifier: client
  PeerOUIdentifier:
    Certificate: cacerts/ca.sampleorg-cert.pem
    OrganizationalUnitIdentifier: peer
  AdminOUIdentifier:
    Certificate: cacerts/ca.sampleorg-cert.pem
    OrganizationalUnitIdentifier: admin
  OrdererOUIdentifier:
    Certificate: cacerts/ca.sampleorg-cert.pem
    OrganizationalUnitIdentifier: orderer
```

The OU roles and their keys are normally included in the *config.yaml* file.

When you drill down on the digitally signed certificate, Example 2-2 shows how it looks and what it includes.

Example 2-2. Drill down into a digitally signed certificate. Adapted from an image in the Hyperledger Fabric documentation (https://oreil.ly/BfXtQ).

```
Certificate:
  Data
    Version: 3 (0x2)
    Serial Number:
      45:6a:4f:01:de:fj:5d:b2:94:18:79:91:26:31:d8:0e:b0:9b:6b:88
  Signature Algorithm: ecdsa-with-SHA256
    Issuer: C=US, ST=New York, O=Hyperledger, OU=Fabric, CN=fabric-ca-server
    Validity
      Not Before: Nov 20 22:13:00 2019 GMT
      Not After : Nov 19 22:18:00 2020 GMT
    Subject: OU=peer, OU=ORG1, OU=DISTRIBUTION, CN=user1 ❶
.
.
.
    X509v3 extensions:
      X509v3 Key Usage: critical
        Digital Signature
      X509v3 Basic Constraints: critical
        CA: FALSE
```

```
        X509v3 Subject Key Identifier:
          17:B0:9B:29:42:F6:44:E0:7D:02:C6:78:96:2D:97:14:7A:D7:FC:CA
        X509v3 Authority Key Identifier:
          keyid:DC:91:B7:85:A4:37:66:D0:D2:B7:62:A9:3F•59:83:D6:EB:01=E8:80
1.234.5.6.7.8.1:

        {" attrs": {"hf.Affiliation":"ORG1.DISTRIBUTION",
        "hf.EnrollmentID":"user1","hf.Type":"peer"} } ❷
```

❶ `OU=peer` is the role (Node OU), `OU=ORG1, OU=DISTRIBUTION` is the organizational unit, and `CN=user1` is the enroll ID.

❷ `"hf.Affiliation":"ORG1.DISTRIBUTION"` is the organizational unit, `"hf.EnrollmentID":"user1"` is the enroll ID, and `"hf.Type":"peer"` is the role (Node OU).

Shown in Figure 2-5 and the list that follows, the MSP folder contains critical certificates and config files.

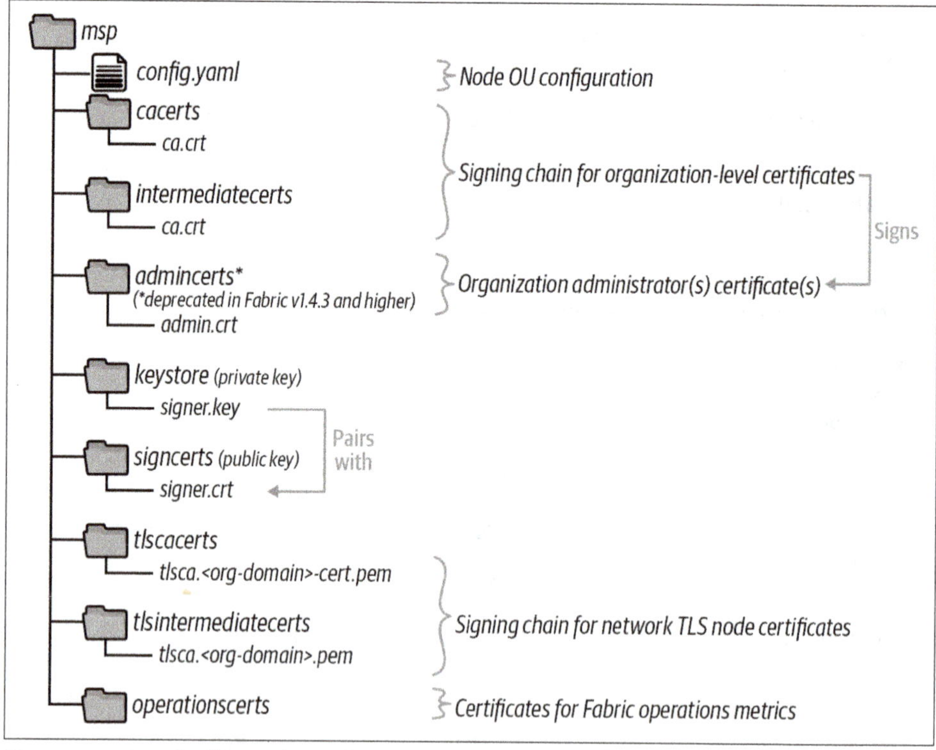

Figure 2-5. Config files and certificates in the MSP folder. Adapted from an image in the Hyperledger Fabric documentation (https://oreil.ly/BfXtQ).

config.yaml
: Enables Node OU and defines the roles.

cacerts
: Contains a list of self-signed X.509 certificates of the RCAs trusted by the organization represented by this MSP. There must be one RCA certificate in the MSP folder.

intermediatecerts
: This folder contains a list X.509 certificates of the ICAs trusted by this organization. The ICA may represent different organization units such as `MANUFACTURING` or `DISTRIBUTION`.

admincerts
: This folder contains the list of identities of participants who have the role of admin for this organization. *admincert* is depreciated from V1.4.3, and in later releases, the admin role is defined in the Node OU by enabling the "identity classification" option.

keystore
: This folder is defined for the local MSP of peer or orderer which contains only one private key of the node to sign the transaction proposal response, as part of the endorsement process.

signcerts
: This folder contains the node's certificate issued by CA. This folder is mandatory for the local MSP, which contains exactly one public key.

tlscacerts
: This folder contains a list of self-signed X.509 certificates of the RCAs trusted by this organization for secure communications between nodes using TLS.

tlsintermediatecacerts
: This folder contains a list of ICAs trusted by the organization, represented by this MSP for secure communication between nodes using TLS.

operationscerts
: This folder contains certificates that are used by the Fabric Operations Service API for operations metrics.

Predetermining Workflow Among Participants

Chapter 1 discussed what sort of workflow takes place in the creation and handling of an AI system. Since blockchain is the single source of truth for your AI, it is important to have all of your workflow mapped out and to design your system in such a way that workflow can be changed by system administrators, because it will likely change often.

Think back to the Chapter 1 discussion of participants, assets, and transactions, and apply this to the workflow involved in generating the AI model. Table 2-2 shows examples of functionality found in an AI-driven web application, where that functionality is a breakdown of the relative participants, assets, and transactions, and the blockchain controls that can be used.

Table 2-2. Examples of participants, assets, and transactions typically found in an AI-driven web application (by functionality)

Functionality	Hosting and/or storage	Participants	Assets	Example transactions	Blockchain control(s)
Web application layer	In the filesystem of the container *or* Code in repository	Web application developers, DevOps engineers, stakeholders	HTML, CSS, databases, filesystems	An application developer makes changes to code and those changes are approved by a stakeholder and deployed to production by DevOps or continuous deployment processes	1. Workflow and identity 2. Tamper evident
AI layer	On network devices	AI engineers, MLOps engineers, stakeholders	Model	MLOps engineer inspects model, artifacts for reproducibility, experiments, and project integrity and approves model for deployment	1. Workflow and identity 2. Tamper evident
ML content	In object store with verification hashes on the blockchain *or* On chain	AI engineers, MLOps engineers, DevOps engineers, database administrators, AI agents	Structured data, unstructured data, databases, tables, libraries, hosts, servers, containers	AI engineer introduces data set; DevOps updates server software; database admin updates data set	1. Workflow and identity 2. Tamper evident

You can expand this table to add functionality and touchpoints for your particular system.

ML pipeline and MLOps

Perhaps the most workflow-intensive area in AI is the ML pipeline, in which models are created, enhanced, and deployed by developers, data scientists, and DevOps.

While it is in the ML pipeline, the prediction problem to be solved is *operationalized* (broken down into meaningful components) and the model is *trained* (influenced with data) and further improved with experiments. Then, system administrators and deployment specialists use traditional DevOps techniques to push the container housing the model live.

In Figure 2-6, blockchain, along with a workflow system, is used to enforce governance of a retrained model that no longer meets established requirements and to record an audit trail of the process. In this example, the trained AI model is represented by a rectangle, while the model's output is represented by either a circle or a triangle; however, stakeholders have previously declared that the output must be a circle or a star. The new version is rejected by the AI team because it outputs a triangle, when only circles and stars are allowed. This keeps the incorrect model from moving forward into production.

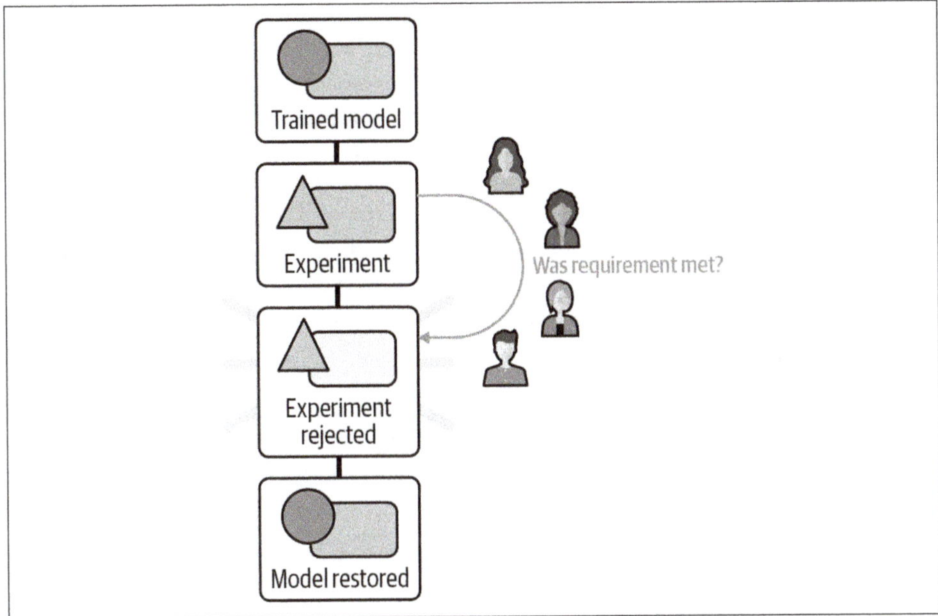

Figure 2-6. Example of how the work of an AI team might be tracked on blockchain

Created to automate this process, *MLOps* is a modern methodology that combines the ML pipeline with continuous integration and continuous deployment (CI/CD). MLOps uses a process similar to traditional DevOps to manage and deploy code, with special steps added for ML projects.

MLOps provides a formalized, automated framework for the steps used to train, deploy, and improve a model. A high-level look at the steps used to validate the model is shown in Figure 2-7.

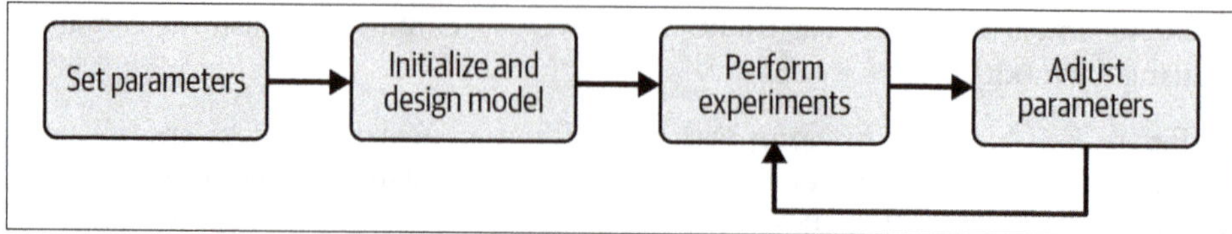

Figure 2-7. The high-level model validation steps from the ML pipeline

Even using MLOps, it is tough to trace the ML *provenance*, which is a record of the journey the AI has taken to get where it is at. Often the ML experiments are run for many iterations on a massive number of nodes, and only models with the desired traits are included in those that go to production.

In the current trend of training AI models, different MLOps methodologies are used to train the model, where logs of each and every activity of a data scientist are recorded in a certain database. Once a training session is completed, the tool locks the metadata and artifacts of the training so one can trace back the history. But again, the whole system is based on a centralized system where a programmer can easily reach and change the content from the database. There is thus a problem in maintaining provenance of a model or data set. Blockchain can be a problem solver for this kind of issue, wherein each stakeholder gets their own node that stores logs of trained models. Only that person has access to the node, and no one can modify it (not even that person).

Figure 2-8 shows an example of a high-level model validation workflow as implemented in the BTA you will build in the exercises. Chapter 5 explores this workflow in depth as we build the model validator example for our blockchain tethered AI project.

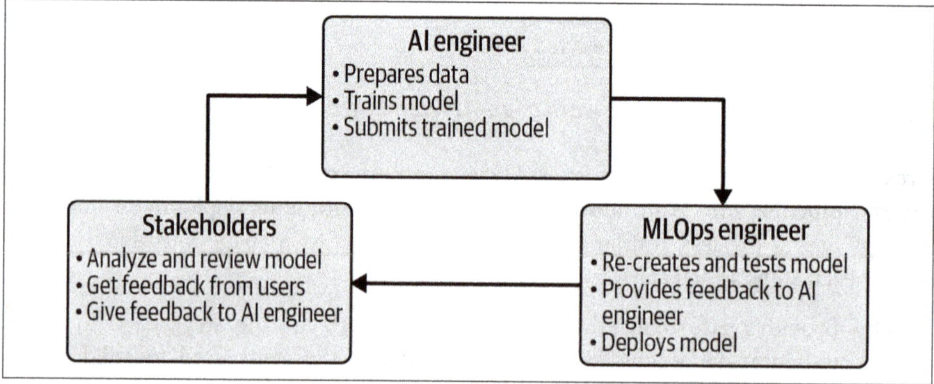

Figure 2-8. High-level model validation workflow to be implemented in BTA exercises

Data cleaning and bias reduction

Data cleaning and AI bias are related issues because bias is often baked into ML training data. This section examines the far-reaching bias problem, as well as some possible approaches for identifying and correcting it by leaving a traversable audit trail that helps people to pinpoint and even reverse the bias.

Bias comes in many forms, and everyone has some biases. One of the first steps in combating bias is to have a clear organizational culture, including guidelines that address bias. However, the bigger issue lies in the data and the algorithms, because if these are biased by nature, even the most well-intended AI system can turn bad. Part of risk management is managing bias.

There are countless types of biases. *Bias* is the product of someone's environment and conditioning. If someone grows up as a vegetarian, they would likely be biased against meals that contain meat. They might not have ill intentions—they may not realize they have a bias at all. But this bias might surface if they are preparing a data set that recommends healthy meals. Here are some common types of biases encountered in ML:

Social
: Within a culture or society, inequities that are introduced into the input data. Our inherent cognitive biases—over 180 have been classified by psychologists—are the brain's attempt to simplify the vast amount of information being received from its immediate environment.

Classifier
: Also known as representation, this is when there are inadequate, unrepresented, or unrealistic classifications, leaving out portions of a group or demographic.

Data selection
: Underrepresentation of lack of realism can bias training data.

Data preparation
: Inadequate cleaning up or preprocessing of data usually results in inadequate or invalid data.

Automation
: A secondary system failure can feed poor training data to the AI.

Reporting
: The occurrence statistics are misrepresented by multiple orders of magnitude due to unrealistic training data.

Data sabotage
: Purposeful tampering with the data, injecting false information.

Time change

As an example, it is problematic if the time to produce data (the throughput) changes drastically and the model sees "faster" as better, without validating the accuracy of the data.

Data shift

A shift in the distribution of data over time produces bias.

Analyzing the output rather than the algorithms keeps intellectual property confidential in terms of sharing information with the customer, but someone will still need to tweak the model. Figure 2-9 shows the data types to look for (*https://oreil.ly/xHidr*).

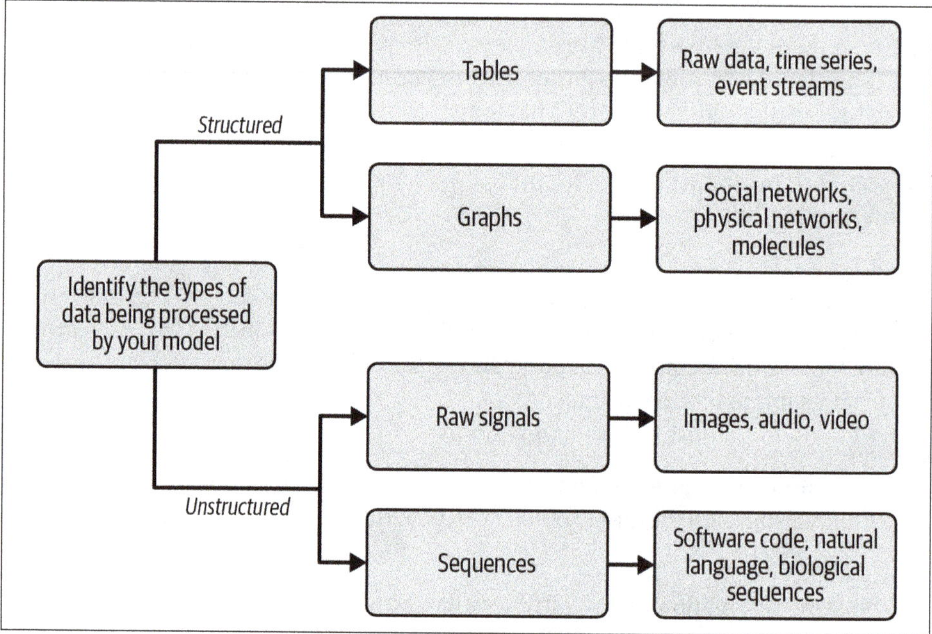

Figure 2-9. Analyzing data begins with identifying the types of data being processed by your model. Adapted from an image in Trustworthy Machine Learning (https://oreil.ly/D0wGB) by Kush R. Varshney.

Here are some best practices for reducing data bias:

- Examine data collection sources. Understand the context in which the data is captured, and then in what contexts AI can correct or exacerbate bias.
- Make sure the training data sets are large enough and taken from all available sources to prevent sampling bias. Analyze whether the algorithms work when used on subsets of the larger population. Monitor results over time—machine learning reveals biases in the output.

- As part of a multidisciplinary strategy to eliminate bias, diversify your organization to get different points of view. This strategy would ideally include ethicists, social scientists, and experts who best understand the nuances of each area of machine learning processes.
- Establish a debiasing policy that includes technical, operational, and organizational strategies. Use a debiasing library from a known source such as Trusted AI (*https://oreil.ly/F625A*). Cultivate data analyzing tools and strive for transparency in policies and operations. This includes improving human-driven processes, which have traditionally driven the creation of models, through process design and cultural training. Then, decide which use cases need human intervention.

Data integrity is the basis for sound machine learning and AI. If your data is tainted in any way, the resulting model will be flawed, and the results of retraining the model will also be tainted. If the data set is incomplete, such as using test data from a small age range or only one gender, the resulting model won't properly represent the real-world data. It is critical that the data set is complete.

Visual recognition AI provides many obvious examples of bias. Flawed results range from the misclassifying and misidentification of a piece of candy as a kitchen tool, dogs as cats or some other mammal, misidentifying a bricked tower as a carrot, or a human as anything but one. In 2020, Harvard University published the results of an audit of five different image recognition technologies (*https://oreil.ly/ZZW5O*), and they all performed poorly when it came to identifying Black women. The National Institute of Standards and Technology (NIST) confirmed these studies across 189 algorithms (*https://oreil.ly/WefV_*): they are least accurate on women of color. Because ML requires both positive and negative examples of the image that is being "learned," it's incumbent upon the data scientist to think of as many things as possible that may look like the image, but are not—such as a wrapped Tootsie Roll being misidentified as a kitchen rolling pin. That covers image recognition, but there are far more complex examples.

Author, technologist, and futurist Jaron Lanier has been quoted in several interviews[1] as saying that, with respect to the internet and particularly social media, the misuse of user data as predictive tools for marketing companies and the subsequent feeding of the response of the same user to marketing efforts by those same companies has pushed the internet into a cycle of manipulation of that user. The third-party internet

1 See his 2018 lecture "How the Internet Failed and How to Recreate It" (*https://oreil.ly/n6838*) or his 2013 talk "Who Owns the Future?" (*https://oreil.ly/rRMFv*) for examples.

company hosting the marketing is just a platform providing "information" and "social interaction" for the user.

But what's really happening is that the user is being manipulated to respond to negative information (words, images) over and over again by playing on their emotions with incendiary content and peppering that with occasional positive feedback to keep the user addicted ("influenced," social media content creators like to say) to the content playing in a similar sequence of events. With *confirmation bias* (agreement with a group), a user will get a dopamine hit from the response and keep coming back. The user seeks and finds information that confirms their viewpoint over and over, getting more and more satisfaction from using social media. It all creeps in so slowly, the user doesn't realize it until someone's bugging them to put down their phone while they're at the dinner table. Attractive content on a convenient device captures the user's attention, and the AI model keeps them engaged. Then the model observes and harvests their reactions so ML can fine-tune its approach.

What happens when AI fails to properly (or at least, confidently) identify a known object because personal, unconscious biases prevent the developer from creating adequate training data sets? What happens when AI has been inadequately trained and is only able to confidently identify a relatively small subset of known variations on that object instead of the full breadth of variations? A comprehensive list of biases (*https://oreil.ly/YUUV8*) was published by Marcus Lu in February 2020. In addition to confirmation bias, he lists 49 more cognitive biases that are commonly found on social media, including the Dunning-Kruger effect and belief bias.

The Role of Smart Contracts

Smart contracts are defined in Chapter 1 and explored in depth in Chapter 3, but they bear mentioning again here. Smart contracts, when used as a controller for an application's workflow, help determine what business logic must be executed before certain actions are recorded on blockchain. For instance, the BTA system you assemble in this book's exercises routes an approval on a new model from an AI engineer to an MLOps engineer before a model is deployed. This type of business logic smart contract interacts with the smart contract that exists at the blockchain level, which checks for consensus and writes blocks to the blockchain, or rejects them.

The *Dunning-Kruger effect* goes something like this: the less you know, the more you think you know because you're filling in the blanks with your own guesses, and the more you know, the less you think you know because you find out that you were wrong in so many ways. *Belief bias* is when we judge the strength of an argument based on how plausible the conclusion is in our minds rather than how strongly it supports the conclusion. Looking at the bias list, there are a number of other biases that might play out in a scenario where participants are making policy or operations decisions and signing them on smart contracts, but their decisions are not sound.

Blockchain Control 2: Distributing Tamper-Evident Verification

Blockchain is *tamper evident*. This means if someone or something changes any of the data by brute force, computing the same hash becomes impossible, which makes the unauthorized changes apparent. Remember that blockchain, which stores verification hashes for data as a series of timestamped, linked units called *blocks*, is a peer-to-peer network that can be shared among multiple stakeholders.

Control 2 can be used with AI to verify that data and algorithms have not undergone tampering or corruption, as analyzed in Table 2-3.

Table 2-3. A breakdown of participants, assets, and transactions for a pre-production model

Functionality	Hosting and/or storage	Participants	Assets	Example transactions	Blockchain control(s)
Pre-production model	In repository with hashes on blockchain	Developers, DevOps, AI agents	Model/ algorithms, repositories, hosts, code origins, contributors, release notes, patches, certifications	Create code, update code, delete code, create new release, receive updates to federated model	1. Workflow and identity 2. Tamper evident

Using Crypto Anchors to Verify Data Sets, Models, and Pipelines

As mentioned earlier in "Establishing Identity" on page 42, the validity of anything on blockchain is only as good as the identity methods associated with the participants and assets. Identity is the foundation upon which all of the transactions are assumed to be authentic—if identity is not robust, then the entire blockchain is in question. Crypto anchors are a way to tie the physical identity of a participant or asset to their digital identity in a way that can be verified.

Hardware items typically have some sort of a unique identifier associated with them, such as an engraved serial number like a vehicle identification number (VIN) on a car. Other goods are more difficult to uniquely identify—for instance, honey or diamonds. These don't come with a unique identifier, but instead have unique characteristics. For example, if honey is watered down during the supply chain voyage, its molecular structure will no longer look the same when examined microscopically. Since crypto anchors are digital, it is possible to create a cryptographic signature of a specimen of honey from a hash of the microscope's output and store it on blockchain, making every block containing every transaction in the supply chain journey carry the signature of the molecular structure of the original product.

Crypto anchors sound more complex than they are. You can easily create a crypto anchor by creating a hash of facts aggregated with a unique identifier, make that crypto anchor the contents of a block (it could be the *genesis,* or very first, block in a blockchain), and every block after will be signed with it. Some suggestions for AI crypto anchors are shown in Table 2-4.

Table 2-4. Ideas for using crypto anchors to tether AI systems

Crypto anchor target	Crypto anchor contents
Training data set	A timestamped hash of data facts, including size, characteristics, and architecture, along with the MAC ID
Model	A timestamped hash of model facts, the model's digital identity from X.509 digital certificates, and the hardware information such as a serial number of the part in which AI is embedded
Pipeline	A timestamped hash of network facts, such as the location of the data center, the type of resources used, and network security policies

To tell if digital content has been modified or if the hardware has changed, you can build a verifier that recomputes the crypto anchor and checks it against the value stored on blockchain.

Using Blockchain to Detect Common AI Hacks

As Chapter 1 addressed, AI models, like any other systems, are subject to hacks and attacks. Common attacks on AI include adversarial data attacks, like poisoning and evasion attacks, as well as model stealing and impersonation attacks. All of the normal security concerns are of consideration, plus a host of new threats on account of the extra steps and mystery of origin involved in ML and the ability for models to change based on input. The following list explains some of the most common hacks from Chapter 1, along with ideas on how to use the blockchain verification to prevent or expose them:

Poisoning attack

Since this attack involves malicious data changing the classifier, one way to prevent a poisoning attack would be to create a smart contract that monitors for classifier mismatches. This could be done by locking down the list of permissible classifiers for data with certain characteristics in a separate channel, so the ML can inquire to blockchain to see if something is permitted without seeing the list of what is permitted.

A poisoning attack could be exposed in a similar way by detecting when a data set has been poisoned and red-flagging it on blockchain as unsuitable for use. The last good data set could be found by reviewing previous data sets that were verified as valid and rerunning the training from the last good set.

Evasion attack

Since this attack distorts production system test samples to push data points beyond the decision boundary, one way to prevent it is to make sure your samples come from a reliable source. For instance, if you are using the Windows ML Samples Gallery (*https://oreil.ly/vrSge*) you will want to record that source as authentic on blockchain, and make sure your MLOps flow checks blockchain before checking samples.

You can flag this type of attack by recording any attempts to use data sets that are not listed on blockchain.

Model stealing

Because the model is stolen and re-created elsewhere in this type of attack, making your models fully dependent on their blockchain node would break this method, since the attacker could not spoof the required blockchain node.

Alerts of attempts to steal models could be monitored by alerting for outside attempts to probe for blockchain nodes.

Impersonation attack

Samples such as faceprints or fingerprints of victims are replaced with wrong samples, allowing unauthorized access to any number of systems. If the original account owner records biometrics to blockchain, then those biometrics can be compared historically to any new biometrics, and any anomalies can be flagged for intervention.

Using blockchain, it would be impossible for the attacker to get rid of the original biometrics.

You might not be able to prevent all attacks immediately, but having a methodology like blockchain verification to chip away at them will give you a more robust system in the long run.

Understanding Federated Learning and Blockchain

In some cases big, real problems could be hiding deep inside the opaque world of AI and ML. *Federated learning* is a special type of machine learning where remote devices train the models, which are later aggregated into the main model without transferring the data. Federated learning is different in that the model resides with the data, while the training takes place remotely. This means that the trained model, absent its data, needs to be trustworthy on its own.

Typically, the training data set is cleaned up and prepared for use and then the model is built using selected ML algorithms. The model is trained and finally rolled into production. A typical federated learning process is shown in Figure 2-10. In this example, you can see the distributed data, the invocation of the training, and finally the remotely trained model being synced with the production model.

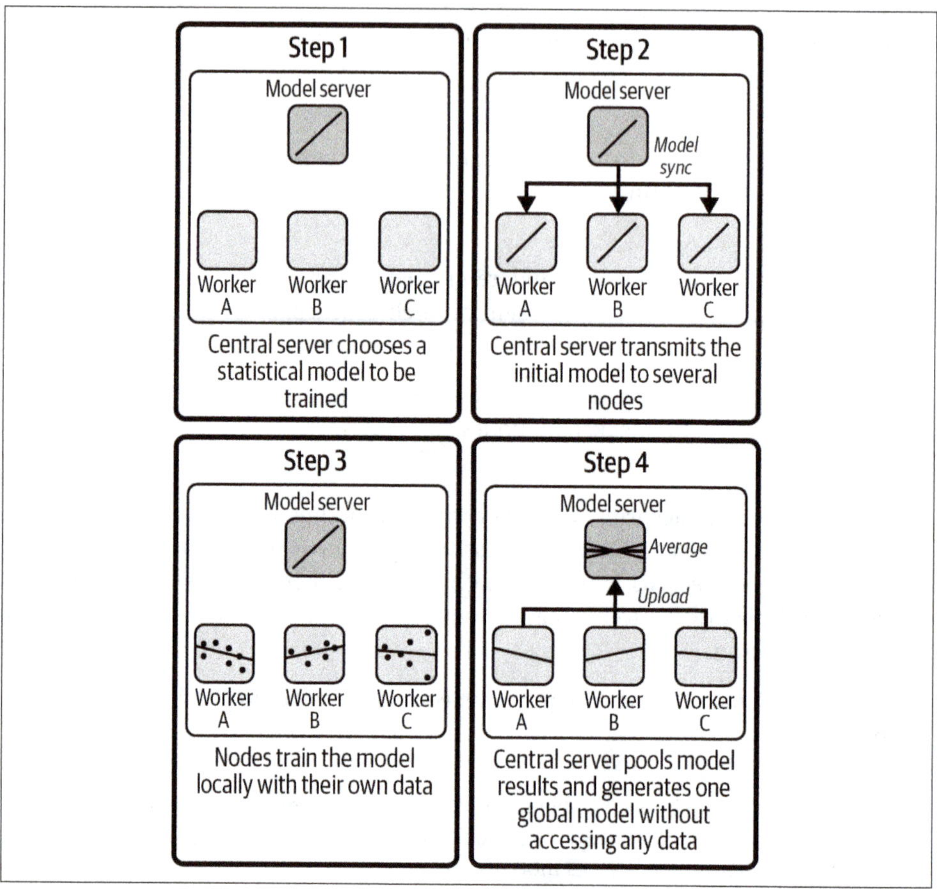

Figure 2-10. Federated learning for visual recognition data. Adapted from an image by Jeromemetronome via Wikimedia Commons (https://oreil.ly/cImei), CC BY-SA 4.0.

Because models that have been trained by federated learning must be trustworthy independent of their data, there could be trust issues if you cannot verify provenance and provide transparency. This can be fixed by recording a tamper-evident ledger of all training events and underlying components, and making a verification available when the model is instantiated.

Understanding Model Marketplaces

Pre-trained models save money and time, and speed up the ML process significantly. Common tasks and domains are addressed, and all the AI engineer has to do is further train the model to fine-tune it. Often these models are hosted elsewhere and accessed via API. Data is pre-cleaned, specifications of the data and intended uses are outlined in data factsheets, and it is often tested for anomalies like bias.

One such site is *huggingface.co*. Hugging Face offers not only pre-trained models via API—more than 20,000 of them—but also offers data sets with accompanying factsheets and tools to automate training. Another model marketplace is run by AWS. In the AWS Model Marketplace (*https://oreil.ly/Zo1db*), models can be selected through a point-and-click interface and be deployed on AWS EC2 instances.

As with any online marketplace, it is advisable for you to proceed with caution. While the marketplaces do some due diligence with their participants, results likely vary and the best practice is to evaluate each supplier yourself before using their models, and keep track of their information in your own factsheet.

Next, consider how to control your AI once it has been released to production.

Blockchain Control 3: Governing, Instructing, and Inhibiting Intelligent Agents

Blockchain can provide proof it followed pre-established technical and business policy criteria by requiring every significant AI event be recorded in a tamper-evident ledger. For example, when a model or training data is modified it would be traceable on blockchain, detailing who approved the change and how (and possibly why) the change was implemented.

Control 3 will become very important when wanting to trace or reverse AI, or prove in court that the output of AI is traceable to certain people or organizations. Table 2-5 shows the breakdown of two governance-related processes into participants, assets, and transactions.

Table 2-5. Breakdown of participants, assets, and transactions for governance workflows

Functionality	Hosting and/or storage	Participants	Assets	Example transactions	Blockchain control(s)
Stakeholder workflow	Cloud container	Managers, investors, system planners	Proposals, contracts, declarations, approvals, agreements, planning documents, specifications, requirements	Stakeholders agree that the system will never fall below 98% accuracy	1. Workflow and identity 2. Tamper evident 3. Govern, instruct, and inhibit

Functionality	Hosting and/or storage	Participants	Assets	Example transactions	Blockchain control(s)
Production model	Content, architecture and model combined, resulting in a genie or sovereign agent. Runs on one or more hosts; could be embedded in products.	Production model, AI agents, developers, DevOps	Rules, intent, logs, predictions, analytics, performance, recalcitrance, interventions, recalls, termination	Performance, behavior incidents, complaints, ratings, reviews, changes made to own code, changes made to own data, errors and outages	1. Workflow and identity 2. Govern, instruct, and inhibit

To think about how to approach AI's fact flow and the ML pipeline, consider a supply chain example where lettuce was tracked through the supply chain from the farm to Walmart's shelf using an RFID sticker that was scanned by authorized personnel and tracked using IBM's blockchain technology at each step along the way. A detailed writeup (*https://oreil.ly/dOXTd*) of the entire project on *Pixelplex.io* runs through all the players, reasons, and risks. IBM has formalized and is offering the software to manage the process flow; this product is called IBM Food Trust (*https://oreil.ly/9paIS*). An overview of this process flow is shown in Figure 2-11.

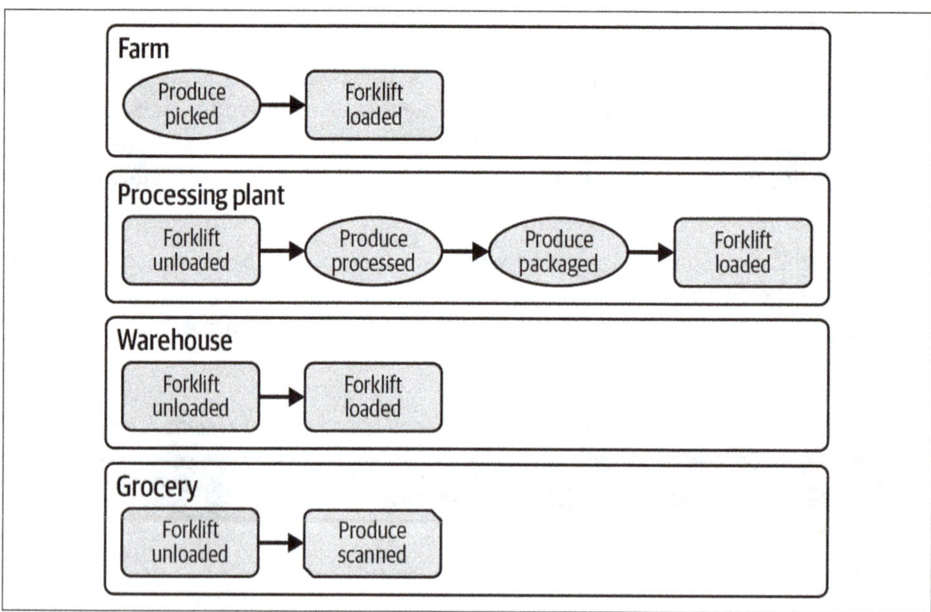

Figure 2-11. The real-world events that make up the product workflow

The predetermined points where the sticker was scanned join the points in the workflow, and the people authorized to approve or reject the scanned-in information are part of the governing group that is signing off the smart contract that's moving through the workflow. This is recorded on blockchain, along with the information for that transaction. In this case, the transaction has two parts: the approval of the information and the consent to move forward in the approval process. Table 2-6 shows how this breaks down in terms of participants, assets and transactions.

Table 2-6. Example participants, assets, and transactions for a supply chain system

Functionality	Hosting and/or storage	Participants	Assets	Example transactions	Blockchain control(s)
Supply chain application	Cloud computing instance	The farmer, the processing plant, the truckers, the grocery store	Unit of produce (crate/pallet)	Movement of unit(s) of produce from one point in the supply chain to the next	1. Workflow and identity 2. Tamper evident 3. Govern, instruct, and inhibit

Another example of an organization where a supply chain blockchain is retraced (*https://retraced.com*) focuses on the fashion industry supply chain. Garments can be tracked and traced all the way from farmer to artisan, and information about the origin of the goods—even how much CO_2 was used to produce the garment—is transparent due to the use of blockchain.

Let's first dive deeper into how to create a group that handles the governance of the blockchain.

Establishing a Governance Group

Governance encompasses the system by which an organization is controlled and operates (called *operations*) and the mechanisms by which it and its people are held to account (called *policy*). The group as a whole has a shared business aim, and the process by which they make decisions is a simple circular process of planning, implementing and evaluating, and then approving. Governance processes are designed to ensure:

- Accountability
- Transparency
- Responsiveness
- Abiding by the rule of law
- Stability
- Equity

- Inclusiveness
- Empowerment
- Broad-based participation

In AI/ML, this also means the group is providing visibility and automated documentation throughout the AI lifecycle, which allows the stakeholders to analyze and make decisions with greater efficacy and enforce their own business policies.

How do you figure out what your policy and operation procedures will be? Your organization, if already established, has policies on everything from how to apply for time off to how to shut down the production servers for software upgrades. For each of these policies, your organization also has a list of steps on how to carry out those policies, called operating procedures. Each policy and operating procedure has to go through a consent and approval process; sometimes both processes are performed at the same time, and sometimes they're separate "rounds" of asking each person. It depends on the size and structure of your governance group. It could be that the upper level of management consents to the policy, and their direct reports approve or reject the policy since they'll be enforcing it among their subordinates. And if the organization is large enough, the direct reports and *their* direct reports should be approving and rejecting it in that case. In every case, everyone knows that they are voting and what they are voting for.

This leads to the question: how do you establish a governance group, size, and structure? First you pick the people, and who you pick depends on what is being decided upon. *Cooperative functioning* (sometimes known as *sociocratic governance*) involves selecting people from top to bottom in an organization; every level of personnel is considered a stakeholder and needs to have a say in policies and operations that they directly affect and are affected by. There will be different people for different policies and procedures, but the feedback must flow throughout the organization.

In our Walmart example, the governance group would be made up of representatives from the suppliers' farms, processing plant, warehouses, transportation company, and Walmart management. Each of these would be at the level of the organization that is involved in the decision making for that policy or operation and would be able to sign off on policy.

Implementing On-Chain Governance

Governance does not have to be strictly manual, which usually involves emails, phone calls, meetings and other manual methods of communication. *On-chain governance* is a system for implementing and managing policy changes using a blockchain-based workflow system. In on-chain governance, there are steps to build consensus among the governance group and steps to gain consent from each of the members. Both procedures can be managed using smart contracts. Participants verify the information in the transaction to make sure it's accurate and that the parameters regarding the transaction have been satisfied. Once participants have completed their verification process, the results are submitted to the network. After review by other participants and consensus has been achieved, a new block is added to the blockchain network. Normally, participants would receive a notification of the transaction, typically an email. The new record appended in the blockchain is also visible to respective participants' interfaces, and different actions can be performed over the record through the screen based on the given permission.

IBM's Approach to AI Governance

IBM is integrating several systems to create an AI governance environment (*https://oreil.ly/dvGwL*) that, according to the company, is needed in order to provide a single source of truth. The single source of truth is needed to keep organizations protected from AI inefficiencies such as not being able to accurately re-create model experiments, financial penalties such as fines for noncompliance due to mistakes made by AI, or even destruction of an organization's reputation and trust due to a misbehaved AI that gives racist or sexist output.

One potential financial penalty is for breach of data protection laws. According to IBM, the EU plans to add AI regulations to the General Data Protection Regulation (GDPR). GDPR infringements currently can "result in a fine of up to €20 million, or 4% of the firm's worldwide annual revenue" (*https://oreil.ly/PDXeb*).

The components that IBM identifies as being part of its AI governance strategy are IBM OpenPages Model Risk Governance (*https://oreil.ly/4GQeN*), IBM OpenScale (*https://oreil.ly/_oSeI*), AI factsheets (*https://oreil.ly/P5FV-*), and an integration of all of these tools.

The BTA system that you will build later in this book could be integrated via API with IBM's AI governance stack to add a tamper-evident audit trail to the single source of truth.

Carrying out the verification process is not like an informal governance system, which uses a combination of offline coordination (meetings, emails, and so on) and online code modifications to implement changes. An on-chain governance system works only online, and changes to a blockchain are proposed through code updates. Typically, on-chain governance involves the following stakeholders:

- The nodes (and their admins) that validate the transactions
- Developers who write the algorithms
- The participants who have a vested interest in the transactions

The participants or nodes can vote to approve or reject the proposed change. In the case where nodes do not have equal voting power, nodes with a greater financial stake will have more votes than nodes that have a relatively lesser amount. If the change is approved, it is included in the blockchain and baselined. In some instances of on-chain governance implementation, if the proposed change is rejected, the updated code may be rolled back to its version before a baseline. In all of these governance procedures, the stakeholders will all know that they are voting and what they're voting for. Transparency is part of the system's integrity.

On-chain governance implementation differs among various blockchains. For example, you could have a form of self-amending ledger where proposed changes are implemented to the blockchain and rolled out onto the chain's Quality Assurance (QA) version, tested, and then deployed to a production version of the blockchain. If not, the changes are rolled back. Another type of blockchain hardcodes the governing algorithm, which will then trigger either passive (changing the permissions for a participant/node) or active (quarantining sections of the network for updates) actions.

Regardless of which type of blockchain you use, on-chain governance is worth the time to implement to allow the supply chain to manage their policies and operations more efficiently online instead of through lengthy meetings and tedious sign-off procedures involving emailing and faxing documents.

Developing Compliant Intelligent Agents

There is no point in time in the process of creating, testing, deploying, and auditing production AI where a model can be "certified" as being fully compliant with some set of rules, or entirely free from risk. There are, however, a host of methods to thoroughly document and monitor agents throughout their lifecycle to keep risk manageable, and to enable organizations to respond to fluctuations in the factors that affect this risk.

At question are two factors:

- The extent to which independence is exhibited by an AI
- The AI's level of expertise—its ability to assimilate and adjust to an environment by means of user requests (through smart contracts) and available assets

Software agents (also called *daemons*) are already a standard part of most non-AI software programs: agents run in the background, polling (listening) for some request from some software program. When the software agent receives a request, it dutifully executes whatever is requested so long as it fits its given rules. The rules are not always hardcoded (often they are passed to the agent in the form of variable perimeters) but the agent doesn't really do any thinking, reasoning, or learning; it either carries out the function or returns an error.

One of the most commonly used types of agents is a mail transport agent (MTA). The MTA runs on the email server, listens for incoming messages, and routes them according to the email address contained in the message wrapper. If the mail is going to another domain, the MTA talks to another MTA (via Simple Mail Transport Protocol, or SMTP) and so on until the destination domain is reached and the message is delivered to a user mailbox by a mail delivery agent (MDA).

Intelligent agents (also called *bots*) are software agents driven by AI. A standard MTA can adjust its routing based on network traffic. However, when you add AI to an MTA, you add the dimension of ML, which means that the MTA can be trained in advance on how to operate best from its own environment and location, balanced against the experience of other MTAs. The ML training data might include the logs of millions of other MTAs and the response from the MTA's own routing attempts. The intelligent MTA might then be capable of accurately predicting how to meet its assigned goals (fastest or most reliable? lowest cost?) for routing messages, and changing its behavior based on its predictions.

When an intelligent MTA receives a request, at first it might be just like a regular agent. It picks up the request, verifies that the request fits its rules, and if it does, the agent processes the request. Otherwise it returns an error. This is where the behavior of an intelligent agent deviates. If part of its intent is to operate "error free," then after getting the error, an intelligent agent might decide to adjust something about its own behavior to avoid getting the error next time. It may investigate the answers to this problem by conducting experiments or research, including learning from other intelligent agents.

If the MTAs and MDAs on other mail servers are also intelligent, then the agents can better learn from one another and perhaps even exchange new methods. When you think about all MTAs and MDAs learning in massive parallel across all mail servers on earth, mail routing could evolve very quickly. When you add program synthesis as Chapter 1 describes, the intelligent agent that we depend on the most could evolve beyond any human programmer's knowledge, because it has modified itself with no audit trail. Without any way to detect the origin of the intelligent MTA or method of finding out what it has been learning and doing, the intelligent agent could slip out of control and become a superintelligent agent.

A network of superintelligent MTAs could make catastrophic changes—hypothetically, given the sole goal of speedy delivery, the superintelligent MTAs could determine that message encryption makes message transport too slow and bypass encryption to speed things up. As a result, every mail message in the world that was handled by these MTAs would be easily intercepted—with a total loss of email privacy—and mail administrators would have a colossal mess on their hands, without much recourse.

By adding blockchain to the technology stack of the superintelligent MTAs, you are adding a requirement for the superintelligent agents to report back, based on your previous rules. You can add rules for when the MTA might have to stop taking advice from other superintelligent agents or when it has to go out of service for retraining (for too high a percentage of failed deliveries or leaked messages, for instance). You could specify in the model's fact flow that it has to record its own code changes on blockchain, along with any significant changes in behavior, in a human-readable form. You could make blockchain part of the superintelligent agent's DNA by coding it to fail if blockchain is not available.

When thinking about making intelligent MTAs and other intelligent agents compliant with organizational policies (for example, "all email messages should be private"), there's a checklist of variables that need to be accounted for in order to manage the information and the risks. Effective risk management is a continuous process. As such, it is critical to have a factsheet for each model that's easily accessible to all relevant personnel, especially when you're using multiple algorithms in multiple agents. Even if you're using only one model, changes to models or underlying data or infrastructure, which commonly occur over time, should also be easily discoverable. Some changes should generate specific alerts that are handled by personnel or possibly by an on-chain governance process once the alert is triaged by smart contract.

Some helpful tethers you can include on your factsheet and blockchain touchpoints include the following:

- Objectives for this intelligent agent
- Risks to avoid and unaccounted for risks
- Assumptions behind the intelligent agent
- Methodologies behind the intelligent agent
- Dependencies, and how they have been taken into account
- How to access or re-create training data
- Notes on any tradeoff between accuracy and explainability
- Expected lifecycle for this model
- Review triggers
- Procedure for feedback from consumers or authorities
- Procedure for recall
- Responsible parties and contact information

If you architect on-chain governance into your software, as discussed earlier in this chapter, you will be able to get far into any ML troubleshooting process by automating the ability to display human-readable results to any user that has permission, helping the user to trust the system.

Blockchain Control 4: Showing Authenticity Through User-Viewable Provenance

Blockchain provides traceability of all important events that took place in a system. A consumer of AI should be able to test AI to determine whether they trust it before deploying it for their purpose.

Control 4 will be especially important in using branded AI that has underlying components that come from distributed marketplaces. A breakdown of participants, assets, and transactions for consumer-facing touchpoints is seen in Table 2-7.

Table 2-7. Consumer touchpoints by participants, assets, and transactions

Functionality	Hosting and/or storage	Participants	Assets	Example transactions	Blockchain control(s)
Consumer touchpoint	Varies; person or agent using variety of devices or scripts; AI could be embedded in a product	B2B or B2C consumer, AI agent, project stakeholders	Reviews and ratings, help inquiries, reports, complaints	Checks to see if embedded AI is safe before using it, complains about unruly behavior in final product	1. Workflow and identity 2. Tamper evident 3. Govern, instruct, and inhibit 4. View provenance

Deciding Whether to Trust AI

When planning ways that the consumers of your AI can decide whether or not to trust it, think in terms of the lock on your web browser when visiting a secure site using *https*. The end user only sees the lock or they don't, and they will likely notice a warning when attempting risky activity. A user support tech troubleshooting a warning for the end user can drill down for more information and find out whether a certificate is valid, when it was issued, and information about the issuing certificate authority. This type of idea, of different consumers needing different levels of proof, may help AI become worthy of trust in all stages of its lifecycle. In Table 2-8, you can explore various consumer types, the type of trust they might need, and examples of how the trust can be proven to them in a form they can comprehend.

Table 2-8. Typical consumers of AI, the type of trust needed, and what proof might look like

AI consumer type	Type of trust needed	Example proofs
End user	Overall assurance done via affiliate organization that is a roll-up of all trust organizations involved in the creation, assembly, training, and deployment of the AI	Check to make sure that proof logo is intact, showing that contributors are acceptable by trust organization.
Broker or marketplace	Trust logos of all their member organizations and those of their dependencies	Check to make sure that proof logo is intact, that AI works in certain conditions and situations, and that components are compatible with one another.
Architect	Trust of all brands selected for AI architecture	Check to make sure that all factsheets of brands supplying components match company policy.
Developer	Trust of algorithm libraries and development environments, as well as trust logos of data scientists, along with trust of architecture	Check to make sure that all suppliers meet policy and that any bugs or issues are surfaced, and that support is available should issues arise.
Data scientist	Trust of data libraries and data tests	Check to see if data meets the policy for readiness, and that biases have been removed.
Chief technology officer	Trust in output of AI, trust in provenance, trust in ongoing control of AI	Check to see if adequate testing is being done to make sure the model stays true to its intent as it learns and morphs.
IoT devices	Trust in security and compatibility	Check for compatibility and recalls.
Intelligent agents	Trust of other intelligent agents and marketplaces for intelligent agents and data	Check the reputation and credibility of other agents before accepting their input for recursive learning.

Keep in mind that some people will want to simply take your word for things and others will want to drill down for proof—this will help you to foster appropriate levels of trust in your system.

Summary

Blockchain helps to keep AI in check and under human control. Though it may seem overwhelming at first to apply blockchain control due to the vastness of AI, making sure the underpinnings of the system are locked down in a single source of truth could be key to unraveling problems in the future.

As you work through planning your own use case and fact flow system, remember to refer back to the four controls for a systematic way of thinking about how blockchain impacts each part of AI's lifecycle:

1. Pre-establishing identity and workflow
2. Distributing tamper-evident verification

3. Governing, instructing, and inhibiting intelligent agents
4. Showing authenticity through user-viewable provenance

In Chapter 3 you will learn about several types of AI user interfaces and how to implement controls along with the interfaces.

CHAPTER 3

User Interfaces

Before creating your own blockchain tethered AI (BTA) that incorporates blockchain tethers for the four AI controls from Chapter 2, consider how the UI of the BTA you create can make or break the system's adoption. Often, people using a new system will be pleased so long as the system has a good look and feel, before they even dig into functionality. Conversely, difficult-to-use or disjointed interfaces will give the user a poor first impression, which is difficult to overcome.

If you have already started to test the sample code that is available for Hyperledger Fabric, you will find that while the examples are great for learning to code smart contracts, the UI for the application you generate from the sample code is very rudimentary. Most users would reject this type of an interface, and you couldn't deploy it in an enterprise, since it is not even as sophisticated as commonly used personal systems like social media, banking, and online stores.

Sometimes, it doesn't make sense to develop a new UI, such as when the system is only supplementing functionality performed by another system (like a continuous integration system that deploys approved trained models). In this case, you can do the integration in such a way that the two systems communicate via API, so the remote system causes a trail to be recorded on blockchain, completely transparent to the user. You may have other users accessing the same blockchain with a custom interface like a smartphone app that has other functionality, such as the ability to track and trace the deployments. Even then, you will still likely need to build a UI so you can administer the system.

Design Thinking

Just like when you plan a road trip, you need to know where you are heading, how long it will take you to get there, and what it will cost. It is the same when you are starting a new system from scratch, such as a BTA. Before you plan the UI to your BTA, you need to first identify who will use it. Remember the participants, assets, and transactions from Chapter 1? The participants, or people who interact with your BTA, are the primary focus for building your UI, as well as for gathering your overall requirements.

Primary users of the BTA project will be organizations that want to write, train, test, and/or deploy their AI model in a blockchain based system that gives an authentic blockchain based report about the history of the AI model. They care about information like who trained, who reviewed and how, what was the data set, and so on. Each user utilizes two kinds of interfaces, i.e., an interface to train their AI model (such as Oracle Cloud–based Jupyter Notebook) and the BTA application where the user can upload or review the AI model.

Requirements gathering should be done before you start designing your UIs. *Design thinking* is a process in which you use a set of techniques to cull from the user group what each user needs from the system, what devices they use to interact with it, and how they would like it to look and feel, which in turn gives you your detailed requirements.

As an alternative to holding a design thinking workshop for the group, you can encourage the project sponsor to share design mockups, process flow diagrams, use case diagrams, and flowcharts with the group before any coding begins, and gain their feedback. An easy way to do this is to record videos of each thing that you want to get feedback on, and drop them into a shared folder for the users. This way the group can respond without being in the same place at the same time.

A bonus of design thinking is the people using the new system have buy-in because they helped to design it. Once you have finished analyzing the information you gather from a design thinking workshop, you should have most of the boxes checked to be ready to code.

Enterprise requirements are not normally obvious. Product managers need to go beyond the normal understanding of the real requirements that resolve the business problems. In enterprise design thinking there is the concept of observing, reflecting, and moving together with the whole team. It's not only the product manager who is engaged in the requirement collection—the whole team becomes engaged with customers. It starts with asking *why*, and the solution of the problem lies in the answer of *why*. Maybe the manager needs to ask *why* several times, at least five, to reach the solution. It is a collaboration between the design team and the business users, where the work is completed and reviewed with the end user and again gets put back in the loop for the adjustment.

The team can also use *sponsor users*—experts in the field—to verify the solution. For example, when this book's BTA was being developed, the team consulted with sponsor users—in our case, top experts in cloud-based ML—to gain insight on what workflow was needed.

Stages of Design Thinking

To learn more about design thinking techniques, you can start by looking at IBM's "Enterprise Design Thinking" web page (*https://oreil.ly/eYlM4*).

The main stages of design thinking considered in the development of this book's BTA system are as follows:

1. *Empathize:* Research your users' needs with some combination of interview, survey, focus groups, and general statistics.
2. *Define:* Analyze the information collected from the Empathize stage that helps you to understand the pain and problems of an organization, and create problem statements. One of the problem statements should focus on the problem of AI models that can be dangerous and harmful if the whole developing, testing, training, and deploying process is not tracked properly and built to maintain the originality of the data set.
3. *Ideate:* Understand problems and create ideas based on the problem statements. Find feasible solutions, and adopt the current most efficient one to solve the problem.
4. *Prototype:* Use a prototyping tool to document the feasible solutions found in the Ideate stage. There are many prototyping tools available, like Adobe XD, Balsamiq, and so on. For the BTA that accompanies this book, Google Sheets was used to design the simple field layouts.
5. *Test:* Being based on the prototype, the product is created and undergoes testing to verify that it adequately addresses the identified user problems. A typical AI project is tested in local, development, staging, alpha, and beta environments by various users to verify the output approved by the AI engineer. Finally, the AI model is launched into production. Each stage can have a monitoring feature that helps to improve the product by looping back to the design thinking stages.

Web Interfaces

Building a robust web interface for your BTA is a good way to leverage standards that your users already know how to use. Just about everyone has used a web interface for something. It could be a personal use like social media or banking, or a work use like filling in forms for human resources or a sales workflow. Many people use web interfaces so often that the basic functionality—and often troubleshooting—comes naturally to them.

On YouTube, as part of a Hyperledger Fabric demo, there's a straightforward illustration of how blockchain works, where a marble is transferred from one person to another (*https://oreil.ly/6O5d2*), and a record is added to the blockchain for each transaction. The screen shows all the users, the marbles each user possesses in their marble bag, the marble moving from bag to bag, and the transaction record. Every display is the same—with no difference in appearance to account for different permissions or roles, because everyone was the same type of user for this example.

In another example video, you can view the lifecycle of a car (*https://oreil.ly/XhOTu*) from manufacturer to owner to scrap metal dealer, with transactions saved on blockchain. There are seven unique participants that log in with their own private key. Each participant registers themselves on the platform; when the platform accepts the registration, it generates a private key for them to use when they log in to the system. The system's framework is Hyperledger Fabric Explorer, which is used to monitor all of the transactions that are saved on the blockchain through the consensus of each participant. Logging in as any of the participants reveals the same basic framework and very similar visuals, with small differences in functional options based on the user's role (but still, very similar).

If this were a real system, a police officer or an insurance company could also log in and check the history and provenance of the car from the information on the blockchain. The owner of the car is in full control of the information of their car. The basic framework and user interface of this system is the same for each participant—they can all see the information for each car that's been saved on blockchain. What changes on the interface is the information they can edit.

Blockchain Tethered AI User Interfaces

In real enterprise situations, users expect better customization. To achieve this, it's most efficient to create a basic framework of an interface with all of the possible features that serve every type of user logged into the system—and then turn features on or off to the user depending on a set of permissions for their particular organization unit, which is used to group participants by common access needs. You can create even more customization of the interface functionality-wise by adding staffings within each organization unit that let you set create, read, and update access for data associated with each feature. (Note that you can't delete from a blockchain, you can only write again with a new status such as Canceled.)

For your BTA design, the basic web interface framework is the same for all roles, with the profile and password change functions found on the righthand side of the top menu bar. All of the features, including actions, workflows, and configuration menus, are found on the lefthand sidebar. The features that are available depend on the role and permission level for that user.

Since the user interface is how system participants will interact with your BTA, it is critical that anyone using the BTA—including stakeholders, AI engineers, MLOps engineers, support specialists, business users, and the general public—are all considered when customizing a design. Consider how the participants will be accessing the BTA; for instance, you could also make the interface be a smartphone app, or you could expose BTA logic via the API from some other system using its interface, such as the control panel of an automated vehicle.

Before creating users in the BTA you build in the exercises, you will first have to have an organization unit and staffing set up for that type of user. Just remember that organizations define sets of features, and staffings define levels of access within each assigned feature. An organization can have multiple staffings, but a staffing can have only one organization. Creating organization units, staffings, and users is covered step-by-step in Chapter 7.

User Interfaces for Technical Users

The UI for the blockchain tethered AI that you will build in the exercises hides the application's technical implementation, including how the blockchain works, even from highly technical users like the AI engineer and the MLOps engineer. Easy-to-use tools like the BTA are needed so the AI engineer and MLOps engineer can keep their focus on maintaining trackable, traceable, transparent models. When you are trying to figure out what might be intuitive for an AI engineer or MLOps engineer, try looking at other tools the engineer uses, and discuss with them what has worked and what hasn't.

Once a BTA is developed and implemented, iterative development and feedback cycles will also be very helpful in improving its UI. A process for gathering feedback and implementing effective changes based on real user experience is detailed by Steve Krug in *Rocket Surgery Made Easy* (New Riders). In Krug's process, users are observed by the system developers and changes are quickly made in response to their observations. The process can help you to create effective UIs for all your system's users.

BTA User Mockups

The BTA used in this book's exercises includes five user personas: super admin, organization admin, AI engineer, MLOps engineer, and stakeholder. Information on each and a mockup of their BTA user interface is covered in this section.

> **How Blockchain Is Used**
>
> Besides the standard profile and password information, the following information is saved on blockchain after each iteration:
>
> - Project information
> - Newly created model and its version
> - Experiments under each model
> - *Epochs* under each experiment, which are full cycles through the training data set
> - Cloud bucket URL
> - Blockchain node
> - Log file location from an Oracle bucket
> - AI artifact information
> - Start and finish timestamps for each iteration of an epoch

Super admin

The super admin is the user in a BTA instance with access to verify and approve organizations that have registered in that instance. Super admin can assign a blockchain node and an Oracle bucket to the organization admin, which is tied to the email address that registers the organization in the BTA.

As shown in Figure 3-1, a super admin's interface needs to have tools that can approve the creation of organizations and their administrators. Once they log in, they will see menus giving them the ability to verify, and accept or reject, organization registration and subscription requests, along with organization information details and the ability to modify and delete organizations.

Super admin profile info

Name	Marie Curie
Email	mcurie@myaitest.com
Phone No	XXXX XXX XXX

Unverified Organization

Organization	Address	Email	Phone	Action
Fast AI	395 Whaley Lane, Milwaukee, 53212	john@...	262-555-1212	Verify
Green AI	652 Orphan Road, Elk Lake, 53212	jen@...	715-555-1212	Verify

Verify

BC node info	https://x.x.x.x/kilroybc/2324324
BC channel Name	Org-admin
Oracle Bucket URL	https://x.x.x.x/kilroybucket/43sdfsd4df

Verify

Figure 3-1. Super admin user interface mockup

Let's say you are running a BTA and you have three clients using it. The BTA you are running would be an instance, and each of these three clients who register in your BTA would be an organization, and the person registering each organization is the organization admin. Super admin is intended to be held by the organization that manages the BTA, not the projects. By keeping this role completely separate from the organization administrators, you can manage multiple organizational tenants per instance of your BTA.

Organization admin

The organization admin is the administrator of the registered organization within the BTA application, and can create projects, add users and roles to the project, and see the details of the projects and AI models. As shown in Figure 3-2, once they log in, the organization admin will access tools that allow them to create organizational units and subunits within an organization, add people to specific organization roles inside the units and subunits, manage permissions for any organizational role, and see all of the blockchain activity.

User Profile

Name	John Doe
Email	john@john.com
BC node info	https://x.x.x.x/kilroybc/sdfsd353sdfsdf
BC channel Name	Global Channel Company Channel
Oracle Bucket URL	https://x.x.x.x/kilroybucket/sdfds423432

Create Project

Project Name	Traffic Signal Detection (TSD)
Project Members	*Participants ID* *Participants AI Engineer, MLOps Engineer, Stakeholder* *Organization current or another org name*
Project Domain	*Finance/Ecommerce*

Project/AI Model Grid

Participant	Project Name	Intended Domain	Status	Action
John Doe	TSD	Transportation	Pending	View || Edit || BC History
	Exp deails		Processing	VDetail || Reviews || Monitoring Report | BC History
	Exp deails		Accept	VDetail || Reviews || Monitoring Report | BC History
	Exp deails		Decline	VDetail || Reviews || Monitoring Report | BC History
Mike Will	MNIST	Ecommerce	Pending	View || Edit || BC History

Figure 3-2. Mockup of organization admin UI showing user profile, a screen to create a new project, and a grid of existing projects and models

User management functionality for your BTA could also be integrated with your existing user management systems such as LDAP.

AI engineer

The AI engineer creates an AI model, writes scripts, and tests, trains, and submits the model for the review; as such, the user interface of the AI engineer role is built for creating and modifying algorithms. The AI engineer will log in to the BTA, select from a list of assigned projects, and view the project details. Next, the AI engineer can create a notebook session and open it in the cloud, where they can write the code for AI model building, training, and testing. They can register the logs of each experiment, as well as the training, testing, and validation metrics to a TensorBoard logger, by following a standard logging mechanism, all from within the BTA interface.

The AI engineer then uses the BTA to submit all training and test data to the MLOps engineer. Some helpful metrics are shown in the UI mockup in Figure 3-3; you may find that you want to include additional details in your BTA.

User Profile

Name	Mike Smith
Email	mike@myaitest.com
BC node info	https://x.x.x.x/kilroybc/sdfsd353sdfsdf
BC channel Name	AI-Engineer
Oracle Bucket URL	https://x.x.x.x/kilroybucket/sdfds423432

Project Grid

Project ID	Project Name	Intended domain	Status	Action
#10001	TSD	Transportation	Pending	View || Edit || BC History
TSD-V1	Review Passed		Processing	VDetail || Reviews || Monitoring Report | BC History
TSD-V2	Deployed		Accept	VDetail || Reviews || Monitoring Report | BC History
TSD-V3	Review Failed		Decline	VDetail || Reviews || Monitoring Report | BC History

Figure 3-3. AI engineer project information

Clicking VDetail next to a line item in the project grid reveals detailed information about the model version, as shown in Figure 3-4. Drilling down into the experiment detail from the Version Details screen will show yet more detailed information, as shown in Figure 3-5.

Version Details

Project Name	TSD	
Created By:	Mike Smith	
Version	TSD-V1	
Submitted Date	06-27-2022	
Reviewed Dated	06-28-2022	
Production Date	06-29-2022	
Exp ID/No	**Date**	**Detail**
exp1	06-27-2022	Experiment Detail
exp2	06-28-2022	Experiment Detail
exp3	06-29-2022	Experiment Detail

Figure 3-4. Drilling down into VDetail shows Version Details

Experiment Detail

Project Name	v1
Experiment version	exp1
Code version	
Code repo link	
NB(NoteBook) version	Python 3.6. 9
Train dataset link	
Test dataset link	
framework	PyTorch Lightning
framework Version	1.6.4
Log file link	

Parameters

depth	64
layer_number	10
filters_numbers	3
etc	

Performance metrics

test_accuracy	0.9751999974
test_f1_score	0.9753184915
test_loss	0.0828124508
Roc_curves	
confusion_matrix	
RMSE	
etc	

epoch	train_acc	val_acc	training_loss	val_loss	train_f1_score	train_precision	train_recall
0	0.4719435246	0.2357966907	0.7348255898	0.4719435246	0.5059391088	0.1790594343	0.7169889957
1	0.4719435246	0.2357966907	0.7348256898	0.4719435246	0.5059391088	0.1790594343	0.7169889957
2	0.4719435246	0.2357966907	0.7348255898	0.4719435246	0.5059391088	0.1790594343	0.7357966907
3	0.4719435246	0.2357966907	0.7348255898	0.4719435246	0.5059391088	0.169889957	0.7357966907

Figure 3-5. Experiment details

Creating a new version of a model begins with the AI engineer completing a New Version form, as shown in Figure 3-6. Once a model has been created and tested, a review can be conducted by the MLOps engineer, a stakeholder, or the AI engineer. Initiating review of a model by creating a Review the Model form is shown in Figure 3-7.

New Version form	
Version	
Log file location	Give log file location
Log File version	V1
Model	Give Model location
notebooks version,	
train datasets,	Give Model location
test datasets,	Give Model location
Code repo	
Code version	
Comment	

Figure 3-6. New Version form

Review The Model	
Genral Info	
Version	V1
Log file location	http://ml.oracle.com/...
Log File BC Hash	dkfjds324wkjsdf9sdfdfdsfdsfs
Log File version	V1
Model	http://ml.oracle.com/model/
Model BC Hash	fhsfs9oaduasdjlasjdlasdsadasdasdas
Notebooks version,	1.7
Train datasets,	http://ml.oracle.com/traindataaset
Traindataset BC Hash	flkjsdlfs9sdfsdjfsdfdfgdf34rwerefy6gdrf3sqwq,dflef
Test datasets,	http://ml.oracle.com/testdataset
Test dataset BC hash	dksadasd80kasldask
Code repo	http://git.com/michael/project-name
Code version	v1
Comment	Keep an eye on accuracy

Figure 3-7. Review the Model form initiates a new review

Once model reviews have taken place, they can be found in the Reviews section, as shown in Figure 3-8.

Reviews

Status	Deployed
Rating	* * *
Deployed URL	beta.runbta.com/v1/dasdasdas
Production URL	runbta.com/v1/2323343
Comments	
Documents	
Created At	11/3/2022 16:14:0
Created By	David Well
Staffing	MLOPs Engineer
Status	Reviewing
Rating	* * *
Deployed URL	beta.runbta.com/v1/dasdasdas
Production URL	runbta.com/v1/2323343
Comment	Model maintained accuracy
Documents	
Created At	11/3/2022 16:14:0
Created By	David Well
Staffing	MLOPs Engineer

Figure 3-8. Review showing the deployed URL, who reviewed it and when, and the name of the engineer

MLOps engineer

The key role of an MLOps engineer is to review the AI model submitted by AI engineers, deploy, and finally launch it to production. During this cycle the MLOps engineer needs to change the status of the model based on the output received from the model. The MLOps engineers compare the accuracy and output submitted by the AI engineer with the output they get during the test of the model. The verification is done using output data extracted from blockchain. If the model performs well, it is pushed into production.

While logged into the BTA, the MLOps engineer can view all details of all projects, including versions of the data sets, algorithms, and artifacts; validate and compare the performance of the models; trade data and model feedback with the AI engineer; perform audits of the models; set residual levels and monitor what triggers exceptions; and create any report required.

As shown in Figure 3-9, when an MLOps engineer looks at the Project Grid, they can see the status of the projects and use the BTA features to take action to move them through the deployment cycle.

User Profile

Name	David Wells
Email	david@myaitest.com
BC node info	https://x.x.x.x/kilroybc/sdfsd353sdfsdf
BC channel Name	Company Channel
Oracle Bucket URL	https://x.x.x.x/kilroybucket/sdfds423432

Project Grid

Project Name	AI Engineer	Version	Status	Details
				VDetail || Reviews Monitoring Report
TSD	Mike Smith	TSD-AI-Model-V1	Deployed	BC history VDetail || Reviews Monitoring Report
TSD	Mike Smith	TSD-AI-Model-V2	Review Fail	BC history VDetail || Reviews Monitoring Report
TSD	Mike Smith	TSD-AI-Model-V3	Reviewing	BC history VDetail || Reviews Monitoring Report
TSD	Mike Smith	TSD-AI-Model-V4	Pending	BC history VDetail || Reviews Monitoring Report

Figure 3-9. User Profile and Project Grid (MLOps engineer)

In the same manner as an AI engineer, an MLOps engineer can drill down into the Version Details, as shown in Figure 3-10. From the Version Details, the MLOps engineer can drill down further to find the details of each experiment, as seen in Figure 3-11.

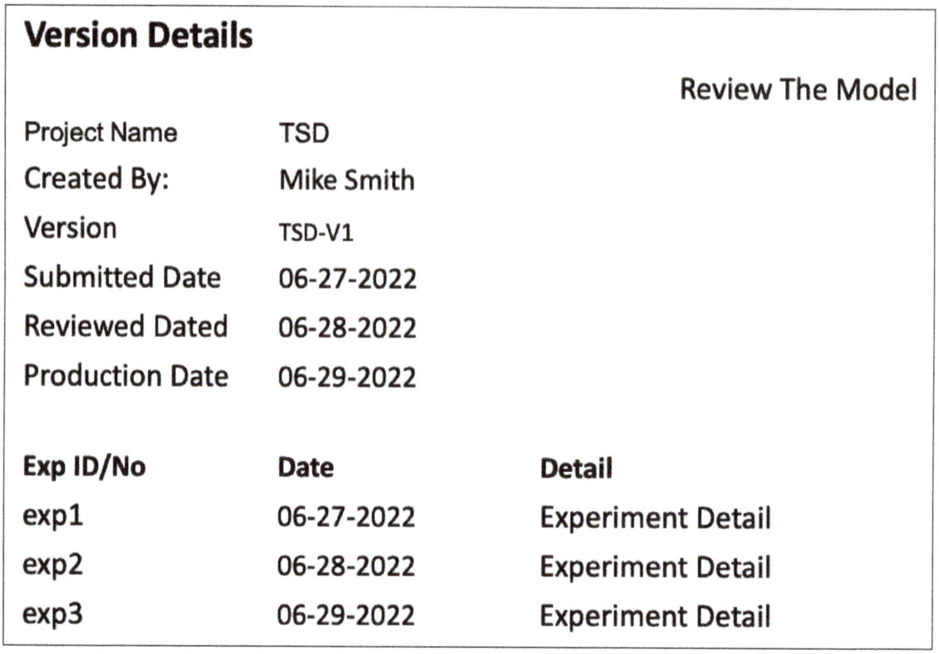

Version Details

Review The Model

Project Name	TSD
Created By:	Mike Smith
Version	TSD-V1
Submitted Date	06-27-2022
Reviewed Dated	06-28-2022
Production Date	06-29-2022

Exp ID/No	**Date**	**Detail**
exp1	06-27-2022	Experiment Detail
exp2	06-28-2022	Experiment Detail
exp3	06-29-2022	Experiment Detail

Figure 3-10. Version Details for MLOps engineer

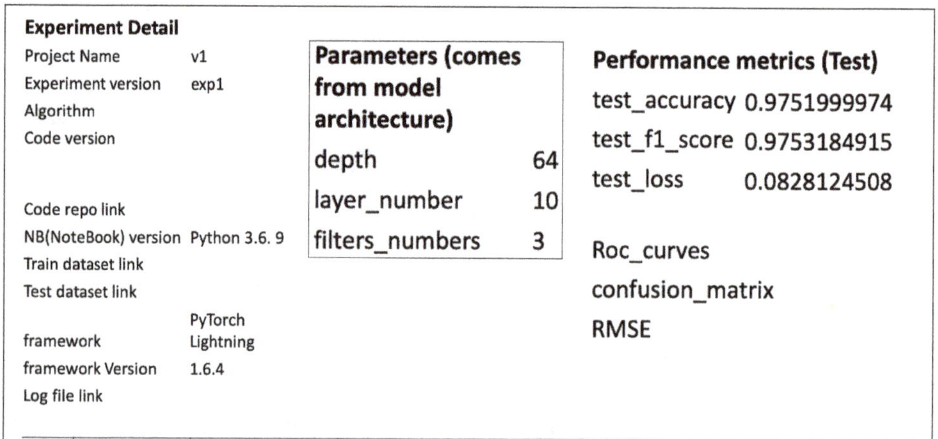

Experiment Detail

Project Name	v1
Experiment version	exp1
Algorithm	
Code version	
Code repo link	
NB(NoteBook) version	Python 3.6. 9
Train dataset link	
Test dataset link	
framework	PyTorch Lightning
framework Version	1.6.4
Log file link	

Parameters (comes from model architecture)	
depth	64
layer_number	10
filters_numbers	3

Performance metrics (Test)

test_accuracy	0.9751999974
test_f1_score	0.9753184915
test_loss	0.0828124508

Roc_curves

confusion_matrix

RMSE

epoch	train_acc	val_acc	training_loss	val_loss	train_f1_score	train_precision	train_recall
0	0.4719435246	0.2357966907	0.73482558	0.4719435246	0.5059391088	0.1790594343	0.7169889957
1	0.4719435246	0.2357966907	0.73482568	0.4719435246	0.5059391088	0.1790594343	0.7169889957
2	0.4719435246	0.2357966907	0.73482558	0.4719435246	0.5059391088	0.1790594343	0.7357966907
3	0.4719435246	0.2357966907	0.73482558	0.4719435246	0.5059391088	0.169889957	0.7357966907

Figure 3-11. Experiment details

The MLOps engineer can view existing Monitoring Reports or create a new Monitoring Report, as shown in Figures 3-12 and 3-13.

The MLOps engineer also has the same screens to add and read reviews as the AI engineer.

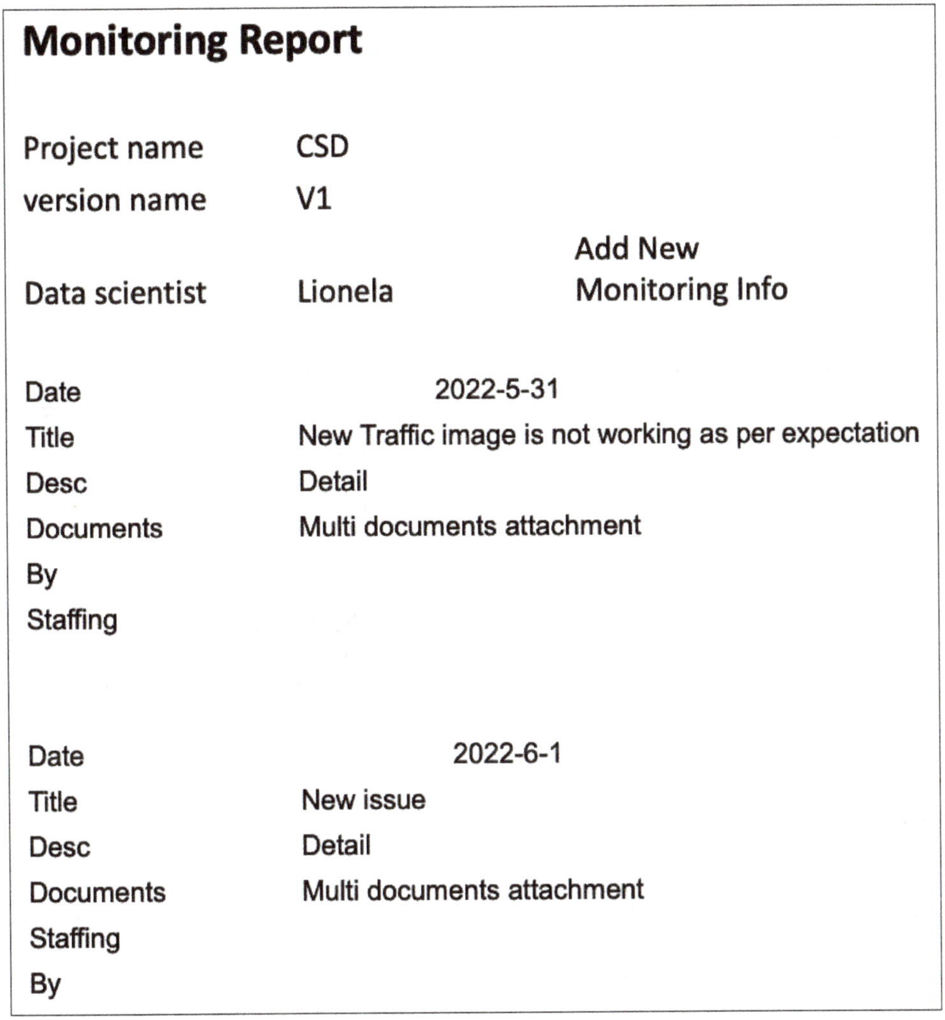

Monitoring Report
Project name
CSD
version name
V1
Add New Monitoring Info
Data scientist
Lionela
Date
2022-5-31
Title
New Traffic image is not working as per expectation
Desc
Detail
Documents
Multi documents attachment
By
Staffing
Date
2022-6-1
Title
New issue
Desc
Detail
Documents
Multi documents attachment
Staffing
By

Figure 3-12. Monitoring Report

New Monitoring Report	
Project name	CSD
version name	V1
Data scientist	Lionela
Title	
Description	
Documents	

Figure 3-13. Adding a new Monitoring Report

Stakeholders

A stakeholder might be an investor or customer or regulator who has a reason for developing the AI model. This user has permission to update the purpose of developing the model either by uploading the documents or writing free text. The user can review the deployed model but cannot change the status of the model. They can monitor the production model and give feedback, but only have the capability to complete the project based on the output of the model.

Once stakeholders log in, they'll see menu options to view details of the iterations, details of the models' performance, and history of the model development. They'll be able to pass along and receive their own comments on the information. Based on feedback and reviews between the AI engineer and the MLOps engineer, the stakeholder will be able to purchase a model from the dashboard through the integrated ecommerce platform.

Functionality

Participants are assigned different functionality based on their responsibilities. The functionality that is assigned to the users often overlaps, since many of the responsibilities are similar. Figure 3-14 shows a super admin creating a newly subscribed blockchain-secured organization by logging in, verifying the organization information, accepting the organization's subscription and modifying it if needed, and setting up the new organization's cloud access and blockchain node.

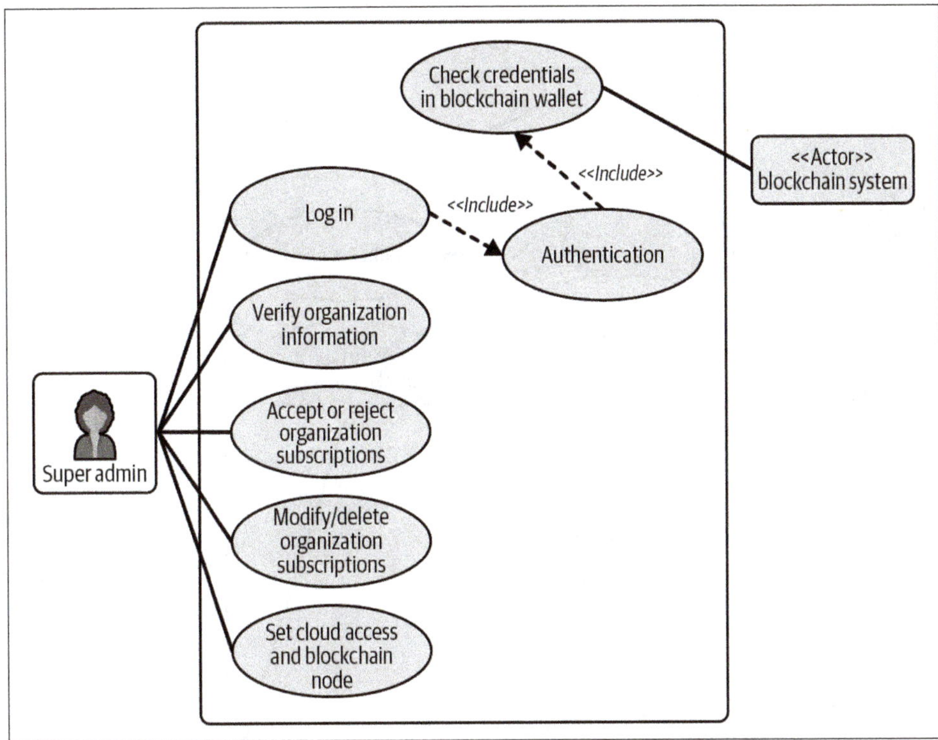

Figure 3-14. Functions performed by the BTA super admin include verifying registered organizations

Figure 3-15 goes on to show the organization admin, who receives their credentials after being approved by the super admin, creating a project and users. The organization admin moves through the BTA workflow, showing the AI engineer setting up the basic AI model and testing and training the model (with the possibility of verifying the model, configuring and tuning on future development cycles). When the AI engineer has finished, the model is submitted to the MLOps engineer, who verifies the model and notifies the AI engineer of its status.

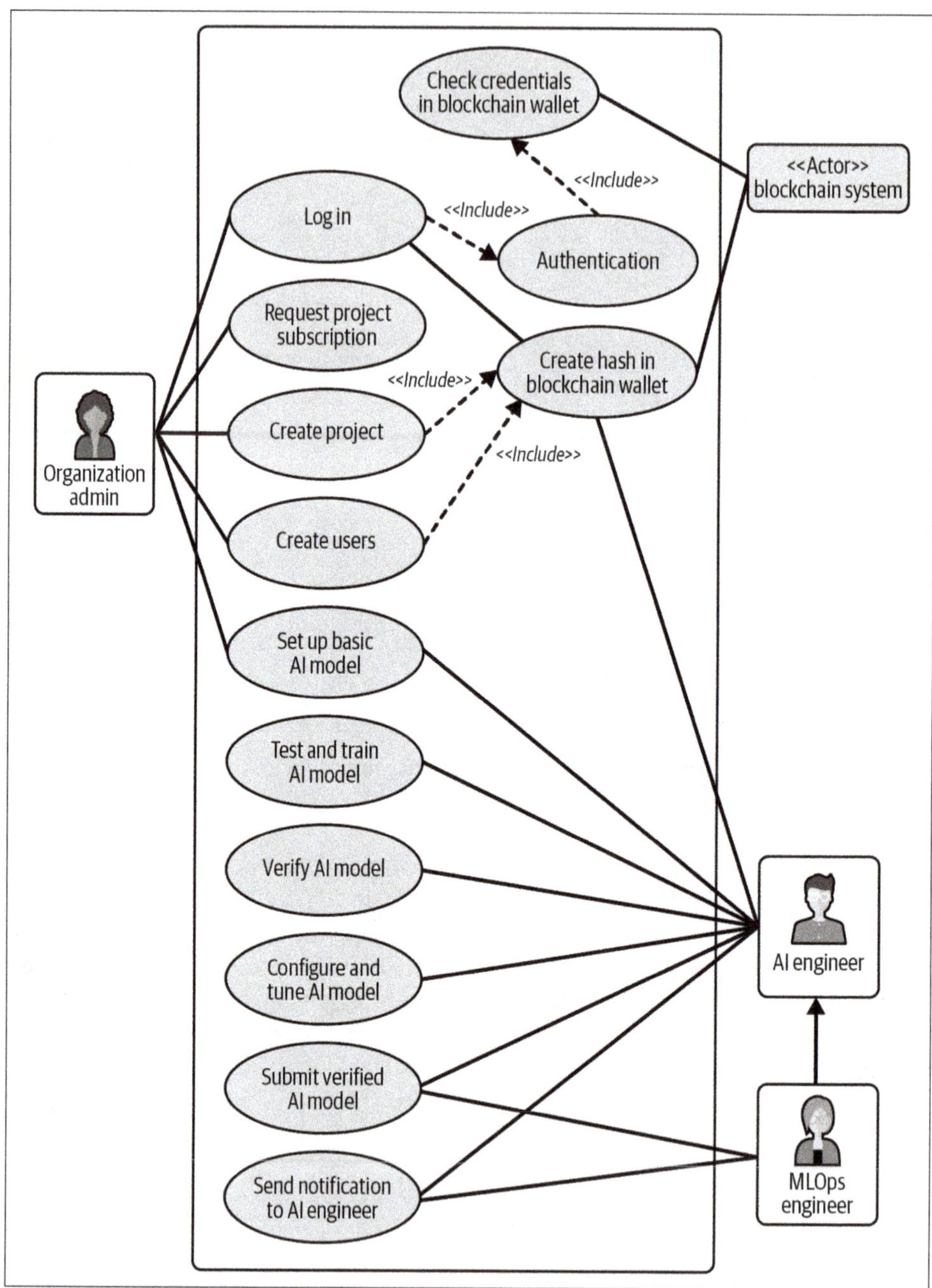

Figure 3-15. AI engineer developing and submitting an AI model, and an MLOps engineer reviewing the model and sending feedback to the AI engineer

Figure 3-16 moves forward in the workflow to show the MLOps engineer deploying the verified model and monitoring it after deployment. The stakeholder then becomes part of the workflow, with privileges that include viewing the model's history, monitoring reports, and providing feedback.

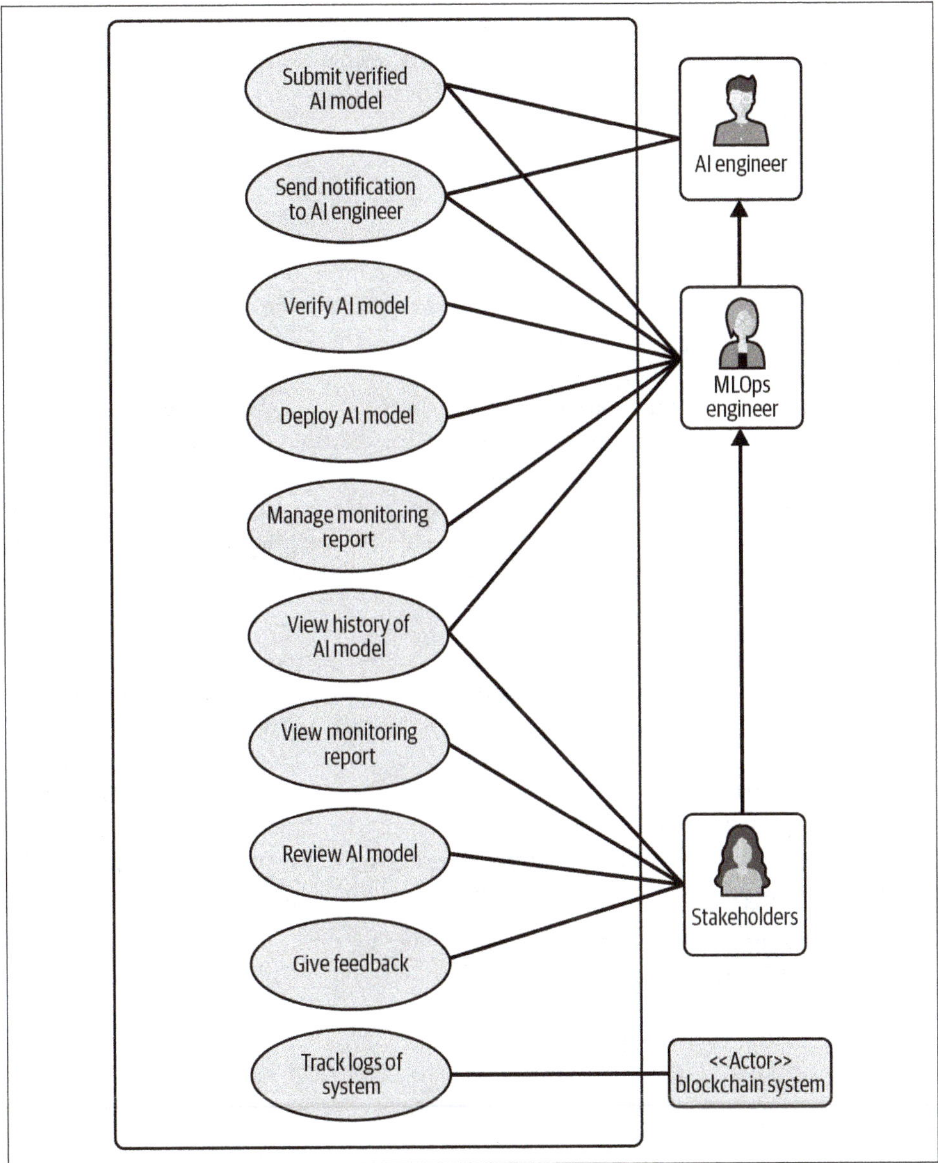

Figure 3-16. The MLOps engineer reviewing and deploying the model, and the stakeholder monitoring the production model and providing feedback

Traceability and Transparency

When considering interfaces, also think about what it will take to give users the transparency that should be present in a trustworthy model. Different users will require different levels of trust. For instance, a casual user of a budgeting system might only need an icon saying the AI is trustworthy, whereas someone rejected for a credit application by AI may want to traverse the chain of exactly what took place, and they may want to determine whether or not the decision to reject the application was based on biased AI training data collected from past unfair practices.

AI supply chain

Supply chains are how we receive most things we use, from toilet paper to automobiles, and as Chapter 2 explained, is the most common use for enterprise blockchain. Any supply chain has upstream steps that have to be completed in order to get the right finished product. For example, there are many different first, second, and third-tier suppliers that create the many parts that are used in an automobile. A certain level of trust and traceability are expected. Blockchain lends itself well to this process due to its tamper-evident nature, its distributed nodes, business-logic managing smart contracts, and ability to prove or disprove an event without sharing the actual data. Supply chain blockchain systems are fairly mature, and generally involve a multiuser, permissioned, cloud-based web interface as the primary user interface. You may find that it is helpful to apply similar principles to the lifecycle of an AI model.

Similarly, there is an *AI supply chain* in which many upstream people and processes are used to create the consumer-facing AI. Many AI models are pre-written and put on public websites from third-party sites. It is hard to tell where the training data came from and whether it was valid, biased or unbiased, and if the resulting models were valid or detrimental. An AI engineer might need to verify the credibility of AI supply chain participants, such as an AI model supplier, before using their products. This process could be like peeling an onion—digging deep into the AI supply chain may reveal the need for further verification.

Consider the supply chain of the data that is being used to train and test the models, and ask yourself these questions:

- Where did the data originate?
- Was it originally structured or unstructured?
- Who touched it?
- Did they clean it up?
- What methods did they use?

- Did they perform any tests on the data?
- Were there modifications resulting from test output?

All of these considerations can form the data's provenance, which should be easily checked by consumers of the AI.

Use Case: BTA

In Table 3-1, you can see blockchain touchpoints in a simple supply chain process versus a simple BTA. Thinking about the AI model building, training, experimentation, and deployment process as a supply chain demystifies the AI opaque box and makes it easier to dissect and explain to others.

Consider the process of a farm that sells eggs as local if the delivery point is 50 miles or less from the farm. Critical points like the mileage of the vehicle will need to be recorded to blockchain. Compare that to the delivery of a trained AI model, and critical points like contracted level of accuracy. In both cases, smart contracts are used to be sure that products are accepted and approved for payment only when the contracted conditions are met.

Table 3-1. Actions that can take place in the workflow of creating and deploying a model, and what could be recorded on blockchain

Action	What could be recorded on blockchain
The engineering team working for an AI company prepares a new model for deployment.	Hash verification of training data sets and algorithms are recorded on blockchain.
The model is optimized for power consumption and accuracy.	Acceptable metrics are recorded on blockchain, such as power consumption not to exceed $5,000 a month and 94% accuracy in results.
The model is ready for deployment.	Prior to deployment, measurements of the current metrics and reviews from the engineering team and input from stakeholders are recorded to blockchain.
The stakeholder approves the trained model and pays the invoice.	Smart contract test: was the threshold of power consumption and accuracy within the original terms of the agreement between the customer and the AI company? If so, approve the release of the trained model and pay the invoice. If not, reject the model and hold the invoice.

You can consider the same type of questions for the AI models, algorithms, and application layer, too. Chapter 2 covered the sort of questions to ask, such as:

- Do you have a positive identity of who engineered this system?
- What is its original intent?
- Where did you get your code?
- Where did your supplier get their code?
- If it is from a marketplace, what credentials are required for a marketplace to be credible?
- What tests can be done to make sure the algorithms remain as intended?
- How was the model trained, and who trained it?
- Where is test output stored, and how is its integrity maintained?
- What administrators can grant access for this code, and what process do they have for approving access to it?

A more casual user might just need to know that the AI engineer is credible, rather than to be able to step back through the entire AI supply chain of things they don't really comprehend. In this case, an icon or trust logo can be used to let the user know that they can trust the system. Trust logos are expected on ecommerce checkouts, and they are an important part of showing that the site can be trusted not to steal your money. Trust logos for AI can be based on blockchain lineage and can be programmed to alert the user not only of the AI supply chain's credibility, but also if the data has undergone tampering.

Building a web interface for your BTA is not only a great way to rapidly develop and deploy the application layer, but also a way to seamlessly include a special interface for system administrators. All of the basic considerations of designing a web application come into play, including appropriate colors, a consistent look and feel, and incorporation of standards such as the location of menus, a responsive design that works across devices and screen sizes, and consistent user management and login/logout functionality. If you have designed your UI so most things are where someone would expect them to be and gathered their input about most other functions, you are well on your way to creating a BTA that users will like.

AI and blockchain are different entities with different flavor and power, and a web interface helps to provide their integrated interface to the end users like AI engineers and stakeholders to work in both platforms seamlessly. The web interface also helps to identify the users who are involved in the training, testing, reviewing, and finally, deploying the model, binding it with blockchain identity.

Hyperledger Explorer

As the name implies, a blockchain explorer like Hyperledger Explorer (*https://oreil.ly/ZY2Ow*) allows you to peer inside your blockchain implementation using a web browser. You can see blocks, transactions, nodes, *chaincodes* (the scripts driving the actions taken on blockchain), the blockchain's data, and you can interact with the blockchain to add blocks or nodes.

When you open Hyperledger Explorer, you see the *DASHBOARD*, which gives you a good overview of the number of blocks, transitions, nodes, and chaincodes that are part of your blockchain network. It also gives you a visualization of metrics such as transaction per organization, and provides a glimpse of the blocks that were most currently written.

Click *BLOCKS* to view the network structure of the blockchain. You will see the peers and orderers created within the network. Also listed is the Membership Service Provider Identity (MSPID) for each peer and orderer.

Click *TRANSACTIONS* for information like the name of the peer where the transaction was created, the name of the channel used to create the transaction, the type of transaction, transaction ID, and timestamp. These details can later help you determine the origin of the record.

Click *CHAINCODES* to learn about the scripts that direct the operation of the blockchain. Chaincodes are Hyperledger Fabric's equivalent of smart contracts. The data is read and written by chaincodes to a *ledger*, which is a sequential record of transactions. You can also see the total number of transactions committed through each channel and chaincode by peer.

Click *CHANNELS* to see details about connections shared among multiple peers. You can see the channel names, along with the number of blocks and transactions that have been shared across each channel, and the timestamp of the most recent transaction.

While this book's exercises do not use Hyperledger Explorer but instead focus on building your blockchain network into a custom web application, you run Hyperledger Explorer alongside the BTA to troubleshoot, or to satisfy your curiosity about the inner workings of your demo blockchain network since it allows you to delve deeper into the blockchain than you can by just using the BTA.

Smartphone and Tablet Apps

As an alternative or addition to a web-based user interface, AI blockchain systems can use a mobile app. Mobile apps are generally platform specific, and are often distributed through platforms like the Apple App Store or Google Play.

In general, it isn't necessary to build an app just to use a web-facing UI on a mobile device. Instead, web interfaces can be built to be fully *responsive*; in other words, able to detect what type of device they are being viewed on, and able to arrange the elements so they are all visible and usable. Your BTA is designed as a responsive web application, so it can be used on any device without modification. If you want to later add extra functionality, such as mobile push notifications, it might be worthwhile to build and maintain an integrated BTA mobile app on one or more platforms.

Email and Text Notifications

Even without a mobile application, you can notify the users of a change in status of some item in the BTA via email and text message. Giving users a way to enable or disable notifications by feature is important for making notifications helpful rather than annoying.

The example BTA you will build in this book's exercises is set up so that email notifications are mandatory when a person registers, and when their registration is either verified or rejected. Notifications are also sent when a user attempts to reset their password or has forgotten it.

Spreadsheets

Frequently, users of the BTA may want spreadsheets because it can be an easy way for them to look for patterns, perform what-if operations, and share the data. Whenever you implement a BTA in production, including a standard way for users to upload and download data in spreadsheets is recommended. You can do this by coding in a button for users that allows them to conveniently generate spreadsheets from the BTA data.

Third-Party Systems

No particular AI can do "everything," despite marketing claims. There can be many reasons why a company needs to integrate the AI with third-party software, and it usually boils down to needing to add a feature that is too complicated or expensive—with respect to time or money—to build from scratch.

Consider the vast number of ways that human beings can interact with AI, and the ways that intelligent agents might interact with one another. For example, your car could contain any number of smart parts that are created and trained by any number of sources. Do the parts work together reliably? Do experiments need to be done to make sure the AI of each part is optimized to work together with the others as one system? When you trust the car to carry you from place to place, do you want to run a check to make sure that everything is working?

The BTA included with this book has used several third-party libraries to accelerate the project development focusing on the end result, which has saved a lot of time and cost, like TensorBoard logger and Oracle bucket. This project has created its own library to connect with blockchain and web applications. The BTA is built using the *MEAN stack* (*https://oreil.ly/37jzX*), which is a development environment that includes third-party systems like MongoDB, Express, AngularJS, and Node.js, and as a result, uses libraries from all of these systems.

You can look at how AI interacts with people today to see how tethering to blockchain can enhance the AI. Here are some examples:

Google search
: Right now, Alphabet's Google is the most popular search engine. Would it be possible to tether blockchain to search results so that the next time you want to go to the same result, a fake version of the website you want doesn't mislead you?

Open your phone or tablet with facial recognition positive ID
: Every instance of you using Face ID would be verified and saved using BTA, so that you can check your mobile device login history in blockchain and look for any attempt to get in that you did not make.

Sending emails or text messages
: When you create an email or message, it can be saved on blockchain and sent out with an attached icon that will let the recipient know that only you sent it.

Social media
: When you browse, comment, or send a direct message (DM), wouldn't you want the recipient to know it's really you, not a spoofed account? BTA can provide a badge or icon as proof.

Digital voice assistants (Siri, Alexa, etc.)
: Login authentication can be handled through BTA so that a spy can't break into your system, eavesdrop on your conversations, send emails without your knowledge, or any number of other things.

Smart home devices
: BTA can provide authentication for login and secure settings on things like home thermostats, indoor and outdoor lighting and other environmental controls, refrigerator-created shopping lists, or any smart appliance.

Work commute
: Starting from an AI-controlled automatic garage door opener to your AI-controlled car, BTA can provide authentication for every aspect of operation that interacts with the outside environment.

Personal banking

Not only logging in to your online accounts, but any aspect of the buying experience flow can be authenticated and compared to your typical buying patterns. These services exist today, but they aren't connected to blockchain; though the banking institutions may use AI to detect or predict fraudulent transactions, it's all behind the scenes. This would be fraud detection that we can see and control from our mobile devices. This could extend to shopping experiences on sites that you use often, like Amazon or Alibaba.

Personal entertainment choices

What you see on Netflix, Hulu, and other streaming services and what you watch at the movies can be somewhat controlled by AI, steering you toward or away from certain selections. BTA can abate that behavior so you have the freedom to search the entire library.

There are many other systems in an enterprise that perform mission-critical functions, and there is a constant need to interact with those systems.

Working with APIs

APIs have transformed the way developers create and write applications. Most businesses using modern technology use APIs at some level to retrieve data or interact with a database for customers to use, creating the industry vertical *platform as a service* (PaaS). The BTA has been integrated with third-party software through internal, custom APIs. There are companies whose main product is an external API with a specific purpose, such as communications, payments, or email, as a PaaS model. These companies enable developers to build applications on their platform, which might perform functions such as hosting web servers or communication applications.

There are businesses whose value comes from connecting different APIs and web services, which are categorized as *integration platform as a service* (IPaaS). IPaaS companies allow users to connect disparate web services and tools, most notably to route data or automate workflows. Both of these verticals have grown tremendously, fueled by the extensibility and ease of use of APIs.

Your BTA is storing log files, testing and training data sets into an Oracle bucket through the APIs provided by the Oracle Cloud. It connects to Oracle Cloud Infrastructure (OCI) through an access key, a secret key, and an endpoint URL. The BTA uses PyTorch Lightning's logger library where the format of the log file that the project needs is created. Chapter 4 illustrates this architecture and dives into it in more detail.

Once the trained and tested AI model is launched into production, the BTA exposes certain web services as APIs, which can be monetized. Such APIs are used in web or mobile or SaaS applications by including provided secret or access keys.

Integrated Hardware

The scenarios for using blockchain tethered AI with integrated hardware are limited only by the imagination.

Since the software that AI engineers build for AI workflow systems can be integrated to include just about any intelligent hardware system, it is important to consider the real-world impact of such devices and make sure there are *soundness checks*, or cross-checks, to ensure that the system is functional and compatible with other components. One very common integration of AI and hardware occurs in today's cars, which have many different components that have to pass individual checks in order to work together, making each car function properly in the current environment.

One methodology used to cross-check components, operational design domain (ODD), determines the multitude of details that determine where and when a vehicle (or similar equipment like a robot) can operate. To understand this, consider that when you drive your own, nonautomated car, you are fully aware of your ODD, considering factors such as time of day and road conditions when you decide how to control the vehicle. You would know you probably don't want to drive on an icy road in rush hour, especially if your tires aren't in great shape. A fully self-driving vehicle, however, would have AI in command of analyzing the ODD without any human needing to be in the loop. Such a vehicle might check the tire pressure, check the temperature, and go into nonoperational mode.

The sample ODD principles used for automated vehicles can be used on robots and hybrids. Imagine a car-robot hybrid that picks your child up from the bus stop or does some other regular nearby errand. Think about the various components that might be talking to one another: a computerized steering system, lighting system, braking system, interior cabin climate, communications system; the list goes on. Using ODD, each component has its own memory stored on an erasable-programmable read-only memory (EPROM) (*https://oreil.ly/DsXBJ*) chip that remembers its optimization data.

If you pull a component from a robot that always runs during the daytime in dry weather, chances are it will have to be reoptimized in order to run at night or in the rain. So it is important that a soundness check is done by the vehicle to make sure the optimization isn't wrong for conditions. This data stays in the vehicle unless the car undergoes diagnostic testing. If the card is pulled to a different vehicle, it will retain the optimization settings in EPROM until they are reset by the new vehicle. Now, imagine introducing blockchain to this scenario as a more permanent form of memory. This means that instead of just analyzing current settings, you have a tamper-evident record showing exactly how and why each part was optimized.

As shown in Figure 3-17, each component could have its own blockchain channel which allows its own chain, stored in the part on its EPROM, that can act as a tamper-evident, auditable, permanent memory bank.

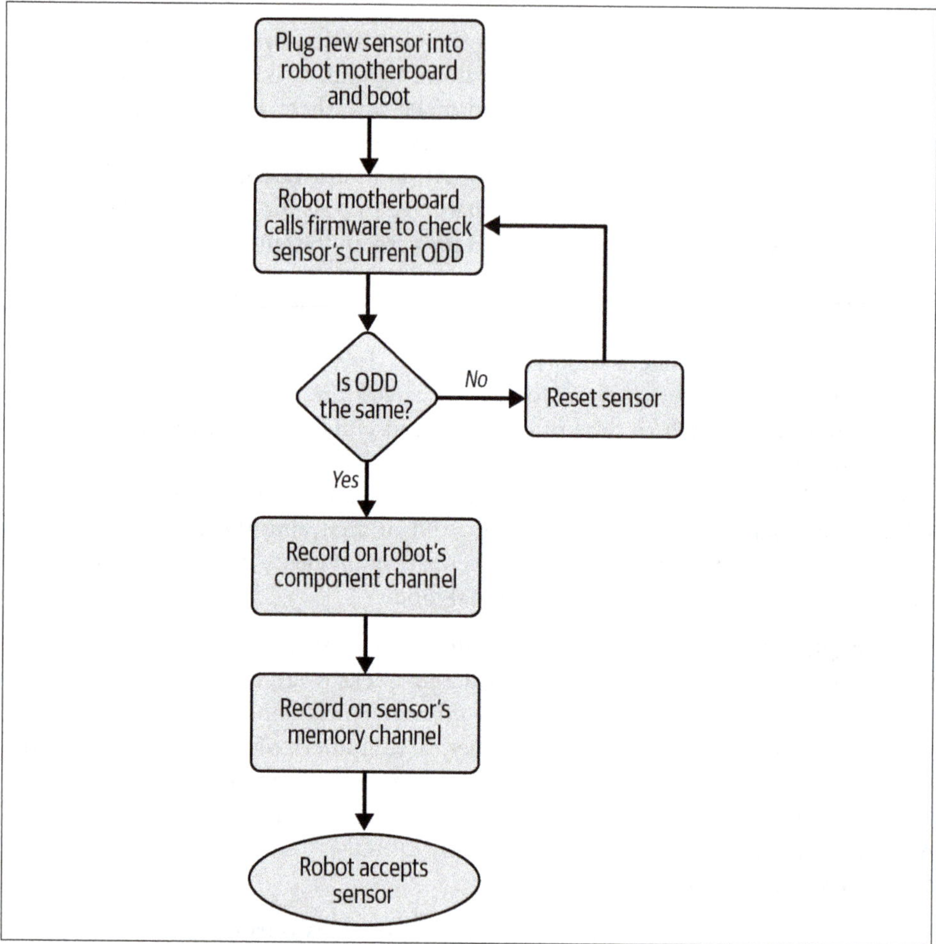

Figure 3-17. Diagram showing how blockchain channels might be used to add a new sensor with reinforcement learning capability into a robotic system

Other nodes of the blockchain can be stored on other stakeholders' systems, such as the workbench used for testing parts. Whenever the part comes into communication with the rest of the blockchain network, the data on that part's ODD channel could be shared with the rest of the blockchain network, either openly or as a zero-knowledge proof. This allows a part to take its entire history with it, including data supporting how and why optimization decisions were made, when it is removed and put into another system.

Bear in mind that much of this integration testing is done digitally through the use of *digital twins*, which are a digital representation of a physical device (or twin), such as a robot. One interesting use case for digital and physical twins is robot reinforcement learning (*https://oreil.ly/3WwSa*). Figure 3-18 illustrates how this process might flow if a part is removed from a robot and placed onto an engineer's workbench. The engineer then does some work on the part—maybe they create 1,000 digital twins and run massive experiments and come up with some new set of optimization data. Those new settings are then loaded onto the card, which is in turn loaded back into the robot. With a blockchain scenario, the new optimization data is stored on the card, along with the details of the model, such as the AI engineer's identity and history of the experiments.

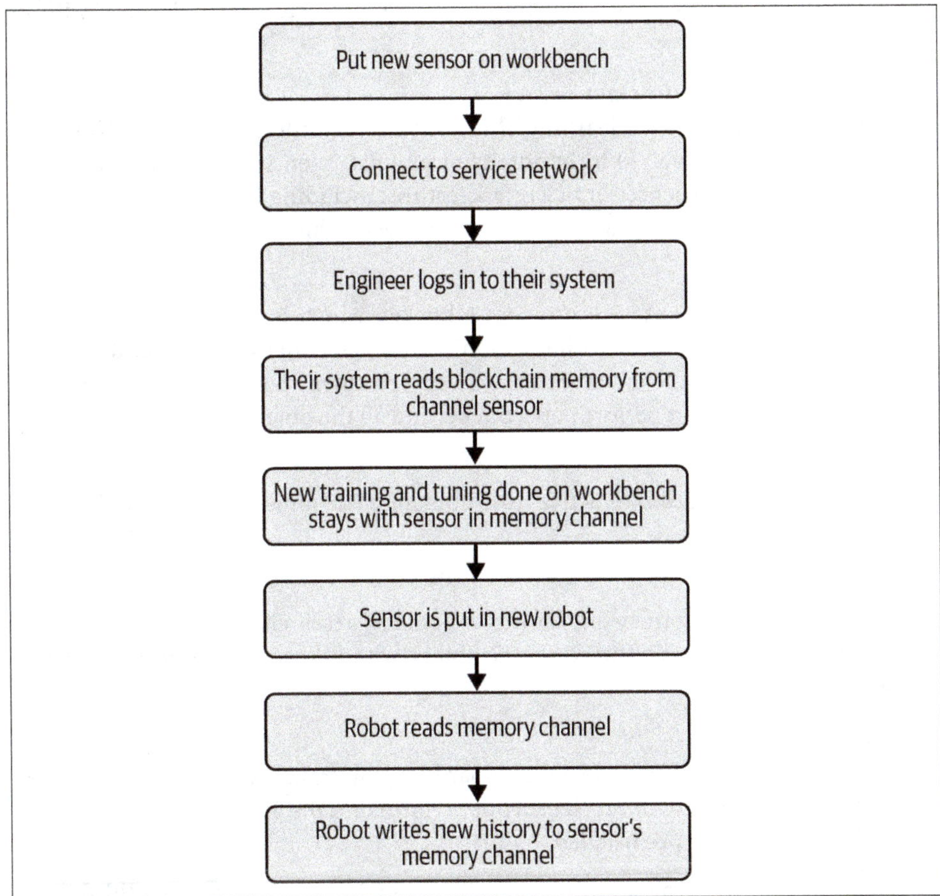

Figure 3-18. Sensor with ML capability remembers its history even when removed from the robot

When the part is placed into the robot, blockchain smart contracts can be used to validate whether or not a modified part meets the robot's ODD requirements, such as maximum speed or operating conditions.

Consider that when integrating hardware with blockchain tethered AI, ODD could be substituted for any number of other checks—a version check, a requirements check, a maintenance check, an intent check, an expiration check, a recall check—and all of these could be various blockchain channels. The checks could also be done in parallel as opposed to always sequentially.

Third-Party Services and Tools

The BTA project employs the following third-party services and tools, each with its own unique user interface:

Oracle Cloud Infrastructure Data Science
: An end-to-end machine learning (ML) service that offers JupyterLab Notebook environments and access to hundreds of popular open source tools and frameworks. The Data Science service offers features including Model Building, Model Training, Model Deployment, and Model Management.

Oracle bucket
: OCI Object Storage service provides a bucket, which is a container for storing objects in a compartment within an Object Storage namespace. A bucket is associated with a single compartment. The compartment has policies that indicate what actions you can perform on a bucket and all the objects in the bucket.

Jupyter Notebook
: Provides a web-based interactive development environment for notebooks, code, and data.

PyTorch Lightning
: The deep learning framework for professional AI researchers and machine learning engineers who need maximal flexibility without sacrificing performance at scale.

TensorBoard logger
: PyTorch Lightning offers the TensorBoard logging framework. Its logs are stored to the local file system in TensorBoard format. This is the default logger in Lightning; it comes preinstalled.

With some additional programming, your BTA could also connect it to a third-party program that analyzes the transparency, explainability, and fit (*https://oreil.ly/sy3JN*) with respect to your business model. Connecting with the right programs helps to validate the AI model by analyzing whether the data might be biased or fair. Opaque box testing can be applied to AI models in order to identify the accuracy level of the model. The MLOps engineer needs to understand the purpose of the project, the hyperparameters (as mentioned in Chapter 1, the run variables that an AI engineer chooses before model training), and algorithms used to train the model. Such an integration would be to overcome the opaque box nature of ML within the system you are building. Additionally, programs like SHapley Additive exPlanations (SHAP) (*https://oreil.ly/cq099*), local interpretable model-agnostic explanations (lime) (*https://oreil.ly/nZgwZ*), or Explainable Boosting Machines (EBM) (*https://oreil.ly/P-_uv*) can be integrated with your ML. These are model agnostic and provide easy-to-understand graphics and terminology explaining the results of the iteration output. Anyone who is validating the model needs to ensure that this type of analysis has been performed and the conclusion from the analysis is aligned with the business problem. When you integrate this type of functionality into your BTA, you will also need to build each new feature into your UI.

The Four Controls by Participant and User Interface

If you take a moment now to think back to the four controls you learned about in Chapter 2, it will help you to apply principles such as traceable identity, workflow, tamper-evident verification, governance, and provenance to your BTA. The controls and the points to consider follow:

Control 1: pre-establishing identity and workflow criteria for people and systems

- Registration: receive system verification from the super admin that can be disabled by one click.
- Log in with the temporary password, then privately change at will.
- Within an organization, there is an organization admin that can add users to the organization and control which modules each user can access, which in turn controls what they see on their user interface.
- Within an organization, the organization admin can control the permissions for each user by turning them on or off for each function based on the user's functional role within each module.

Control 2: distributing tamper-evident verification

- Each change of information by a validated user is recorded as a transaction and saved in the blockchain: create, edit, undo, or delete.
- Each transaction's information is given a transaction ID and saved in a block with a unique hash and a timestamp, and added to the blockchain.
- With any attempt to tamper with a block, the fraudulently generated hash will not match the authentically generated hash, and it will be evident immediately. An error message will be generated and sent out to a predetermined distribution list, including the super and organization admins.

Control 3: governing, instructing, and inhibiting intelligent agents

- The transactions are conducted by verified users and by consensus, recorded, and stored on blockchain.
- The workflows can be set up to instruct the user what to do if there is a deviation from the established workflow, such as a rejection of output data.
- The models can have an alarm to trigger if selected parameters of the output exceed a set difference level between the validation data and the predicted data (the residual).

Control 4: showing authenticity through user-viewable provenance

- Present an icon or other indicator alongside the data to show that its provenance has been tracked on blockchain, and that the proof recorded on blockchain matches up with the actual data.
- You can also display e-signatures or images of actual signatures that the stakeholders have made, on approval workflows, such as for final models. Each signature can display the aforementioned blockchain-verified icon alongside the signature (but as a separate object).
- Allow all users on the system to see the blockchain history of every blockchain-verified information that they have permission to see.

System Security

Since two different platforms (blockchain and AI) are being integrated through a web application, security needs to be checked at all levels, including AI, database, blockchain, and additional security points, as explained in the following sections.

AI Security

In the example BTA, the AI is created in the Oracle Cloud using different available resources in the cloud like OCI Data Science resource, Oracle bucket, and Jupyter Notebook. With adequate permission, the user can get access to the Oracle Data Science tool, from where the notebook is accessible. Users also need to get access to the bucket so that artifacts and log files can be placed there. So when all required access and permissions are given, the AI engineer starts to write code to create, train, and test the AI model.

This book refers to an account using OCI Data Science. The user begins at the login page by typing in their tenancy identification (the Cloud Account Name), which is set up by the organization admin when the account is purchased. Only users authorized by that admin can log in to the system. Once the tenancy and the service location in the cloud has been verified, the individual login screen appears.

After the username and password are verified, the user enters their dashboard. Along with the username and password, BTA is providing an extra security layer that comes out of Hyperledger Fabric. The BTA algorithm encrypts user credentials that exist within the wallet of the Hyperledger Fabric network using the SHA-256 algorithm, and the encrypted key is sent to the user after the registration is successfully saved in blockchain. The user has to enter the encrypted key in the BTA application after the normal username and password are verified.

Database Security

The example BTA uses two databases, which are stored in MongoDB. Make sure that none of the DB ports are opened so outside access is not possible. Use a bcrypt algorithm, which is used to encrypt the user's password, so the real password remains with the real user.

Blockchain Security

Hyperledger Fabric is used as a blockchain platform in this project where the user's credentials are stored in the secured blockchain environment. BTA has also added an extra layer of security by creating a blockchain-based password and using it during user login. So the user needs to pass login credentials across the blockchain as well, not only in MongoDB.

There are additional blockchain security considerations, like making sure updates are routinely and properly applied. Using a third-party version of Hyperledger Fabric, like Oracle Blockchain Platform, can help prevent problems like this because updates are automatically applied.

Additional Security

Below are some additional steps taken to secure the example BTA. These are suggestions, and when going to production with your BTA, you can perform your own security review that is appropriate for your deployment:

- JSON Web Token (JWT) authorization with refresh token.
- Google reCAPTCHA on signup/login with backend validation.
- API response and body need to be as per the data transfer object (DTO); otherwise, it will throw an error.
- API guard along with organization and feature guard for proper access flow (nobody can use the API except the user with proper access).

Summary

As you move on to Chapter 4, you will find it handy to think of what types of UI you will want to implement for each user persona. If you plan to fortify your BTA demo and use it in production, keep in mind that, as with any other software development effort, it is not possible to get every requirement correct without getting feedback from the people who are trying to use your new system. Before developing a version of the BTA that you will take to production, make sure you hold a design thinking session with someone representing each user persona.

The people using the system, and your response to their requests, will be a big factor in its success.

CHAPTER 4

Planning Your BTA

After reading Chapters 1 through 3, you are now prepared to start building your own blockchain tethered AI system (BTA). This chapter helps you get the scope for setting up your Oracle Cloud instance and running your model (Chapter 5), instantiating your blockchain (Chapter 6), running your BTA (Chapter 7), and testing the completed BTA (Chapter 8).

The BTA is built by interweaving the MLOps process with blockchain in such a way that the MLOps system *requires blockchain to function*, which results in the AI being tethered. To do this, the BTA integrates blockchain with MLOps so that a model must be approved in order to proceed through the cycle of training, testing, review, and launch. Once a model is approved, it advances to the next step of the cycle. If it is declined, the model goes back to the previous steps for modifications and another round of approvals. All of the steps are recorded in the blockchain audit trail.

To plan for a system like this, you need to consider the architecture of the BTA, the characteristics of the model you are trying to tether, how accounts and users are created and how permissions are assigned, and the specifics of how and why to record certain points on blockchain.

BTA Architecture

The BTA has three major layers in its architecture: the BTA web application, a blockchain network, and the buckets.

Alongside the BTA, you will use a Jupyter Notebook, which is a Python development environment that helps you to build and test models on your local system. The BTA architecture provides you with cloud-based buckets to store and share logs and artifacts that are generated when you run the code that is contained in your Jupyter

Notebook. Figure 4-1 gives you a high-level overview of the architecture that this book's exercises use.

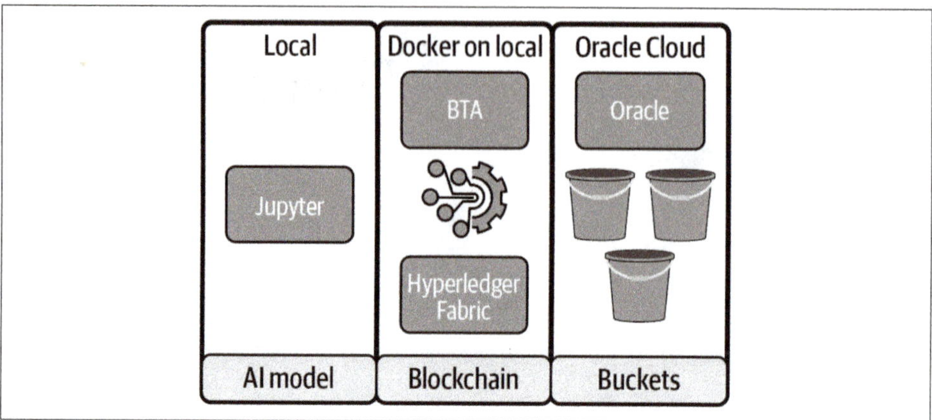

Figure 4-1. High-level architecture used for this book's exercises

These environments work together to allow AI and MLOps engineers to route and approve a new or modified model, or store objects like models and logs in buckets, while recording cryptographic hashes of the objects onto blockchain.

When the users are created in the BTA, the organization admin also issues them Oracle Cloud credentials. These credentials are stored in the BTA web app under each user's configuration. The users log in to the BTA, and the Oracle Cloud and blockchain are seamlessly connected to the system with no further action from the users. Chapter 5 explains the Oracle Cloud integration and setup process in detail.

While the stakeholders will not take an active role in model development, they still need the Oracle Cloud access because their logged-in user requires access to blockchain and the archives in the buckets.

Sample Model

To test your BTA, you need a model to tether. This book's accompanying code provides a sample Traffic Signs Detection model, which is a good model to test because it has features that allow you to try all four blockchain controls, as Chapter 2 describes.

The completed AI factsheet in the next section details the Traffic Signs Detection model. There could be many more facts on the factsheet, but this is enough information for testing purposes.

AI Factsheet: Traffic Signs Detection Model

Let's define some of the terms we'll be using:

Purpose
: Detect traffic signs based on input images.

Domain
: Transportation.

Data set
: The data set is divided into training data and test data. The data set is collected from the German Traffic Sign Recognition Benchmark (GTSRB) (*https://bit.ly/3QLpiQI*). This data set includes 50K images and 43 traffic sign classes.

Algorithm
: Convolutional neural network (CNN).

ML type
: Supervised learning.

Input
: Images of traffic signs.

Output
: Identify input images and return text containing names of traffic signs and probability of successful identification.

Performance metrics
: Accuracy of the model based on the F1 score and confusion matrix.

Bias
: Since the project uses 43 classes, each class has 1K to 1.5K images, so data skew is minimized. No known bias.

Contacts
: MLOps and AI engineers, stakeholders, and organization admin are the major contacts of the project. (In this case, all of those contacts are you.)

How the Model Works

To try the sample model, you can browse to its user interface using a web browser and upload an image of a traffic sign. If the model thinks it recognizes the sign, it will return the name of the sign. Otherwise, it will indicate that the sign is not recognized. This model is similar to visual recognition used in vehicles to recognize traffic signs. This is illustrated in Figure 4-2.

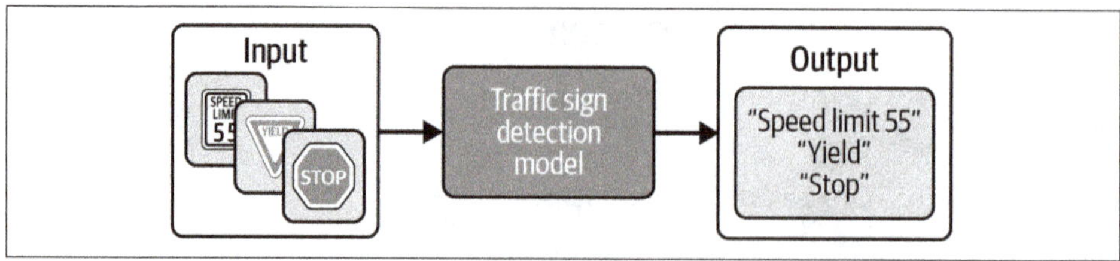

Figure 4-2. Sample inputs and outputs of the Traffic Signs Detection model

A simple visual recognition model like this is built by training the model with thousands of images that contain street signs, and thousands of images that contain items that look like street signs but aren't. This has already been done in the example model that is included with this book.

If this were a production model, AI and MLOps engineers might continue to attempt to improve its accuracy. They may introduce new sets of training or testing data, or they might modify an algorithm to do something like consider the context of the traffic sign (Is it covered by a tree branch? Is it raining?). The AI and MLOps engineers routinely run controlled experiments with modified variables, then weigh the results of the experiments against the results of previous tests and look for measurable improvements.

The modifications to the Traffic Signs Detection model itself, which are explained in depth in Chapter 5, are made using a Jupyter Notebook that runs on your local computer. Now that you are somewhat familiar with the model, you can consider how to tether it with blockchain.

How to use the Jupyter Notebook to modify the Traffic Signs Detection model is explored in the exercises in Chapter 5.

Tethering the Model

The BTA keeps track of how various approvers impact a model, such as how a stakeholder affects the model's purpose and intended domain; how an AI engineer collects and manages training data and develops models using different algorithms; how an MLOps engineer tracks and evaluates inputs and outputs and reviews performance metrics, bias, and optimal and performance conditions; and how AI and MLOps engineers create explanations. The BTA's scope could be expanded to include additional user roles, like an auditor.

The AI engineers can log in to the BTA and record details about model training events and experiments. This triggers workflow to MLOps engineers who are involved in the approval and deployment of the model. The workflow is such that an AI engineer can create a model in the BTA, record the results of certain experiments, and submit the model for review and approval. Then, the MLOps engineer user can test the model, review the results of the AI engineer's experiments, and give feedback. Once the MLOps engineer approves the results, the model is presented to the stakeholder for a final approval.

When submitting a model for approval, the BTA will prompt the AI engineer for a unique version number. As you can see in Figure 4-3, the BTA collects URLs for the log files, test and training data sets, model URL, notebook version, and code repository at the same time, which become tied to this version number.

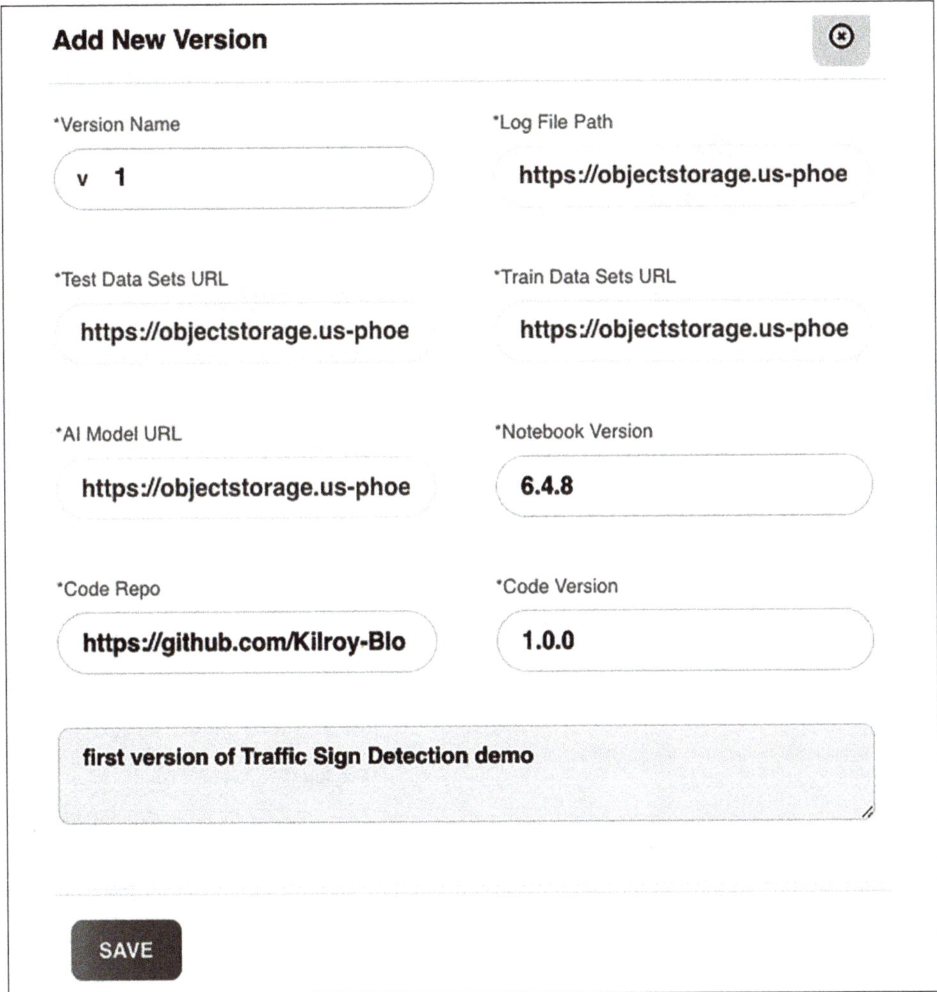

Figure 4-3. AI engineer assigning a version number to a model in the BTA

When the Add New Version form is submitted, cryptographic hashes are created from this information and stored on blockchain, which creates a tamper-evident trail of the origin of the model.

Next, the experiment is run and the detailed outcome is recorded by the AI engineer. When the model arrives at the next step—review by the MLOps engineer—they will receive an email notification. When the MLOps engineer opens the link, they will access the Version Details screen, which contains information they need to perform their own testing and form their own feedback about the model. The Model Details section, as shown in Figure 4-4, shows the MLOps engineer at a glance the basic information about the model, such as its code version, notebook version, and the URLs of the data sets used to train that version. Along with the details of the model are *hyperparameters*, which, as you may recall from Chapter 1, are the run variables that an AI engineer chooses before model training, and test *metrics*, or analytics, for the model for the most recent and past epochs. The MLOps engineer can review these details before deciding whether to approve or reject the model.

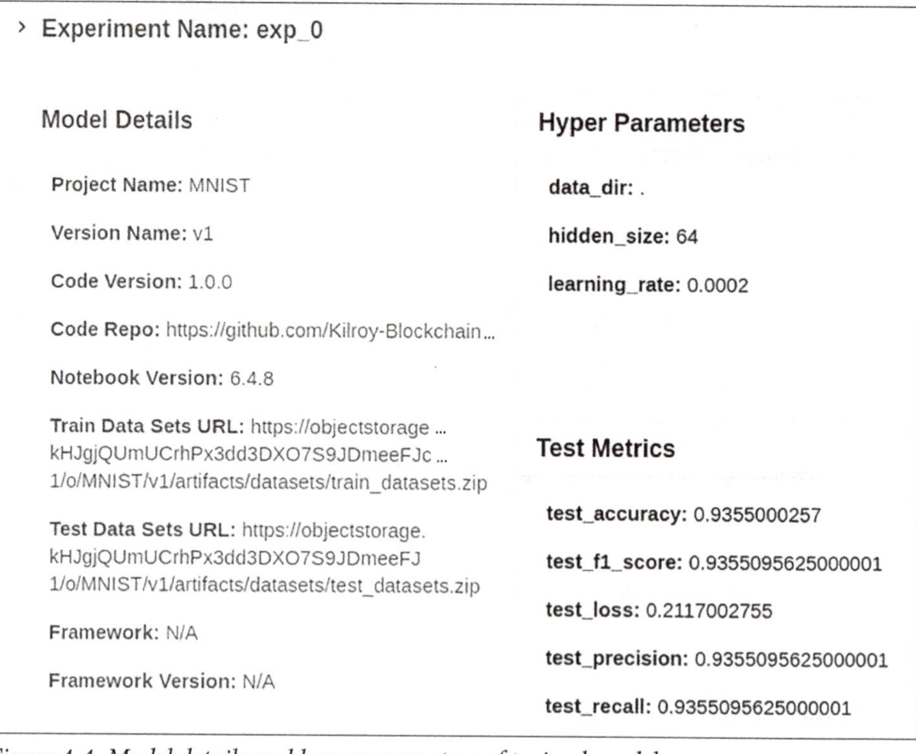

› Experiment Name: exp_0
Model Details
Project Name: MNIST
Version Name: v1
Code Version: 1.0.0
Code Repo: https://github.com/Kilroy-Blockchain...
Notebook Version: 6.4.8
Train Data Sets URL: https://objectstorage ... kHJgjQUmUCrhPx3dd3DXO7S9JDmeeFJc ... 1/o/MNIST/v1/artifacts/datasets/train_datasets.zip
Test Data Sets URL: https://objectstorage. kHJgjQUmUCrhPx3dd3DXO7S9JDmeeFJ 1/o/MNIST/v1/artifacts/datasets/test_datasets.zip
Framework: N/A
Framework Version: N/A
Hyper Parameters
data_dir: .
hidden_size: 64
learning_rate: 0.0002
Test Metrics
test_accuracy: 0.9355000257
test_f1_score: 0.9355095625000001
test_loss: 0.2117002755
test_precision: 0.9355095625000001
test_recall: 0.9355095625000001

Figure 4-4. Model details and hyperparameters of trained model

Next on the Version Details screen is a list of epochs that are associated with a particular version. The list shows metrics for each run through the data set that has been done in this version, as shown in Figure 4-5.

Epoch No	train_acc	train_f1_score	train_loss	train_precision
0	0.8082908988	0.8083999753000001	0.6439025402	0.8083999753000001
1	0.9128363729000001	0.9128391147	0.292299062	0.9128391147

Figure 4-5. List of epochs of an experiment

Further down on the Version Details screen, as shown in Figure 4-6, are details that help you to verify the results of the experiment and the steps taken to achieve the results. These details include the path to the log file, a link to test and training data and blockchain hashes which can be used to verify that the data has not undergone tampering, the URL of the model, a hash that can be used to verify its code, and a link to the code repository.

Project Name:	MNIST
Version Name:	v1
Log File Path:	https://objectstorage.us-phoenix-1....axutkjfnpof3/b/ds-1/o/MNIST/v1/logs
Test Data Sets URL:	https://objectstorage.us-phoenix-1....rtifacts/datasets/test_datasets.zip
Test DataSets BC Hash:	9a44cbbe04b208e212a21157b71b051ec14e9178d6134371f354287c00bfaa88
Train Data Sets URL:	https://objectstorage.us-phoenix-1....tifacts/datasets/train_datasets.zip
Train Data Sets BC Hash:	1096f55547a3d7ad1931ee32cb25bf10f8cf41857610b6f64cedaec7c7e4f018
AI Model URL:	https://objectstorage.us-phoenix-1....3/b/ds-1/o/MNIST/v1/artifacts/model
AI Model BC Hash:	09f78ff847efa3434e92f6481b70f1f87783d84db68c7538cd7cde29529a66ff
Notebook Version:	6.4.8
Code Repo:	https://github.com/Kilroy-Blockchain-corporation/bta-aimodel.git

Figure 4-6. Version details

The status of the version and details about its origin are also displayed on the Version Details screen, as shown in Figure 4-7. This status indicates whether the version is still a draft or if it has been put into production, along with information about when it was created and the name of the AI engineer who created it.

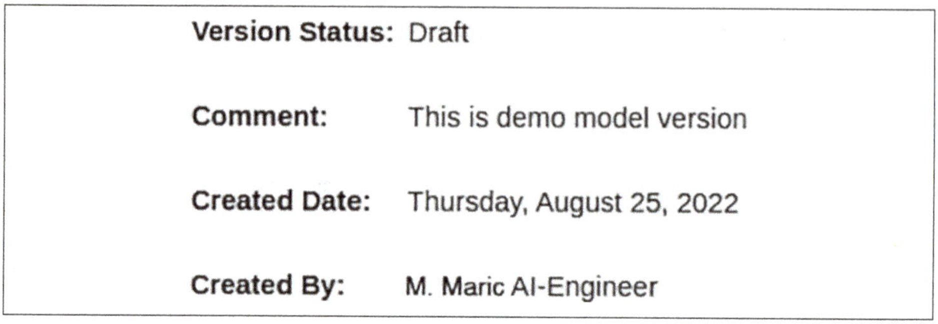

Version Status: Draft

Comment: This is demo model version

Created Date: Thursday, August 25, 2022

Created By: M. Maric AI-Engineer

Figure 4-7. Version status and origin details

As shown in Figure 4-8, the Version Details page displays a Log File BC Hash. This is the value stored on blockchain that can be used later to prove the log file has not undergone tampering.

Log Hash: 9275e1a764a87d19b5a9be57a7b87e79af1a724b9dd20dc97054a9b92289febd

Figure 4-8. Log file hash that will only compute to the same value if the log has not changed

The MLOps engineer completes their review, as shown in Figure 4-9, using the Add Monitoring Report form.

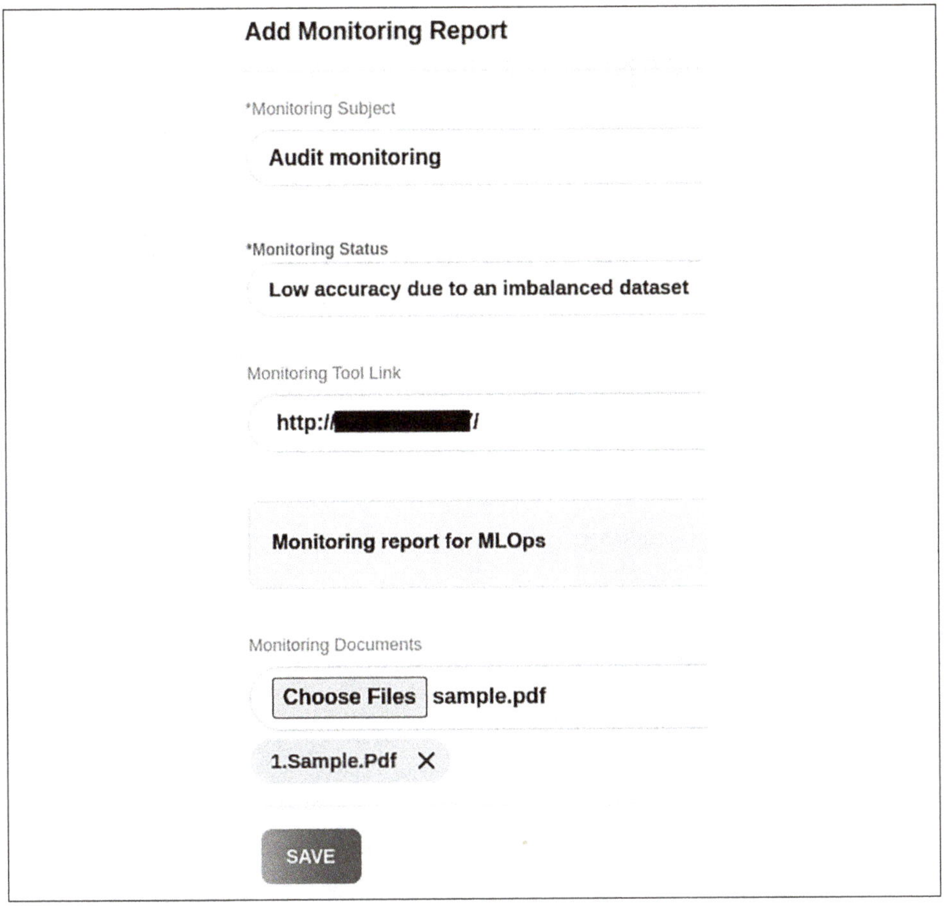

Add Monitoring Report

*Monitoring Subject

Audit monitoring

*Monitoring Status

Low accuracy due to an imbalanced dataset

Monitoring Tool Link

http://[redacted]/

Monitoring report for MLOps

Monitoring Documents

Choose Files sample.pdf

1.Sample.Pdf ✕

SAVE

Figure 4-9. Adding a new monitoring report in the BTA

The AI engineer can gather input from the MLOps engineer by reviewing the Monitoring Report, as shown in Figure 4-10.

› **Project Name:** MNIST

› **Version Name:** v1

› **Data Scientist:**M. Maric AI-Engineer

All Reports

Title: Audit monitoring

Status: Low accuracy due to an imbalanced dataset

Description: This is monitoring report by Mlops

Documents:

Sample.Pdf

Monitoring tool link: http://[redacted]/

Staffing: MLOps Engineer-1

Created By: M. Maric-MLOps engineer

Created At: 2022-23-25

Figure 4-10. BTA monitoring report interface

If this were a real scenario, you would want to also include *peer reviews*, which means that in addition to the MLOps engineer and the stakeholder, other AI engineers could add their reviews of a model.

The AI engineer reviews and implements the required changes and submits the model again for the review. This cycle continues until the stakeholder accepts the product or until some other limitation, like permitted time or budget, has been reached.

How Blockchain Tethers the Model

The model is tethered by permanently storing cryptographic hashes of every approval, log of the model, and links to versions of the model. This is done starting from the time of the model's submission for review and through testing the model and validation, as many times as the model might go through this cycle. The blockchain technology allows someone to later prove whether or not the model is properly trained by tracking and tracing the model's provenance through the BTA audit trail.

Any objects, like the model itself or the logs, are stored off-chain in an object store. A link to the object is stored on-chain, along with a timestamp and a cryptographic hash that can be recomputed to provide proof of the object's integrity.

A system like this could be built without blockchain, using the other workflow layers without the tamper-evident audit trail that blockchain provides. By adding the blockchain layer to the stack, any changes made by bad or sloppy actors to the model, whether the actors are human or AI, will be exposed. This is because if one block's data is changed, it will be evident to everyone using the blockchain, as you observed in Chapter 1.

In Figure 1-6 you could see that the chain breaks because the hash representing the data in the block will no longer resolve to its previous value. Figure 1-7 showed that you have multiple copies, or nodes, of the blockchain distributed amongst the participants of your blockchain network, which means no person or system can wipe out the record of what took place. As a result, your audit trail is tamper evident, which only blockchain makes possible.

After the model is reviewed and approved, it is deployed onto a production server and closely monitored by the MLOps engineer and stakeholder in a continuous feedback, improvement, and maintenance loop.

The BTA's records help users with an oversight role to be certain of the provenance of the model, including who has trained the model, what data sets are used, how the model got reviewed, the model's accuracy submitted by the AI engineer compared to the model's accuracy submitted by the MLOps engineer, and the feedback given by peers. The BTA can be used to produce a blockchain-based audit trail of all steps and all actions done during the development and launching of the model, which is helpful to stakeholders and auditors, and which Chapter 8 explores in detail.

People may switch jobs, organizations may change policies; still, the current policies need to be evaluated in order to allow or disallow a model from passing into production. Building these requirements into a BTA will help to catch, or even prevent, mistakes that result from organizational changes.

Four Controls

As part of planning how to tether the traffic sign model, consider how your BTA meets each of the four controls mentioned in Chapter 2:

Control 1: pre-establish identity and workflow criteria for people and systems
: Control 1's criteria is met, because your users all have certificates tied to their identity and the workflow is built into the BTA.

Control 2: distribute tamper-evident verification
: Control 2's criteria is met because the AI engineers, MLOps engineers, and stakeholders all have access to whether or not the current model and components match up with what was stored when the blockchain was updated, which would prove the model has not undergone tampering.

Control 3: govern, instruct, and inhibit intelligent agents
: The criteria set by Control 3 is met because the AI engineers, MLOps engineers, and stakeholders review the deployed model, govern it, and provide feedback. If the review meets the requirements the team sets for it—for instance, if the latest model exceeds the confidence score of the previous iteration, and the accuracy is rated higher than the model currently running in production, then the new model can be launched into production and will undergo monitoring.

Control 4: show authenticity through user-viewable provenance
: The criteria for Control 4 is met because the lifecycle of the model is recorded on blockchain. The model can be used in a commercial application, and a programmatic method of verification can be added that displays authenticity and enables the consumer to retrieve a detailed trace.

Subscribing

The BTA is *multitenant*, which means that different organization accounts, with different users, can exist in one implementation without impacting one another. Brand new BTA accounts are created by adding a new subscription. Subscription requests are initiated by the new organization admin on the BTA signup page, as Chapter 7 explains.

When you create a new subscription in your test BTA, make sure you do it with the email address that you plan to use for the organization admin. For your test, use any organization name and any physical address that you like. After you submit your request for a new subscription, the *super admin*, or built-in user who oversees all subscriptions, will be able to approve it and allow your organization admin to use the BTA to create users, upload and approve models, check the audit trail, and delegate these functions and features to other users.

At the time of subscription approval, the super admin adds an Oracle bucket to the new subscription, and creates the required blockchain node, using the Oracle Cloud account for the organization. Chapter 7 explains the complete steps for adding and approving a subscription, and for integrating it with the Oracle Cloud. Now that the account is set up, the organization admin can start working access control and create organization units, staffings, and users.

Controlling Access

Access control by way of user permissions is the cornerstone of a multiuser, multi-tenant software as a service like the BTA. When different users log in, they can see different features and perform different functions within the BTA. This is accomplished through creating organizations and staffings that define the level of access, and assigning them to users. Chapter 7 has more detail on how to set up access control and users. This section provides an overview to give you a high-level understanding of how access is managed.

Organization Units

Organization units are intended to be logical groupings of features that are assigned to people with similar roles. In your BTA, you have an organizational unit called AI engineers, another called MLOps engineers, and another called stakeholders. Within these organization units, sets of features that fit the role are selected, making these features available to any user assigned to this organization unit.

Staffings

Staffings fall within organization units and are intended to mitigate users' create-read-write-update access within the features. For this BTA example, we only have one staffing for each organization unit. In a production scenario, you may have multiple staffings within each organization unit.

If you don't see a feature in the staffing list, make sure it is enabled in the staffing's organization unit.

Users

The BTA offers role-based access control (RBAC) implemented via units called organizations and staffings. This way, the depth of the information displayed to any individual user can be controlled by placing that user in an organization and staffing appropriate to their level of authorized access. It is critical to create traceable credentials and well-thought-out permission schemes to have a system that lets the right participants see the right information, and keeps the wrong participants out.

As you have read throughout this chapter, there are five types of users that you will use in your test BTA: super admin, organization admin, stakeholders, AI engineers, and MLOps engineers.

When a user is added, they get login credentials from the BTA application. These details include a username, a password, and a blockchain key generated at the blockchain end using the SHA-256 (*https://oreil.ly/_nbTK*) hashing algorithm as a *collision resistant* hash function that hashes the user's wallet info and creates the key. A collision resistant hash function means that it is unlikely to find two inputs that will hash to the same output.

If this were a production project, some good questions to ask yourself when determining participants are: Who is on the team? How are they credentialed? What sort of organizations and roles should they be grouped into? What is the procedure when someone leaves or joins?

Super admin

The super admin is a special user that is automatically created when you instantiate your BTA. The super admin can inspect any subscriber's authenticity and either verify or decline any organization's subscription. The super admin is assigned their own blockchain node, where all approved or declined subscription requests are stored.

Organization admin

Once the subscription is approved by the super admin, the BTA allows the new organizational admin to log in. An organization admin has permission to manage the users for their subscription by assigning the correct roles and permissions. The organization admin plays an important role in using the BTA by creating the project, organization units (departments), staffings, and users.

The organization admin creates all required organization units and permissions before creating the users. While different kinds of permissions for model creation, submission, review, deployment, and monitoring can be set in the BTA, these exercises suggest that you follow the steps outlined in Chapter 7 for setting the user permissions so you have a system that will work properly; then you can safely make changes to test new ideas.

It is important to understand that after creating all required permissions, the organization admin needs to create at least one AI engineer, MLOps engineer, and stakeholder to start a project. Since these users must approve or reject a model, a project cannot be created unless one of each type of user is created. In order to let the user work with the blockchain, a blockchain peer and channel name should be assigned to each user by the organization admin.

Revoking Access and Privileges

The organization admin can revoke a user's access and privileges from the entire project. They can disable the user in both the BTA application and Oracle Cloud account, and remove the permission (staffing) from the user account.

However, it is just a soft delete; the user's data is not deleted anywhere from the application, nor does the blockchain node get deleted. Instead, the user is added to the revocation list, which means the user will not be able to access the node if they try. Access in the blockchain is only possible if the user passes out of the revocation list.

AI engineer

After the organization admin creates the AI engineer, the user receives an activation email. The email contains the username and password. It also contains the blockchain key created using the user's blockchain wallet info like a public key. The SHA-256 algorithm is used to create the key. In the sample project in this chapter, the user needs to first enter their credentials on the login page, as shown in Figure 4-11.

Figure 4-11. Login page

Next, the user is asked to supply their blockchain key to pass the second layer of security of the application, as illustrated in Figure 4-12.

This feature is built to address blockchain control 1 (pre-establish identity and workflow criteria for people and systems). The identity created in blockchain is used in the web application through the Blockchain Key Verification page.

When the account in Oracle Cloud is created by the organization admin, it sends an email to the user which includes Oracle Cloud login credentials. These details have to be entered into the user's configuration so they can be passed to the cloud by the BTA.

After the activation of the BTA application account and Oracle Cloud account, the user logs in to the BTA application where all AI projects assigned to them are listed. The engineer should be able to start model development using Oracle Cloud–based data science resources. After a model is created, the engineer can log in to the BTA web application, select a project assigned to them, and start creating a new version of the recently built model. In the sample project, the user can create a new version of the model but keep it as a draft. Draft status allows the user to come back and change the model info in the web application. Once the model is ready to submit, the user can submit it for review by the MLOps engineer. After submitting the model, the user cannot change anything in the submitted version.

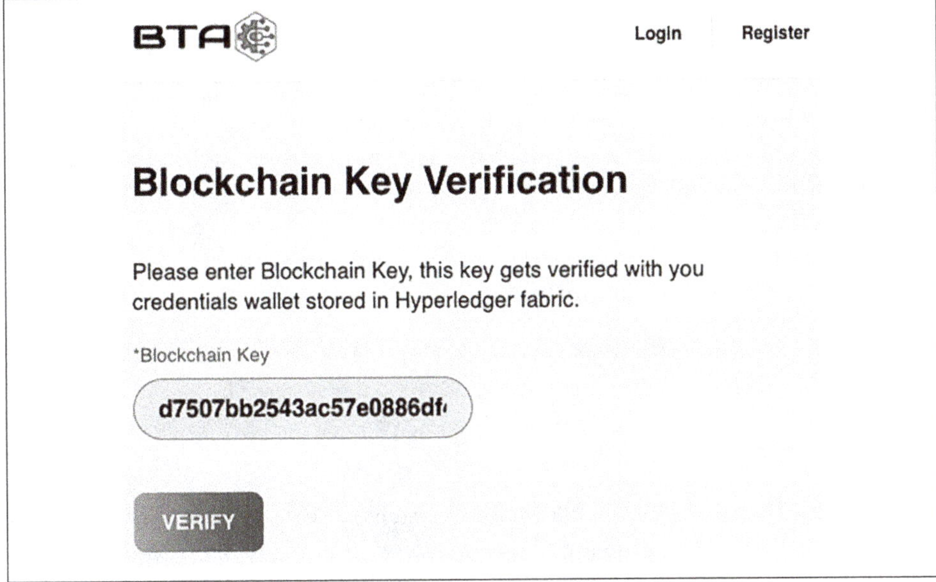

Figure 4-12. Blockchain key verification page after passing first login

After creating a model, the log file should be stored in the user's bucket in the folder hierarchy shown in the following list:

- Project Name
  - Version Name (V1)
    - Artifacts
      - Train Data Set
      - Test Data Set
    - Log
      - *Exp1.json*
      - *Exp(n).js*

MLOps engineer

The MLOps engineer reviews and deploys the submitted models, and can see all projects in the BTA, including multiple versions of each project. The MLOps engineer downloads the model and runs it in their own data science environment, where test data and logs are stored in the user's own bucket following the folder format discussed in the AI engineer's role.

Before the review process starts, the MLOps engineer makes sure that the data set submitted by the AI engineer has not changed by comparing the hash of logs and artifacts between the current version versus before the run. Figure 4-13 shows basic information about the project such as the name, version, engineer's name, and the blockchain membership service provider, or MSP, verifying the identity of the version's creator.

Project Name: MNIST
Version Name: v1
Created By: Mileva+ai_eng@kilroyblockchain.com
Creator MSP: Peer05AIEngineerBtaKilroyMSP

Figure 4-13. Model details

The Verify BC Hash section of the Model Blockchain History screen in BTA compares blockchain hashes of the log file, test data set, training data set, and AI model against the hashes of current bucket data to prove that data tampering has not taken place, as shown in Figure 4-14.

Type	Submitted Data Blockchain Hash	Bucket Data Blockchain Hash	Status
Log	9275e1a764a87d19b5a9be57a7b87e79af1a724b9dd20dc97054a9b92289febd	9275e1a764a87d19b5a9be57a7b87e79af1a724b9dd20dc97054a9b92289febd	Verified
Test Data	9a44cbbe04b208e212a21157b71b051ec14e9178d5134371f354287c00bfaa88	9a44cbbe04b208e212a21157b71b051ec14e9178d6134371f354287c00bfaa88	Verified
Train Data	1096f55547a3d7ad1931ee32cb25bf10f8cf41857610b6f64cedaec7c7e4f018	1096f55547a3d7ad1931ee32cb25bf10f8cf41857610b6f64cedaec7c7e4f018	Verified
AI Model	09f78ff847efa3434e92f6481b70f1f87783d84db68c7538cd7cde29529a66ff	09f78ff847efa3434e92f6481b70f1f87783d84db68c7538cd7cde29529a66ff	Verified

Figure 4-14. The Verify BC Hash section of the Model Blockchain History screen in BTA

If the hash verification passes, it proves that artifacts and logs have not been tampered with, thus addressing blockchain control 2.

As with the AI engineer, the MLOps engineer should activate two accounts before starting. These are the Oracle account and the BTA application account. With successful account activation and login, the user gets access to the OCI Data Science resources, the BTA application, and the blockchain peer.

MLOps Tools

Like most emerging technologies, machine learning has a variety of platforms to support automation. Three popular platforms, which work together, are DVC, MLflow, and DagsHub.

DVC (Data Version Control) (*https://dvc.org*) is an open source version control system for machine learning. DVC began as a way to control versions of training data, but has evolved to becoming more of a catchall for details needed to re-create experiments. DVC, according to its website, now includes "full code and data provenance (which) help track the complete evolution of every ML model."

While repositories like Bitbucket and GitHub are standard for most software developers, they are not used consistently in the MLOps world. Even using repositories when sharing experiments—as opposed to file sharing spreadsheets and zip files—is considered to be MLOps. However, this is being taken a step further by using a machine learning *data set auto generator* (DAG). A DAG combines a model, its data, and code into a single deployable pipeline.

MLflow (*https://www.mlflow.org*) is an open source platform designed to handle the workflow behind machine learning. MLflow integrates with both DVC and DagsHub to help engineers with reproducing and deploying experiments, and it provides a central registry for AI facts.

DagsHub (*https://oreil.ly/NLTOr*) is a platform that looks like a repository, and uses DAGs to integrate your Git, DVC, and MLflow remotes. It helps you version and push your data, models, experiments, and code. DagsHub is useful for sharing code, data, and experiments with another engineer or for transferring a model to another environment, such as development, staging, or production systems.

The BTA that you build in this book's exercises overlaps some of these features. Your BTA can be integrated with any of these tools to provide a tamper-evident audit trail on blockchain.

When the review process starts, the MLOps engineer can change the status of the model to "Reviewing" so that the other project participants know that the review process has begun. After reviewing the model, the MLOps engineer can change the status of the model to "Review Passed" or "Review Failed." (A model gets "Review Passed" if the accuracy of the model reviewed by the MLOps engineer is greater than the AI engineer's accuracy retrieved from the submitted log file.)

Once the review passes, the MLOps engineer changes the status to "Deployed" and releases a testing/deployed URL for the rest of the users. After the model is reviewed, the MLOps engineer can change the model's status to "Deployed." They can add ratings of the model, production URLs, and review the version number, or add a log-and-test data set that is pulled by the script based on the version number. By adding review details from a MLOps engineer, the stakeholder or end user knows why the model was approved and deployed. This helps in governance and auditing of the AI model, which addresses blockchain control 3.

Additionally, a team review helps to make the model more authentic. Screenshots of a bug or issue with the model can be compiled into one document and uploaded to the BTA. The model's status can be set to QA to indicate it is under review, which is noted on blockchain. This creates a tamper-evident audit trail of deployment issues. The MLOps engineer can then launch the model to production if reviews after deployment are positive. The engineer should then change the status of the model to "Production." They can also update the status to "Monitoring," which allows for feedback if bugs or other issues are found in the launched AI model.

Stakeholder

Stakeholders pass through the registration and account activation process in a similar fashion to the AI and MLOps engineers, but with different staffing assignments. Stakeholder users get the staffing permissions that allow the user to review, complete, or cancel the AI model. The stakeholder gets access to the blockchain node, but it is not necessary to get access to the Oracle Cloud account as the user is not going to develop an AI model. The stakeholder user, as the decision maker, can either cancel or complete the project.

The stakeholder is able to review the deployed model and monitor the production-based model. The stakeholder is able to see who has submitted the model, the accuracy of the model, and compare the hashes of the logs and artifacts before and after they deploy to prove the provenance of the artifacts. All this information is pulled from the blockchain node along with the transaction ID and timestamp, so it addresses blockchain control 4.

The stakeholder can add or update a purpose for the model, as shown in Figure 4-15, and review, monitor, audit, and approve or decline the model.

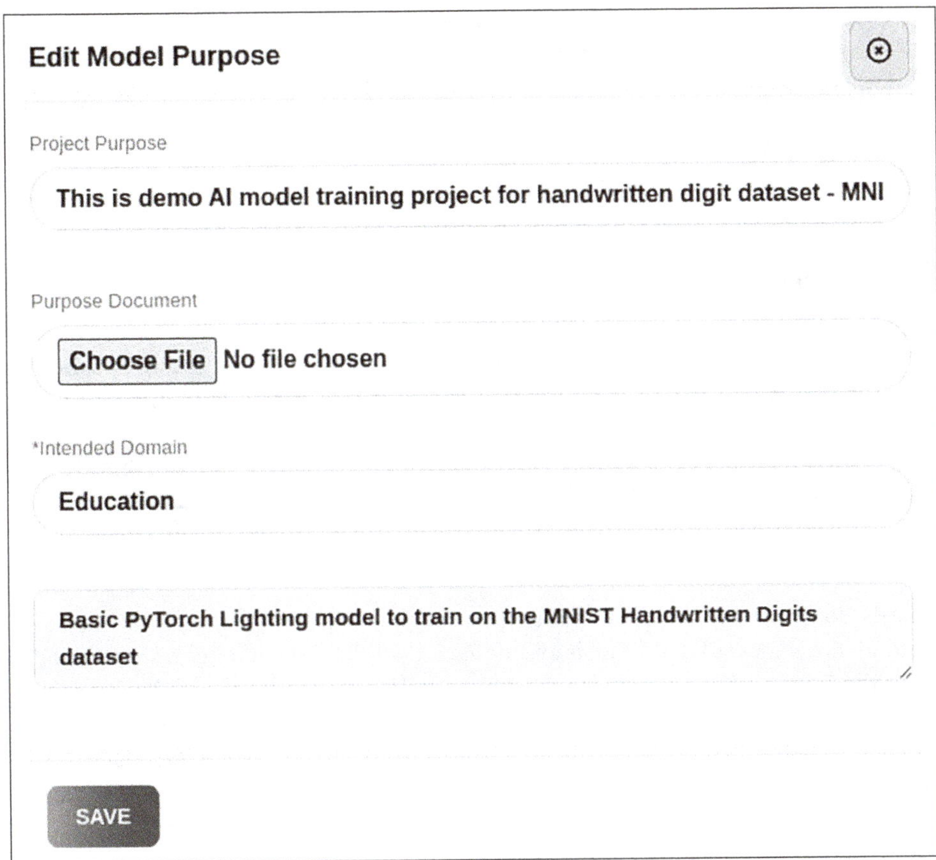

Figure 4-15. A stakeholder updates a purpose for a model in the BTA

Analyzing the Use Case

Chapter 1 discussed defining your blockchain use case. Figure 1-13 illustrates how to determine the participants, assets, and transactions for blockchain networks. Now you can apply this process to your BTA use case, and determine how to address both the business logic and the technical requirements of the BTA's blockchain component.

> ### Blockchain as a Layer of User Security
>
> The access control, privacy, and confidentiality mechanisms allow for confidential sharing, so that no unintended user can access restricted data or models. Blockchain brings an added feature to user management, in that it can record and also enforce security by means of smart contracts and agreed upon governance protocol. Tracking the order of exchanges helps to enable fair assessment of user contributions. Blockchain can be used to track ownership and usage across complex provenance chains.

Participants

A *participant* does some action that involves writing to the blockchain, while a *user* is anyone who logs in to the BTA web user interface. As such, an AI engineer is both a user of the BTA and a participant in the blockchain network because their approvals and comments need to leave a tamper-evident trail. An auditor user may not need to leave such a trail, because they are only reading records and auditing them. In this case, the auditor is a user of the BTA, but not a participant of the blockchain network.

Assets

Models, code repositories, logs, artifacts, and reports are the assets you will use when building the example BTA. Models are the AI models before and after training epochs and experiments. Repositories are where the code is stored. Logs are the temporary historical records that are produced during the epochs, similar to text logs found for any other computer system. Artifacts are defined as training and test data sets that have been used in previous training and testing. Reports are produced by the BTA or by supporting systems.

You might think that the BTA is supposed to log all data for each and every activity on blockchain. However, your BTA does not require that all data be logged *on* blockchain and it does not record each and every transaction. There is a good reason for not storing all assets like logs and artifacts into blockchain and into applications: the files themselves are too large and numerous, and storing the objects there isn't a good use for blockchain. Also, because there might be millions of objects like these in an ML system, storing them on blockchain distributed nodes will ultimately slow down the blockchain network and affect the performance.

It is better to put objects into a cloud-based object store with a pointer to the object and a hash of the object stored on blockchain. To make sure that the data set or log produced is tamper evident (the info has not been changed from the date of submission), the BTA stores the hash of those files (log and artifacts) in blockchain using the SHA-256 hashing algorithm, as detailed in Chapter 2.

At the time of model verification, the MLOps engineer makes sure the hash of the log or data set they get while running the model in their instance matches the hash of those files submitted by an AI engineer. If the hash is not the same, it indicates that the data set or log info has been changed outside of the accepted workflow. In that scenario, the MLOps engineer will not deploy the model. Instead, the model gets the status "Review Failed" and the AI engineer gets a chance to amend it based on this feedback.

When the MLOps engineer or stakeholder reviews the model, the channel (*global-channel*) receives the data and sends it to the stakeholder, MLOps engineer, and AI engineer's peers. In this way, data gets shared among different peers. This architecture is created for a project where each participant belongs to different organizations and grows when new projects are added. This architecture is responsible for achieving all four blockchain controls mentioned in Chapter 2.

Transactions

As discussed in Chapter 1, a transaction is what occurs when a participant takes some significant action with an asset, like when an MLOps engineer approves a model. When other participants comment on the model, those are also transactions, and are recorded on blockchain.

Usually, when you think through your transactions is where you will find the information that you need in the audit trail that you will store on blockchain, or blockchain touchpoints. Think of them as important points within the lifecycle of your model, timestamped and recorded on the blockchain sequentially so they can be easily reviewed and understood.

Smart Contracts

As you learned in Chapter 1, the term *smart contract* is used to refer either to functions within the chaincode that drive the posting of blocks to the blockchain, or the business logic layer of the application that drives workflow. In your BTA, smart contracts are used to automate the acceptance or rejection of the results of a model training event, and to kick off rounds of discussion about why the model is being accepted or rejected and what to do about it.

The workflow smart contracts used in your BTA only require any one participant to move something into a different status such as QA. In a nontest scenario, this workflow can be as complex as the business requirements, requiring a round of voting or for some other condition to be fulfilled (e.g., QA has to be performed for two weeks before the model can be put into production).

Audit Trail

Chapter 1 explained in detail how to determine and document blockchain touchpoints. This section guides you through how to design the audit trail for your BTA.

The purpose of adding blockchain to an AI supply chain is to create a way to trace and prove an asset's provenance. Therefore, it is very important to make sure all of the critical events are recorded onto blockchain. The BTA project allows AI engineers to develop the AI model using whatever toolsets, frameworks, and methodologies they prefer. Their development activities are not logged into the blockchain because there would be tons of trial and error in the code, which may not make sense to record because it would make the blockchain too big and unwieldy.

For this reason, the sample BTA focuses on the participants, assets, and transactions surrounding the model submitted by the AI engineer to the MLOps engineer for review. Some project information from the AI factsheet, such as its purpose and key contacts, are part of the BTA-generated audit trail, as shown in Table 4-1. In this table, you can see a timestamp of when each transaction was posted to blockchain, a transaction ID, an email address associated with the participant that created the transaction, which Hyperledger Fabric MSP was used for identity and cryptography, a unique ID for the project, detail about the project, and its members.

Table 4-1. Project info storing in blockchain

Timestamp	TxId	Added By	CreatorMSP	projectId	Detail	Members
2022-07-10T16:44:24Z	52628... 6d2365	OrgAdmin @...	PeerOrg1Mainnet BtaKilroyMSP	628b6c2... fa45625	Project: TSD Domain: Transportation Traffic sign detection is the process...	aiengineer@..., mlopsengineer@..., stakeholder@...
2022-04-11T16:44:24Z	726b7... 6d2369	OrgAdmin @...	PeerOrg1Mainnet BtaKilroyMSP	428b6c... 562569	Project: HDR Domain: Education The handwritten digit recognition...	aiengineer@..., mlopsengineer@..., stakeholder@...

The BTA also stores transactions that relate to when the model was tested, along with hashes of the log file, test data set, and training database, as shown in Table 4-2. By adding version status, this becomes an easy-to-understand audit trail of the training cycle of the model.

Table 4-2. AI models retrieved from blockchain

project id: 428b6c252a41ae5fa4562569

Timestamp	TxId	CreatorMSP	versionId	Version	logFile BCHash	test Dataset BCHash	train Dataset BCHash	version Status
2022-07-11T15:24:24Z	933d0... c7573	PeerMLOpsEngineer MainnetBtaKilroyMSP	60e6... 55298	1	68878... 99ce91c6	e5af4... 385dd	1dd49... 9107d	Review Passed
2022-07-11T14:24:24Z	d091a... 9221	PeerAIEngineer MainnetBtaKilroyMSP	60e6f... 55276	2	bef57... 892c4721	7d1a5... d4da9a	4fb9... 1f6323	Pending
2022-07-10T19:24:24Z	75bc... 52946	PeerStakeHolder MainnetBtaKilroyMSP	62ca8... 7562	3	88d4... f031589	ba78... 0015ad	36bb... 4ca42c	Complete
2022-07-08T19:24:24Z	2e6b... 9a4b	PeerMLOpsEngineer MainnetBtaKilroyMSP	60e6f... 5255	4	ab07... 9ju6a97	1b60e... ca6eef	179e... 98b72c	Review Failed

The status of a trained model, its version details, and the corresponding URL are also recorded in your BTA. Table 4-3 shows how this might look to a participant using your BTA to audit the AI.

Table 4-3. Model audit trail with timestamps and transaction ID hashes

Version ID: 62ca8a8b3c1f1f70949d7562
versionName: v3.0
logFileVersion: v1.0
logFileBCHash: 88d42...31589
testDatasetBCHash: ba781...015ad
trainDatasetBCHash: 36bbe...ca42c

Timestamp	TxId	CreatorMSP	Deployed URL	Model ReviewId	Production URL	version Status
2022-07-10T19:24:24Z	75bc7c8094... 5c3d652946	PeerStakeHolder MainnetBtaKilroyMSP	-	-	-	Complete
2022-07-10T17:44:24Z	6c4a63e39f... 2b7463cdf8b	PeerMLOpsEngineer MainnetBtaKilroyMSP	-	-	-	Monitoring
2022-06-15T13:45:24Z	17fa18dcab... df34rsdf984	PeerMLOpsEngineer MainnetBtaKilroyMSP	-	-	http://productionurl.com	Production
2022-06-27T13:45:24Z	27fa18dcab... 76224d3b7	PeerStakeHolder MainnetBtaKilroyMSP	-	-	-	QA
2022-06-25T13:45:24Z	sdfsdf3dc... 3234nisdfms	PeerMLOpsEngineer MainnetBtaKilroyMSP	-	-	-	QA
2022-06-23T13:45:24Z	34dfd32j... 324234sdf32s	PeerMLOpsEngineer MainnetBtaKilroyMSP	-	-	-	Deployed
2022-06-16T16:44:24Z	476254942... 9b55efe32	PeerMLOpsEngineer MainnetBtaKilroyMSP	-	-	-	Review Passed

Timestamp	TxId	CreatorMSP	Deployed URL	Model ReviewId	Production URL	version Status
2022-06-15T12:40:24Z	6685c676bd...4ad39c17	PeerMLOpsEngineer MainnetBtaKilroyMSP	-	-	-	Reviewing
2022-06-10T11:45:24Z	da23812033...670c3146f45	PeerAIEngineer MainnetBtaKilroyMSP	-	-	-	Pending

Part of auditing a blockchain is having the ability to check the hashes and request a change. This is addressed in Chapter 8, where you can also find more screenshots that show how the BTA is intended to look and work.

Summary

In Chapter 4 you learned about your AI model and what it does by reviewing its factsheet. You took a look at the various user personas in more depth, as well as how system access is controlled for each. Finally, you started looking at the BTA blockchain use case in more depth, analyzing the participants, assets, and transactions, and exploring the sort of audit trail that is possible with blockchain.

In Chapter 5 you will move on to setting up your Oracle Cloud instance and running your model.

CHAPTER 5
Running Your Model

In order to have a blockchain tethered AI, you first need an AI to tether. This book's code repository includes a Traffic Signs Detection model (*https://oreil.ly/KVKGp*) that you can run, test, and change.

In this exercise, you will set up the Oracle Cloud that will be used to integrate your model with blockchain (Chapter 6) and the BTA (Chapter 7). You will also prepare your local environment for running Python, PyTorch, and Jupyter Notebook.

Finally, you will clone the repository that contains the sample model, gain an understanding of what files are used, and use a Jupyter Notebook to bring the model to life.

Exercise: Oracle Cloud Setup

Setting up Oracle Cloud Infrastructure (OCI) is the first step to building the BTA. This is because the cloud resources are used to securely manage and share the files shared by an AI engineering team and its stakeholders. When you set up OCI, you will create a bucket used to store objects, and then assign access to that bucket by creating groups that correspond with the staffings you will create in your BTA application. Remember as you proceed through the examples that you need to create OCI resources for each of your BTA team staffings: ai-engineer-staffing, mlops-engineer-staffing, and stakeholder-staffing.

Keep a notepad file with the information that is noted as being needed later, such as the bucket connection URLs, so you don't have to search through OCI for it again. Be sure to use a plain-text notepad so your certificates don't break.

Creating a Cloud Provider Account

The blockchain, BTA, and model all share access to a single Oracle bucket (referred to as *the bucket*) which is used as a shared object store for training data, testing data, log archives, and model code. You read about the Oracle bucket in Chapter 4. It is extensively used during experimenting, submitting, and reviewing a model for storing and sharing logs and artifacts.

To follow these instructions to create and use buckets, you will need to have access to an Oracle Cloud account. If you do not have one, you can set up a free trial account by visiting *cloud.oracle.com* and clicking Sign Up.

You can use a different cloud provider, in which case you will need to correlate these steps to that provider's instructions.

If you are creating a free trial account on *cloud.oracle.com*, you will fill out a short form providing your name and email address. After Oracle verifies your information, you will be sent a link to complete the account information screen, where you set a password, select whether your account is corporate or individual, and set your cloud account name and home region. When you complete all the items and click Continue, you will be asked for an address and payment verification. After you supply a credit or debit card number to Oracle to verify your identity, and agree to Oracle's terms, click Start My Free Trial. Your card will be charged some small amount which will be promptly returned. When you add your payment verification method, Oracle states that you will not be charged unless you upgrade your account. After you click the button to proceed with payment verification, stay on the page. The payment verification section of the page will update with a message thanking you for verifying your details, and you will need to click the box in the Agreement section once more before clicking Start My Free Trial.

Make sure that when you sign up for your account, and each time you sign in, that you choose *cloud.oracle.com* and not *oracle.com*. The accounts are different, and an *oracle.com* account does not give you access to cloud services.

Creating a Compartment

OCI allows you to create logical groups of resources in units called *compartments.* To create a compartment, from the OCI menu choose Identity > Compartments. Click Create Compartment and then name the compartment "BTA-staffings." In the description, indicate resources for BTA staffings. Accept the rest of the defaults and click Create Compartment.

Creating a Bucket

To create an Oracle bucket under your OCI tenancy, go to the OCI Console menu and choose Storage. Next, in the Object Storage & Archive Storage section of the Storage menu, choose Buckets. This will bring you to the Buckets screen. On the left side, you will see a section for List Scope, where you can choose the compartment for your bucket, BTA-staffings, which you created in the previous step. This will display the Create Bucket screen, as shown in Figure 5-1.

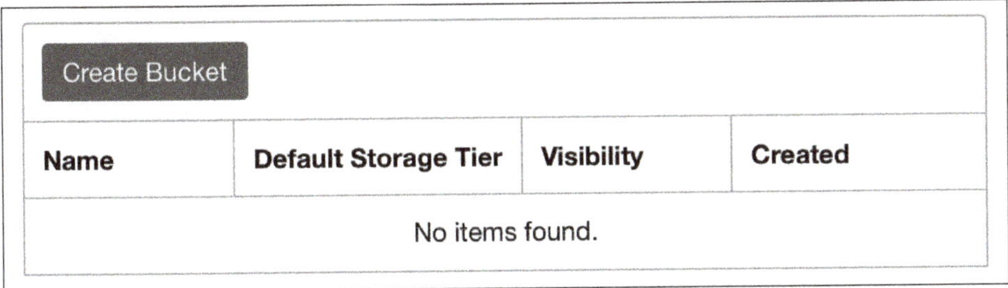

Figure 5-1. Create Bucket screen

Click the Create Bucket button and name the bucket "ai-engineer-staffing." Leave default storage at Standard, and accept all of the other defaults. Scroll to the bottom and click Create to create the bucket.

Click the link on the bucket name to open the bucket that you created, as shown in Figure 5-2.

Create Bucket

Name ▲	Default Storage Tier	Visibility	Created
ai-engineer-staffing	Standard	Private	Sat, Nov 12, 2022, 14:45:55 UTC

Figure 5-2. Click the link on the bucket name to open the bucket

When you open the bucket, you can display information about your bucket, as shown in Figure 5-3.

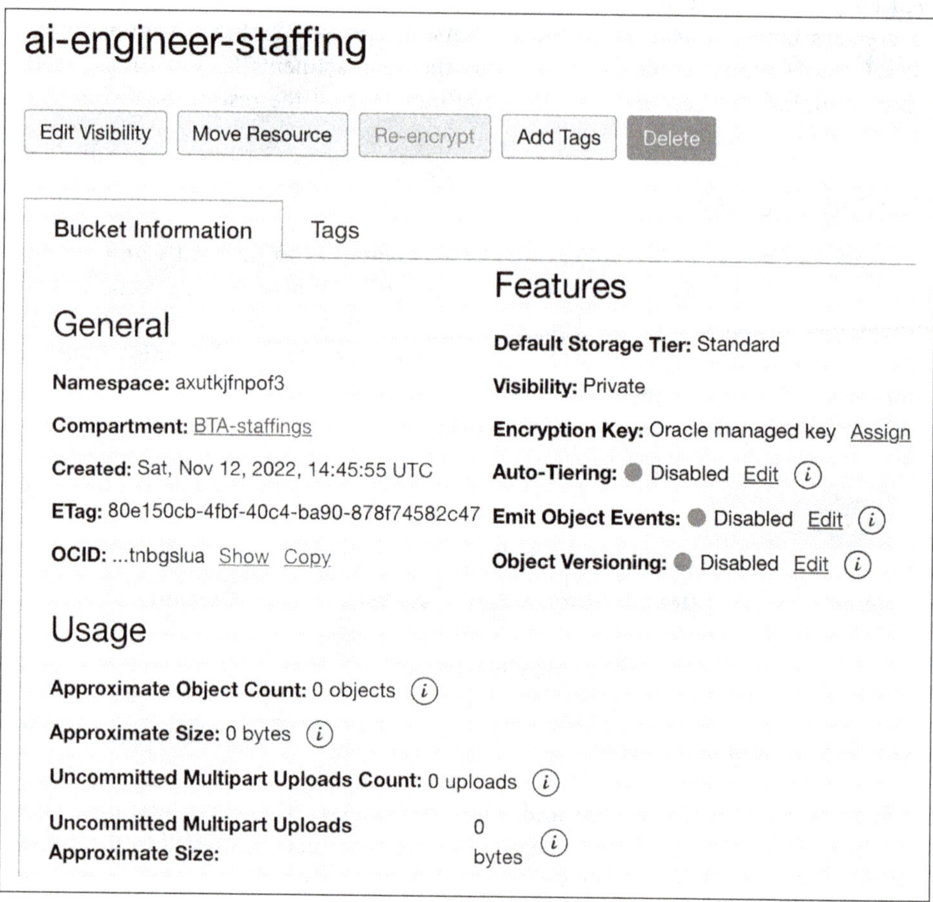

Figure 5-3. Displaying bucket information

Repeat this process for the MLOps engineer staffing and the stakeholder staffing, using the descriptive bucket names "mlops-engineer-staffing" and "stakeholder-staffing."

Creating a Pre-authenticated Request

Now that the buckets are created, create pre-authenticated requests so each type of user can access their bucket directly through their BTA login.

To do this, display the Bucket Information screen for ai-engineer-staffing again and scroll to the bottom of it. On the left, in the Resources menu, click Pre-Authenticated Requests. This brings up a Pre-Authenticated Requests screen. Click Create Pre-Authenticated Request and name it ai-engineer-staffing. Scroll to the bottom and click Create Pre-Authenticated Request to create the request.

After you have created the request, a screen appears to show you the pre-authenticated request details, as shown in Figure 5-4. This is very important since it gives you the pre-authenticated request URL, which will not be shown again. Copy this to a notepad and save it. You will use this URL while creating each staffing in the BTA, as it provides user access to the bucket data from the web application and from the blockchain.

Name *Read-Only*

ai-engineer-staffing

Pre-Authenticated Request URL *Read-Only*

https://objectstorage.us-phoenix-1.oraclecloud.com/p/rcEsd5vzrl2fRcSecq

Copy this URL for your records. It will not be shown again.

Figure 5-4. Pre-authenticated request details showing the URL

Repeat this process by opening the bucket details for mlops-engineer-staffing, scrolling to the bottom and choosing Pre-Authentication Requests from the menu at the left, and then do the same for the stakeholder-staffing bucket.

Creating Oracle Groups

You have created buckets for the AI engineer, MLOps, and stakeholder BTA staffings. Next, you need to add Oracle groups that correspond to each of the staffings. To create groups, from the OCI menu click Identity > Groups. Click the Create Group button and name your group "ai-engineer-staffing," with a description of AI engineer staffing. Click Create to create the group. Repeat the process for your other groups, mlops-staffing, and stakeholder-staffing.

These Oracle group names must match exactly the staffings you will set up for the BTA web application in Chapter 7. For this demo, you can make this easy by using ai-engineer, mlops-engineer, and stakeholder as your group and staffing names.

Creating IDCS Groups

Next, you need to create *federated* groups for each of the staffings, which allow you to share credentials across multiple systems. Still in the OCI menu's Identity and Security section, choose Federation. Click the link on the name of the provider, probably OracleIdentityCloudService, as shown in Figure 5-5.

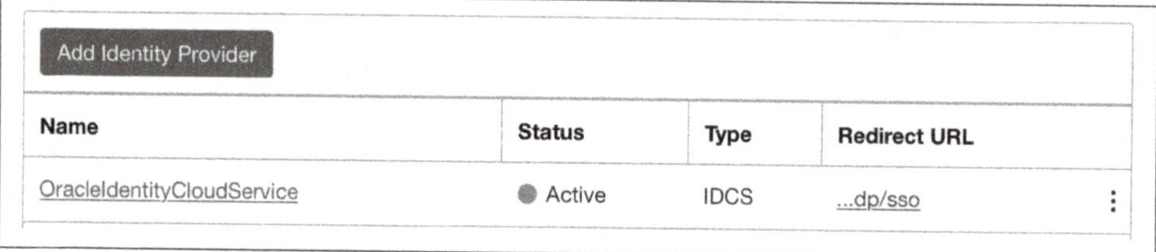

Figure 5-5. List of identity providers showing OracleIdentityCloudService

From the Identity Provider Information screen, scroll to the bottom and, from the Resources menu on the left, click Groups. Click Create IDCS Group and complete the name, which is the same as those you used for the other groups.

Create an IDCS group for each of the BTA staffings that have buckets. Name the first IDCS group "ai-engineer-staffing." Accept the defaults for the other fields and click Create. Repeat the process to create IDCS groups for mlops-engineer-staffing and stakeholder-staffing.

Mapping Oracle Groups

You have now successfully created OCI and IDCS groups. The next step will be creating the mapping between the groups. To map the OCI groups to the IDCS groups, create a group mapping that corresponds to each group.

From the OCI menu, choose Identity and Security > Federation. Click the link to open the details of the OracleIdentityCloudService identity provider, scroll to the bottom and, from the Resources menu, click Group Mappings. Click the Add Mappings button. Select an Identity Provider Group on the left and match it with the corresponding OCI Group on the right, as shown in Figure 5-6. Click Another Mapping and repeat for each staffing. After you have all three mapped, click Add Mappings to create them.

Your new mappings will now appear in the group mappings list.

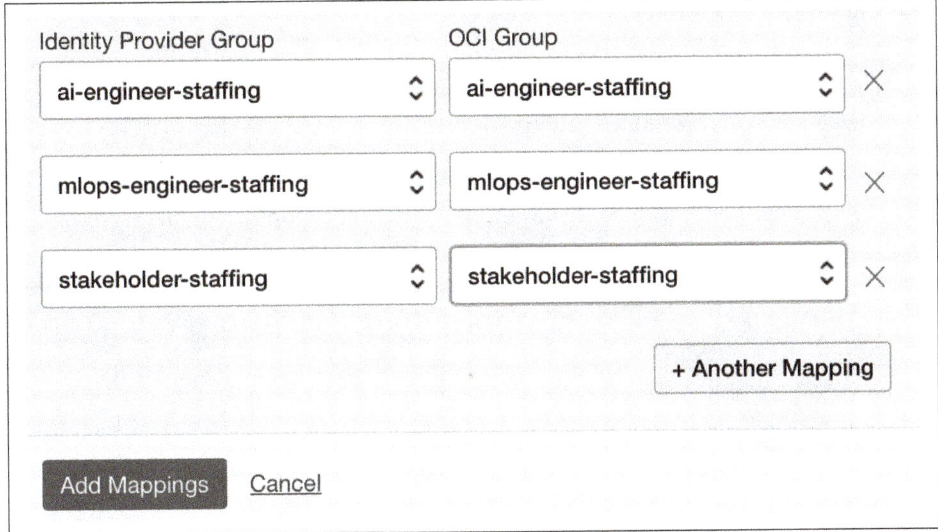

Figure 5-6. Mapping an Identity Provider Group to an OCI Group

Creating a Policy

The next step is to create security policies that correspond with each of the BTA staffings. To begin, open the OCI menu and click Identity & Security > Create Policy. Name the first policy "ai-engineer-staffing." For Compartment, select BTA-staffings from the drop-down. Toggle the switch to hide the Policy Builder and show the manual editor, and paste the code shown in Example 5-1 into the policy builder box for ai-engineer-staffing.

Example 5-1. Policy statement for ai-engineer-staffing

```
Allow group ai-engineer-staffing to read buckets in compartment BTA-staffings
Allow group ai-engineer-staffing to manage objects in compartment BTA-staffings where
target.bucket.name='ai-engineer-staffing-bucket'
```

Click Create to create the policy statement.

Repeat for mlops-engineer-staffing and stakeholder-staffing, using the code shown in Examples 5-2 and 5-3.

Example 5-2. Policy statement for mlops-engineer-staffing

```
Allow group mlops-engineer-staffing to read buckets in compartment BTA-staffings
Allow group mlops-engineer-staffing to manage objects in compartment BTA-staffings
where target.bucket.name='mlops-engineer-staffing-bucket'
```

Example 5-3. Policy statement for stakeholder-staffing

```
Allow group stakeholder-staffing to read buckets in compartment BTA-staffings
Allow group stakeholder-staffing to manage objects in compartment BTA-staffings where
target.bucket.name='stakeholder-staffing-bucket'
```

When you are finished, you should have policies for AI engineer, MLOps engineer, and stakeholder staffings inside the BTA-staffings Compartment, as shown in Figure 5-7.

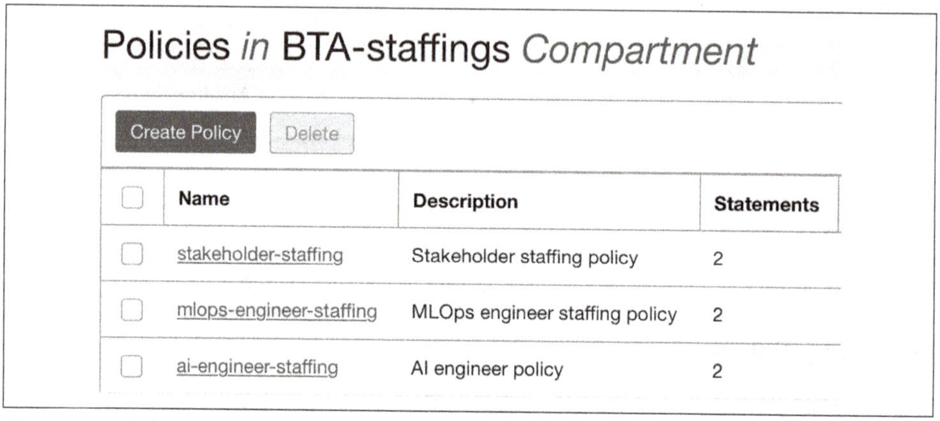

Policies *in* BTA-staffings *Compartment*

Create Policy | Delete

Name	Description	Statements
stakeholder-staffing	Stakeholder staffing policy	2
mlops-engineer-staffing	MLOps engineer staffing policy	2
ai-engineer-staffing	AI engineer policy	2

Figure 5-7. Policies in BTA-staffings compartment

Generating a Secret Key

A secret key is needed to make a secure connection from the Jupyter Notebook to OCI Object Storage. This key provides privileges for the user to perform updates to the target bucket. To generate the secret key, while still signed in to OCI, click the Profile icon at the top right corner of the screen. From the Profile menu, select User Settings to open the User Details page. In the User Details page, scroll down to the bottom. From the Resources menu on the left, click Customer Secret Keys, and then click Generate Secret Key. Specify a name for the secret key (for example, ocisecretkey), and then click Generate Secret Key. Copy and save the secret key to a safe place, because it won't be shown again. The OCI secret key will be used as the value for the `aws_secret_access_key` variable when configuring bucket access for the model in "Configuring Boto3" on page 145.

As mentioned, you will need your secret key when you configure your model to use the bucket in the next exercise. You will also need to supply a value for the `aws_secret_access_key_id` variable, which is the OCID in each bucket's information screen on OCI. The OCID for the bucket can be copied at any time, as opposed to the OCI secret key, which is only shown once when it is generated and must be saved in a safe text file at that time. If this secret key is lost, a new one will need to be generated.

This completes the configuration of OCI and the creation of buckets. In the next section, you will download the model and load the data into the buckets.

Exercise: Building and Training a Model

The Traffic Signs Detection model, also referred to in our notebook as MNIST, allows a user to upload images that might contain traffic signs. Then the model returns a text value describing any traffic signs the image contains. The model is simple and when it is running, it looks like Figure 5-8.

Figure 5-8. Traffic Signs Detection is a simple, free convolutional neural network image recognition model

This model is a *convolutional neural network* (CNN) (*https://oreil.ly/DZqcc*), or a type of highly effective neural network model that uses three layers of increasing complexity to narrow down and eventually identify details in an image, as shown in Figure 5-9.

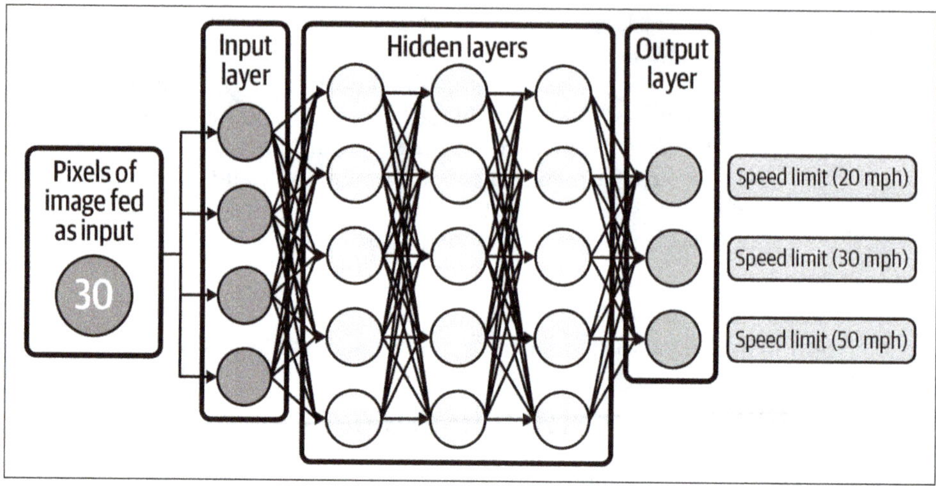

Figure 5-9. The multilayered approach to image recognition using a CNN

Exploring the Model Repository

To get the code for the Traffic Signs Detection model, from your project directory, clone the repository as follows:

```
$ git clone https://github.com/kilroyblockchain/bta-aimodel.git
```

Make sure you review the *README.md* file for any updates to the installation steps.

Your model can be set up to run either on the local server, as described in these steps, or in the cloud. The important thing for either situation is to know that the cloud-based bucket is a common tool where AI training logs and artifacts are stored. A copy of your model and artifacts is stored in the bucket so they can be shared with different participants through the BTA. To review the main facts about your model, refer to Table 4-1.

Inside the *bta-aimodel* folder you cloned, you can see five additional folders: *data*, *finallogfile*, *formattedjson*, *model*, *tb_logs*, and *zipdatasets*, along with two other files, *MINST_AI_MODEL.ipynb* and *Readme.md* (there is also a *.gitignore* file from GitHub).

The folder *bta-aimodel/data/MNIST* contains two additional folders: *raw* and *processed*. The folder *raw* contains image files that are used as training and testing data for your experiment. The folder *processed* contains two files representing the machine learning model produced by the PyTorch library: *training.pt* and *test.pt*. These files, which contain algorithms that perform AI tasks, aren't meant to be directly opened, but instead are called by functions in your scripts.

The folder *finallogfile* contains folders for each version of the model, and those folders contain log files. If you are looking at this folder when you have just pulled the repo, you will see one folder, *version_0*. Inside that folder is a JSON-formatted log file containing the output of the last experiment done on the model.

The folder *formattedjson* is used to store JSON-formatted log output. It contains a folder for each version of the model, and those folders contain the folders *train_log*, *test_log*, and *metrics*. Inside the *train_log* folder is *val_loss.json*, which logs the *loss* metric, or the value that the neural network is trying to minimize, such as the distance between the *ground truth*, or information known to be accurate, and the predictions.

Also in *train_log* is *val_acc.json*, which logs a metric that gives the percentage of instances that are correctly classified, and several other JSON files—*train_recall.json*, *train_precision.json*, *train_loss.json*, *train_f1_score.json*, and *train_acc.json*—that are used to store training metrics. The *test_log* folder has the same files, related to model testing instead of training. The *metrics* folder contains two files: *hparams.json*, which is a JSON formatted log of hyperparameters, and *hp_metric.json*, which is a JSON-formatted log of metrics pertaining to hyperparameters, as shown in Examples 5-4 and 5-5.

Example 5-4. Contents of hparams.json

```
{"total_epochs": 5.0, "algorithm_name": "Convolutional Neural Network", "data_dir":
"./data", "batch_size": 64.0, "learning_rate": 2e-05, "hidden_size": 64.0}
```

Example 5-5. Contents of hp_metric.json

```
[{"wall_time":1667792641.1799952984,"step":0,"value":-
1.0},{"wall_time":1667792739.9472017288,"step":0,"value":-
1.0},{"wall_time":1667792742.9905362129,"step":0,"value":-1.0}]
```

The folder *model* contains folders for each version of the model, and those folders contain *pickle files* (represented by a *pkl* extension). An object is *pickled*, or turned into a pickle file, when it is compressed and moved across a network, then *unpickled* when it is loaded into a computer's memory during runtime. When first installed, the only subfolder of the *model* folder is for *version_0*.

The folder *tb_logs* contains a folder called *my_model_tensorboard*. Inside there are folders that correspond to your model version, and those folders contain a file called *hparams.yaml*, which creates a record of your hyperparameters that were used in the experiment when these logs were generated. The contents of this file are shown in Example 5-6. The actual log files are also stored in this folder, have long filenames, and are not human readable. Each version folder also contains another folder called *checkpoints*. The *checkpoints* folder contains a file that isn't human readable that pertains to epoch details.

Example 5-6. Contents of hparams.yaml

```
algorithm_name: Convolutional Neural Network
batch_size: 64
data_dir: ./data
hidden_size: 64
learning_rate: 2.0e-05
total_epochs: 5
```

The folder *zipdatasets* contains two ZIP files: *train_datasets.zip* and *test_datasets.zip*. As their names imply, these are ZIP files containing training and testing images.

The *MINST_AI_MODEL.ipynb* file in the root folder is the one you will use to open your Jupyter Notebook, where you will modify and test the model's code. The *Readme* file, also in the root folder, contains the latest updates about the code, and it is a good idea to look through it before proceeding. When you are finished exploring the code, move on to installing Python.

Installing Python and PyTorch

Python is used to create the AI model together with experiment logs that get pushed to the bucket. Python code is also pushed to repo at the time of new AI model submission or review. Once your Jupyter Notebook session is created, you can write and execute Python code using the machine learning libraries in the JupyterLab interface to build and train models.

To set up your model's environment, you need to install Anaconda (a package and environment manager and a Python distribution that contains a collection of many open source packages) as well as set up a bucket on Oracle. To install Anaconda, follow the instructions shown on the Anaconda website (*https://oreil.ly/Eeg_E*) that are specific to your operating system.

The first time you start Anaconda Navigator, it will ask if you want to update; follow the prompts and update to the latest version.

If you already have Python installed, proceed to installing PyTorch. You will use PyTorch Lightning Trainer to train your model. To do so, visit the Anaconda website and follow the instructions for installing PyTorch (*https://oreil.ly/PsOtR*) for your operating system.

If you already have PyTorch installed, proceed to starting the notebook.

Starting the Notebook

Open Anaconda Navigator, find Jupyter Notebook, and click Launch. After writing a secret cookie to your local drive, the Jupyter Notebook home page will open in your default browser and display a list of your local files. Navigate to the folder that you used to install the `bta-aimodel` code that you downloaded earlier in this chapter and click *MNIST_project.ipynb* to open it in the notebook.

Configuring Boto3

With your notebook open, scroll down to section 4, which contains the code for Boto3 used by the model to access the bucket resources. Modify the notebook to reflect the secret key and access key, bucket name, version number, and project name.

Since in our demo, the AI engineer staffing always initiates new models and experiments, this configuration is specific to the AI engineer staffing's bucket.

As explained when creating your secret key earlier in this chapter, the secret key you saved in that step is used as the `aws_secret_key` in the Boto3 configuration. The `aws_secret_access_key_id` used in Example 5-7 can be located by clicking Object Storage > Bucket, then on the bucket name ai-engineer-staffing. On the Bucket Information tab, look for OCID and click the Copy link next to it. This key can be pasted into your notebook as the `aws_access_key_id`.

Example 5-7. Configuring bucket resources in the notebook

```
import boto3

# Configure Boto3 for Oracle Cloud instead of AWS. Region name and endpoint URL
# change if you are using a different OCI region.
s3 = boto3.resource(
 's3',
 region_name="us-phoenix-1",
 aws_secret_access_key="YOUR OCI SECRET KEY",
 aws_access_key_id="YOUR BUCKET'S OCI_ID",
 endpoint_url="https://xxxxx.compat.objectstorage.us-phoenix-1.oraclecloud.com"
)

# Here each AI Engineer defines required parameters for the project.

# Write the version number for the project
VERSION_NO = "v1"

# Define the project name here
PROJECT_NAME = "MNIST"
```

```
# Define Object Storage Bucket name here
BUCKET_NAME = "ai-engineer-staffing"

# Define the maximum number of epochs
MAX_EPOCHS = 5

# Please write the name of the Algorithm that you are using for this project
ALGO_NAME = "Convolutional Neural Network"

#Define a batch size
BATCH_SIZE = 256 if AVAIL_GPUS else 64

# Folder for storing tensorboard logs and checkpoints
logger = TensorBoardLogger("tb_logs", name="my_model_tensorboard")
```

Writing Your Own AI Model

You can also write an AI model on your own. If you do, you need to make sure that you have the BTA AI model script that changes the TensorBoard native log files into the format that the BTA project needs, and that you also have the code that uploads the logs and artifacts into the Oracle bucket structure:

- Project Name
  - Version Name (V1)
    - Artifacts
      - Train Data Set
      - Test Data Set
    - Log
      - *Exp1.json*
      - *Exp(n).js*

We recommend you use the included model first, and after you get that working, try the BTA with one of your own models.

Running Your Notebook

Now that you have your notebook up and running, take a few minutes and read the entire notebook contents, start to finish. Reading the instructions in the notebook will help you to understand the intent of the code contained in each of the cells, and provide helpful tips. The code contains detailed comments and can help you thoroughly understand your model and how it functions, as well as how it interacts with the BTA. Once you have reviewed the notebook, run it by choosing Run All from the Cell menu at the top of the notebook.

If your notebook doesn't run, make sure that you have configured it as trusted for running scripts. Trusted or Not Trusted status is indicated on a button to the right of the top menu. Click the button to trust the notebook.

Training the model will take some time. You may see configuration warnings as shown in Figure 5-10, which are OK to ignore, along with a blue progress bar showing the current epoch and the status. Once the cell has run successfully, the progress bar will be green.

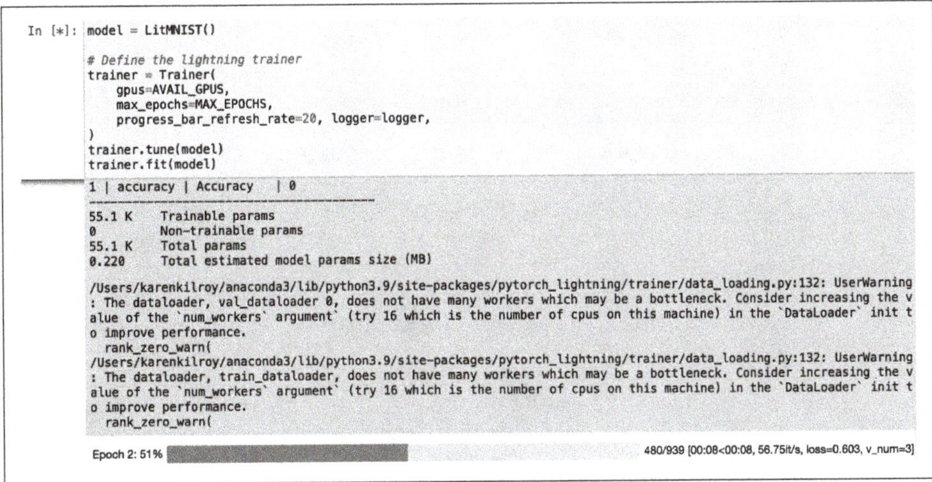

Figure 5-10. Training the model in the notebook

Each cell of the notebook will execute in order. The training and testing cells will contain a progress bar, while others will simply echo a message to the notebook upon completion. The echoed messages, or errors, are found beneath each cell.

Once you have successfully run the notebook, below the final cell which uploads the zipped data sets to OCI, you will see a message reading "Zip datasets upload completed." This means you have done everything correctly, and your zipped data sets are now copied to the ai-engineer-staffing bucket on OCI.

Checking the Bucket

After building, training, and testing the model, log back in to OCI, and from the menu choose Storage > Buckets to look in the bucket to make sure that artifacts and log files are there, as shown in Figure 5-11.

TSD	-	-	-
v1	-	-	-
v2	-	-	-
artifacts	-	-	-
datasets	-	-	-
test_datasets.zip	Fri, Oct 14, 2022, 07:37:22 UTC	1.57 MiB	Standard
train_datasets.zip	Fri, Oct 14, 2022, 07:37:23 UTC	9.41 MiB	Standard
model	-	-	-
TSD_model_0.pkl	Fri, Oct 14, 2022, 06:21:06 UTC	99.18 MiB	Standard
TSD_model_1.pkl	Fri, Oct 14, 2022, 07:37:19 UTC	99.18 MiB	Standard
logs	-	-	-
log_exp_0.json	Fri, Oct 14, 2022, 06:21:03 UTC	5.96 KiB	Standard
log_exp_1.json	Fri, Oct 14, 2022, 07:37:17 UTC	7.08 KiB	Standard
v3	-	-	-

Figure 5-11. The model and its artifacts are stored in a bucket

Understanding Lightning Trainer and Lightning Logger

Pre-trained models, like the one shown in Example 5-8, are neural network models trained on large benchmark data sets like DeepAI's ImageNet (*https://oreil.ly/bZ85X*). PyTorch Lightning Trainer (*https://oreil.ly/CGZAc*) fully automates the training of your model.

Example 5-8. A pre-trained model, automated by PyTorch Lightning

```
class LitModel(pl.LightningModule):
        def __init__(self, n_classes):
        super().__init__()
        self.net = torch.hub.load(
            'pytorch/vision:v0.6.0',
            'mobilenet_v2',
            pretrained=True
        )
        self.net.classifier = torch_nn.Linear(
            in_features=1280,
            out_features=n_classes,
```

```
            bias=True
        )
        self.save_hyperparameters()
```

PyTorch Lightning TensorBoard logger (*https://oreil.ly/7X3VM*) is used to create the standard log file required for the project because the native log created by TensorBoard is raw data. The data is processed by the logger library to create a JSON-formatted log file.

Congratulations! You have completed the second exercise. You have successfully run your model training and testing from your notebook, and verified that the resulting files were uploaded to the ai-engineer-staffing bucket on OCI.

Optimizing Hyperparameters

Hyperparameters, as Chapters 1 and 3 touched upon, are variables in ML experiments that are defined and set by the AI engineer before the learning process begins. They aren't part of, nor can be trained by, the training data. Rather, they help set the environment in which the learning process takes place. Some examples of hyperparameters are the AI learning rate, the number of epochs, the size of training batches, and the number of branches in a decision tree. In a neural network, for example, one hyperparameter might be how many layers are in your model. Every time any hyperparameter is changed and there is another ML run, your version tracker will save that as a new training set version.

The process of choosing which hyperparameters to use to create the ideal model architecture is called *hyperparameter tuning*. It's important to set the right hyperparameters prior to training because optimizing these variables increases the accuracy of the AI model being created. The best value for each hyperparameter needs to be determined either by historical rule of thumb, or by trial and error. Unfortunately, there isn't one specific way to calculate how to modify a hyperparameter to optimize your model architecture.

Learning Rate for Training a Neural Network

For optimization algorithms, one of the hyperparameters is the *learning rate*. The learning rate determines how much the algorithm can change for each iteration, while keeping the loss of accuracy of the model at a minimum. In other words, it determines how fast the machine "learns." It also controls how frequently the other hyperparameters are cross-checked. It can be difficult to choose the optimal learning rate; if it is too low, the training process may slow down too much; if the learning rate is too high, the model may not optimize in an appropriate amount of time.

In the best-case scenario, the user would draw on prior experiences (or other types of learning material) to develop an idea of the appropriate value to utilize when establishing the learning rate.

For the Traffic Signs Detection model, the learning rate we used is 0.0001.

Number of Training Epochs Used

If you don't know where to start with setting the number of training epochs, there's a rule of thumb that the hyperparameter can be initially calculated as three times the number of data columns. The ultimate number of training epochs will depend on the complexity of the model. If the model is still improving after all the epochs are completed, then try another run with a greater number of training epochs.

Data sets are usually grouped into batches (especially when the amount of data is very large). If the batch size is the whole training data set, then the number of epochs is the number of iterations. The selection of the optimum number of epochs must be done to avoid underfitting and overfitting of the curve in the graph seen in Figure 5-12.

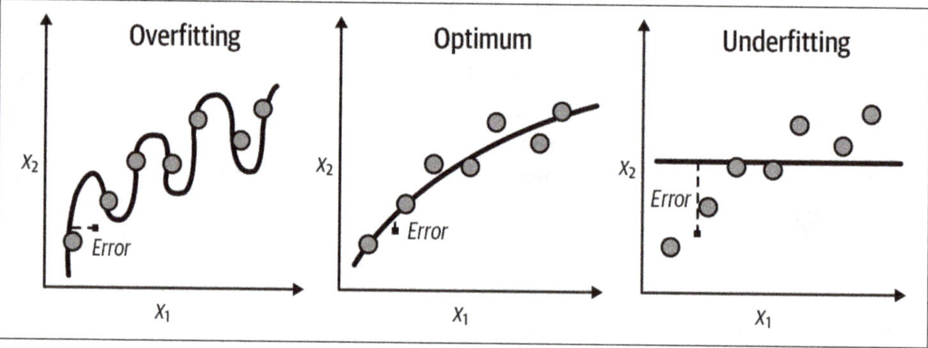

Figure 5-12. Learning curves in machine learning. Adapted from an image in Paperspace's AI Wiki (https://oreil.ly/23EyU).

Size of the Training Batches

The hyperparameter *batch size* defines the number of data samples that are fed into the algorithm at any one time. A full training data set is made up of one or more batches. Let's imagine we want to train our algorithm to recognize different dog breeds using 1,000 images of dogs and that we choose a batch size of 10. This means that at one moment, the network will get 10 images of dogs as a batch. If each epoch consists of a single run of all data over the network, an entire epoch will consist of 100 batches:

$$\text{Batches in an epoch} = \frac{\text{Training set size}}{\text{Batch size}}$$

For the Traffic Signs Detection model, `train_batch_size=4`, `valid_batch_size=1`, and `test_batch_size=1` were defined.

Size of the Hidden Layers

In an artificial neural network, a *hidden layer* exists between the input and output layers, where artificial neurons take in a set of weighted inputs and produce an output through an activation function. It is a typical part of nearly any neural network in which engineers simulate the types of activity that go on in the human brain. If the network is not that complex, there might be only one or two hidden layers between the input and output. If the data has large dimensions or complex features, then there might be three to five layers in order to reach an optimum solution. Figure 5-9 illustrated a neural network with three hidden layers.

The Traffic Signs Detection model uses ResNet-50, a CNN that goes 50 layers deep.

Understanding Metrics

To forecast the target class of the data sample in classification problems, classification models are used. The classification model predicts the probability that each instance belongs to one class or another. It is important to evaluate the performance of the classifications model in order to reliably use these models in production for solving real-world problems.

Most of the time we use classification accuracy to measure the performance of our model; however, it is not enough to truly judge the accuracy of the model. The metrics are logged first when training the model, then the same metrics are used to evaluate the performance of the model on a test data set.

To determine the classification accuracy of the model, we use accuracy, loss, precision, recall, and F1 score.

Accuracy

Accuracy represents the identification of independent images that were not used in training the AI model. The test data sets are used to evaluate the performance and progress of your algorithm's training and adjust or optimize it for improved results. In data science, it's typical to see your data split into 80% for training and 20% for testing.

Loss

Loss value implies how well or poorly a certain model behaves after each iteration of optimization. The model is said to be *underfit* when the training loss is way more significant than the testing loss and *overfit* when the training loss is way smaller than the testing loss. The model performs very well when the training loss and the testing loss are very close.

Precision

The percentage of positively predicted labels that are really correct is represented by the model *precision* score. The *positive predictive value* is another name for precision. To balance false positives and false negatives, precision is utilized in conjunction with recall. Class distribution has an impact on precision. The precision will be lower if there are more samples in the minority class.

Consider precision as a metric for exactness or excellence. When the classes are very unbalanced, the accuracy score serves as an effective indicator of prediction success.

Recall

The model *recall* score shows how well the model was able to anticipate positive results from actual positive results. This differs from precision, which counts the proportion of accurate positive predictions among all positive predictions given by models. The *sensitivity* or *true positive rate* are other names for recall. A high recall score shows how well the model can locate examples of success.

F1 Score

The model *F1 score* serves as a representation of the model score in relation to the precision and recall scores. A machine learning model's performance is measured using the F1 score, which equally weights precision and recall to assess accuracy. The F1 score is employed as a metric in situations when picking either the precision or recall score can result in a compromise in terms of the model producing high false positives or false negatives, respectively. The F1 score is the *harmonic mean* of the precision and recall score.

The sum of a set of data values divided by the number of those values is known as the *arithmetic mean*, or more commonly, the *average*. If, however, those data values are ratios of two variables with different measurements, such as velocity, then it would be appropriate to calculate the harmonic mean. The harmonic mean is the number of the data values divided by the sum of the reciprocal (1 over each value) of the values.

Summary

You now have a running model in an easy-to-use Jupyter Notebook. Its logs, training, and testing data, along with its code, are stored in a shared bucket that can be reached by the model, the blockchain, and the BTA. You have an understanding of how to train the model by manipulating data and hyperparameters.

Now you are ready to take the steps to tether it to blockchain. In the following chapters, you will create the blockchain network, set up the BTA front and back ends, and use the BTA system to simulate collaboration among members of an AI team.

CHAPTER 6

Instantiating Your Blockchain

Now that you have a copy of your model and its artifacts in a bucket, you are ready to implement the blockchain that you will use to tether it. You will use Hyperledger Fabric as your blockchain system, which Chapter 2 explained in detail.

In the next section, you will instantiate a Hyperledger Fabric blockchain instance, test it, and implement chaincode. You will set up a single node that will be used, through the BTA interface, by each of your users as a tamper-evident record of their AI experiments.

Finally, you will set up an OCI connector so your blockchain can reach your bucket.

Exercise: Setting Up Hyperledger Fabric

Setting up the blockchain network is the next step. When you run the scripts for this exercise, you will create a node for each participant, simulated in Docker, which consists of a *blockchain connector*, a certificate authority, a network peer, and chaincode, as shown in Figure 6-1. You will also create channels, which allow the nodes to communicate with one another and play an important role in choosing which peers receive which data.

The blockchain connector is a Node.js script that is installed in each peer, which exchanges data between a web application and the peers. In Figure 6-2, the demo BTA network is shown with all of its participants, revealing how the peers interact using the channels. The *o5-ai-engineer-channel* is a personal channel of an AI engineer that stores the draft model. Another channel, *c1-channel*, receives a newly submitted model by the AI engineer and sends it to the MLOps engineer.

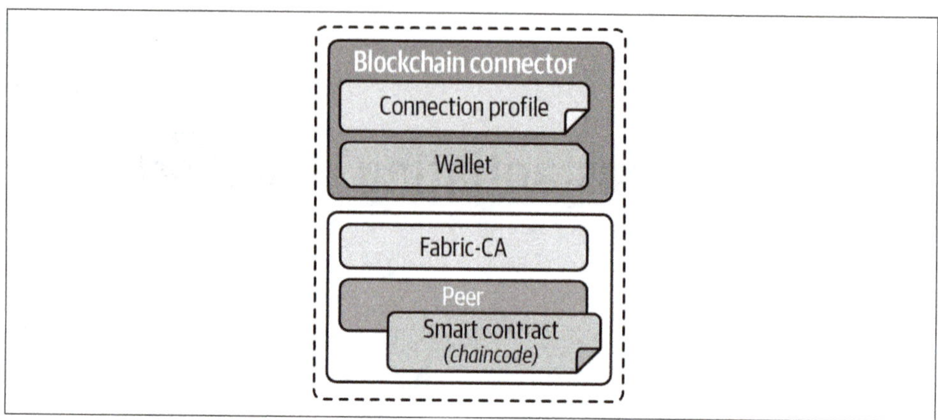

Figure 6-1. Hyperledger Fabric blockchain network architecture for a single node

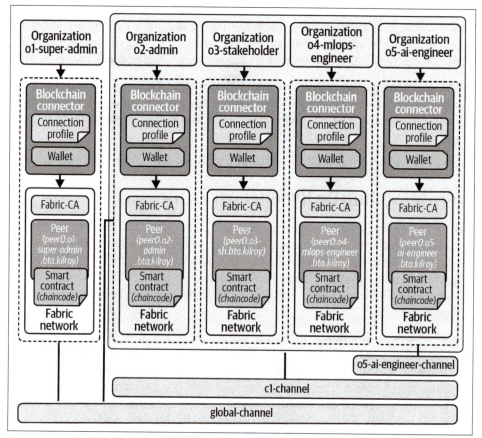

Figure 6-2. Blockchain architecture for BTA shows nodes communicating across channels

Installing Node.js, npm, and NestJS

Node.js includes npm, and both are needed for this book's exercises. Follow the instructions on the Node.js website (*https://oreil.ly/-iZ5w*) to download and install Node.js and npm for your platform.

NestJS is a JavaScript framework used for building Node.js applications. To install it, follow the NestJS website instructions on how to download and install NestJS (*https://oreil.ly/Ej-Cy*) for your platform.

Understanding Hyperledger Fabric 2.0 Required Nodes

Hyperledger Fabric 2.0+ is used to create your blockchain network. The blockchain network is composed of network peers, or *nodes*. Hyperledger Fabric requires certain nodes in order to run. These nodes have their own responsibilities:

Orderer
: The *hyperledger/fabric-orderer:2.4* node is responsible for receiving the transaction, adding those transactions into blocks, and distributing them to peers across the network.

Peer
: The *hyperledger/fabric-peer:2.4* peer nodes are responsible for holding ledgers and smart contracts. All the smart contracts are installed on those peers.

CLI
: The *hyperledger/fabric-tools:2.4* node provides a CLI, which is used to interact with Fabric networks. All the channel creation, channel join, chaincode installation, and other transactions on the network are done through the CLI.

Intermediate CA
: The *hyperledger/fabric-ca:1.5.1* node provides an intermediate certificate authority (CA) that is used for registering users to the blockchain network. The certificates created by the intermediate CA allow the users to interact with the blockchain network.

Go (*https://go.dev*) version 1.18.2, often referred to as *golang*, is the programming language used for the BTA chaincode development. Go was already installed when you set up Hyperledger Fabric, since it is bundled with its accompanying tools.

Installing, Configuring, and Launching the Blockchain

To set up the blockchain environment, from your project directory clone the *bta-blockchain* repository using the following command from your project folder:

```
$ git clone https://github.com/kilroyblockchain/bta-blockchain.git
```

Make sure to look at the repo's *README.md* for any updates to the installation steps.

The *bta-blockchain* folder that you cloned contains folders called *bin, script, bta-network, bta-chaincode, bta-bc-connector*, and *bta-ca*. The *README.md* file in the root directory might contain last-minute updates, so be sure to read it. The *bin* folder contains the binary files you will need to run Hyperledger Fabric. The *script* folder contains shell scripts that help you stop and start your nodes, remove certificates and artifacts, create and join channels, install and instantiate chaincodes, and perform other critical functions to running your blockchain network.

The *bta-network* folder contains several folders: *orderer, ica, peers-c1, cli-c1, channel-config*, and *base*. The *orderer* folder contains a file called *docker-compose.yaml* that is used to run the container that holds the ordering peer. The *ica* folder contains YAML files used to run the certificate authority containers for each type of user, including the super admin and organization admin, as well as for the MLOps and AI engineer roles, and stakeholders. The *peers-c1* folder contains YAML files used to launch blockchain nodes for each type of user. The *cli-c1* folder contains a *docker-compose.yaml* file that launches the Hyperledger Fabric CLI. The *channel-config* folder contains a *configtx.yaml* file that is required to build a channel configuration that contains information of all the blockchain network entities. The *base* folder contains a *base.yaml* file that is used to supply default information for the other YAML files.

The *bta-chaincode* folder contains other folders pertaining to the smart contracts, or *chaincode*. The folders found here are *project, project-version, model-version, model-review, model-experiment*, and *model-artifact*, along with files called *go.sum* and *go.mod*. Because the chaincode is critical to how your AI and your blockchain integrate, this chapter explores the chaincode files found in the *bta-chaincode* folder in depth. The *project* folder contains a Go source file called *project.go* that constructs the blockchain so it expects the type of transactions sent by the BTA. There is also a file called *project* that is a compiled version generated by the script in *project.go*. In the folder called *project-version*, there is a file called *project-version.go*. This script integrates blockchain with the BTA's model versioning features. The folders *model-version, model-review, model-experiment*, and *model-artifact* are all similar in that they tie blockchain to these features in the BTA, and each contains a corresponding Go file that accomplishes the integration.

The *bta-bc-connector* folder contains a variety of types of code used to connect your nodes to the blockchain connector that you will configure later in this chapter, in the next exercise. The *bta-ca* folder contains files necessary to configure a certificate authority for your blockchain, as described in detail in "Blockchain Control 1: Pre-establishing Identity and Workflow Criteria for People and Systems" on page 42.

In the sections that follow, you will generate the certificate files, genesis configuration files, channel configuration files, and anchor peer configuration files, and you will finally download, install, and run the blockchain nodes.

Installing Hyperledger Fabric binaries

All of this section's shell scripts are run from the *bta-blockchain/script* folder. If they don't execute as shown, you can either use `sh` before each command name or `cd` to the *script* folder and run `chmod +x *` to set the script files to executable.

First, change directories to point to the folder containing the shell scripts, and set all scripts to executable:

```
$ cd bta-blockchain/script
```

Next, run this script to download and install the required Hyperledger Fabric binaries to your local system:

```
$ ./downloadBinaryFiles.sh
```

This will return a response of:

```
----------------------------------------------------
Successfully downloaded and installed HLF binary files
----------------------------------------------------
```

Generating certificate files

We are using Fabric CA to generate all the necessary certificates. Run the following script from the *bta-blockchain/script* directory to download all required certificates for different users:

```
$ ./generateCertificates.sh
```

When you run this script, it takes a minute or so to complete. There is a lot of text that scrolls by quickly. You will see a line that confirms as each certificate is installed. Once the script has finished running, you will see a final status:

```
----------------------------------
Successfully generated certificates
----------------------------------
```

Running Scripts

Shell scripts, or the *.sh* files included in the *script* folder of the *bta-blockchain* repo, run in your operating system's terminal window. If you make a mistake or want to try this part of the exercise multiple times for some reason, run `./removeCertificates.sh` to remove any certificates you previously generated and try again. Also, if you have experimented with installation and want to start over, you can always remove the *bta-blockchain* repo and clone it again without impacting the configuration you have already done in *bta-aimodel*. If you want to troubleshoot the script or review it before you run it, you can either open it in your editor or use a terminal command such as `less` (*https://oreil.ly/8wDrY*) to quickly type the script's contents out on the screen:

```
$ less<generateCertificates.sh
```

As each page of text pauses, you can press your space bar to bring up the next page. Typing **q** will stop the display and return your command prompt.

Also note that these shell scripts run by using `./` before the script name because they have been set to be executable (`chmod +x`). Alternatively, you can use `sh` before the name of the script, e.g., `sh generateCertificates.sh`.

As Chapter 2 described, the script generates certificates for the CA for transport layer security (TLS), also known as Secure Sockets Layer (SSL). It generates the organization CA for the blockchain orderer; organization and intermediate CAs for the super admin, organization admin, AI engineer, MLOps engineer, and stakeholder; along with Membership Service Provider (MSP) certificates and TLS certificates for the blockchain's orderers, the super admin, organization admin, AI engineer, MLOps engineer, and stakeholder peers.

The TLS CA secures communications between all the nodes on the network. The organization CA is an organization's identity enrollment CA that is created for each organization which enrolls the identities participating in the blockchain network. Intermediate CAs are used to hide the exposure of the root CA (organization CA in our case). The intermediate CA enrolls the identities participating in the blockchain network on behalf of the root CA.

Generating the genesis block for the orderer peer

Before installing the Hyperledger Fabric network, you will generate the orderer's genesis block, which is its first block. While every channel has a genesis block, the genesis block for the orderer is special since it defines the configuration for the other channels. If you would like to fully understand how genesis blocks are used in Hyperledger Fabric, visit their "Channel Configuration" documentation (*https://oreil.ly/zUDAe*). Run the following script to create the genesis block for your orderer:

```
$ ./generateGenesisBlock.sh
```

After the genesis block has been generated, you will see a confirmation message:

```
----------------------------------
Successfully generated genesis block
----------------------------------
```

Generating channel configuration files

The next step is to generate the channel configuration files. Run the channel configuration generation script:

```
$ ./generateChannelConfiguration.sh
```

After the generation, a confirmation message will pop up on the terminal:

```
-------------------------------------------------
Successfully generated channel configuration files
-------------------------------------------------
```

Generating anchor peer configuration files

Next, generate anchor peers using the following script:

```
$ ./generateAnchorPeer.sh
```

After the generation, the confirmation message will be displayed:

```
----------------------------------------------------
Successfully generated anchor peer configuration file
----------------------------------------------------
```

Running the blockchain nodes

The last step is to download the Docker images for all the nodes and run those nodes on the Docker container.

Starting Docker

If you do not have Docker up and running already, install Docker (*https://oreil.ly/-0x66*) and start it before trying to run your nodes. If you install Docker Desktop for Mac, be sure to make this critical change—otherwise, your o2 node will not start. Open Docker and go to the gear icon to open Settings. On the General tab, uncheck the box that reads "Use gRPC FUSE for file sharing." Use the legacy *osxfs* instead, as shown in Figure 6-3.

Figure 6-3. Docker settings, General tab, showing "Use gRPC FUSE for file sharing" deselected

If Docker is already installed, make sure it is running. (This book's exercises have been tested using Docker v. 20.10.12 and *docker-compose* v. 1.29.2, but more current versions may also work.) All of the configurations are written on a *docker-compose* file.

Now that Docker is running, run the script that starts the blockchain nodes:

```
$ ./runNodes.sh
```

The following output will be shown after the nodes are running:

```
Starting peer0.o4-mlops.bta.kilroy       ... done
Starting peer0.o1-super-admin.bta.kilroy ... done
Starting peer0.o3-sh.bta.kilroy          ... done
Starting peer0.o5-ai-engineer.bta.kilroy ... done
Starting peer0.o2-admin.bta.kilroy       ... done
---------------------------------------
Successfully installed and started nodes
---------------------------------------
```

Troubleshooting

If you see this warning after running `./runNodes.sh`, your blockchain network won't start because Docker isn't installed or isn't running:

```
Cannot connect to the Docker daemon at unix:///var/run/docker.sock. Is the
docker daemon running?
---------------------------------------
Failed to start an Intermediate CA node
---------------------------------------
```

If you see this warning, everything will still work, but you can run `./removeArtifacts.sh` to clear the problem, and then use `./stopNodes.sh` and `./runNodes.sh` to restart the nodes with no errors:

```
WARNING: Found orphan containers (ica.o2-admin.bta.kilroy, cli.o5-ai-engine
er.bta.kilroy, cli.o3-sh.bta.kilroy, orderer1.org.bta.kilroy, orderer2.org.
bta.kilroy, cli.o4-mlops.bta.kilroy, orderer0.org.bta.kilroy, ica.o3-sh.bta
.kilroy, ica.o1-super-admin.bta.kilroy, cli.o2-admin.bta.kilroy, ica.o4-mlo
ps.bta.kilroy, ica.o5-ai-engineer.bta.kilroy, cli.o1-super-admin.bta.kilroy
) for this project. If you removed or renamed this service in your compose
file, you can run this command with the --remove-orphans flag to clean it
up.
```

If you see other warnings when you run your scripts and you want to start this exercise again, run `./stopAndRemoveNodes` (if they started; you can also see them in Docker), `./removeCertificates.sh`, and `./removeArtifacts.sh`.

Now, if you want, you can check the running nodes using the following command, which displays a list of your running Docker containers (you can also look inside the Containers tab of your Docker Desktop if you are running it, and see lots of other information):

```
$ docker ps
```

The list returned contains the Docker container ID, the Docker image name upon which the session is based, the last command that was executed, when the container was invoked, its status or time running, and the ports used.

Hyperledger Fabric version 2.2 is used as the blockchain platform of the BTA, where smart contracts are written in Go and a blockchain connector is created in an application layer based on NestJS. The connector is quite flexible and connects a proposed transaction to the right node through the right channel, validating the accesses in the nodes.

Creating and Joining Channels

The *blockchain connector* is a Node.js module that sits in the application layer but connects to the particular blockchain node through the connection profile and wallet created within the blockchain network. The code in the following sections is driven from the `bc-user` module.

To instantiate our BTA's Hyperledger Fabric blockchain instance, you need to create channels, join the channels, configure the anchor peer, and install and deploy the chaincode. This part of the exercise includes two scripts to help you create and join the channels.

Creating Channels

Channels are used for private and confidential communication between different members of the blockchain network. The channel creation step creates three channels in our scenario—the global channel, C1 channel, and AI engineer channel:

global-channel
: Global channels are the default channels created for super admin users. Super admin organization (*Peer01SuperAdminBtaKilroy*) and organization admin (*Peer02AdminBtaKilroy*) participate on this channel.

c1-channel
: C1 channel is the company channel created for the users associated with that company. In our case, you focus on a single company, called C1. All the users associated with the company join this channel. According to the sample network you are setting, organization admin (*Peer02AdminBtaKilroy*), stakeholder (*Peer03ShBtaKilroy*), MLOps engineer (*Peer04MLOpsBtaKilroy*), and AI engineer (*Peer05AIEngineerBtaKilroy*) can all join this channel.

o5-ai-engineer-channel
: The AI engineer channel is the private channel of the AI engineer of C1 Company. This channel is created to share the AI engineer's private data to the blockchain. Model versions created by AI engineers will be created only on this channel, where only AI engineers of the particular company will have access to it, and the model version status on the application level will be set as "draft." After an AI engineer confirms their channel is the final one—and is ready to submit the model version so that other users including MLOps, stakeholders, and the company admin will have access to it—the AI engineer submits the model version to the company channel (*c1-channel* in our case). The submitted model version then will be accessible by all the users joined on this channel.

To create these channels, run the following script:

```
$ ./createChannel.sh
------------------------------------
Successfully created channels
------------------------------------
```

Joining Channels

For different nodes of the organization to participate on the channels, each peer node of the organization should be joined to that channel. The peers mentioned in "Creating Channels" on page 164 will be joined to the respective channels.

Channels can be joined using this script:

```
$ ./joinChannels.sh
------------------------------------
Successfully joined channels
------------------------------------
```

Configuring Anchor Peers

After joining the channel, each peer needs to update its channel configuration with the anchor peer configuration file *configtx.yaml* (*https://oreil.ly/ZmgHB*), which is a Hyperledger Fabric file available for developers to define anchor peers. Updating anchor peers will define the anchor peer for each organization. Run the following script to update anchor peers:

```
$ ./addAnchorPeer.sh
------------------------------------
Successfully added anchor peer
------------------------------------
```

Using Chaincodes

Chaincodes are the Hyperledger Fabric equivalent of smart contracts used by other blockchain systems, and are used to read and update the ledger. Chaincodes need to be installed on every peer for the peer to execute the transaction. The chaincodes discussed in the following sections, written in Go, are installed on the blockchain network.

Unified Modeling Language (UML) is a standard for modeling software development through a series of diagrams. While the BTA code was not written using this technique, it is possible to model your projects in UML and then use it to generate code (*https://oreil.ly/uoUJa*). One UML diagram that is particularly useful to explain code is a UML class diagram, which is a type of structure diagram that shows a system's classes, attributes, operations, and relationships among objects.

A free utility, go-plantuml (*https://oreil.ly/T37F9*), was used to generate UML class diagrams for this chapter from this book's accompanying Go code. (go-plantuml is the Go version of the PlantUML utility.) In the top bar of each diagram, there is either an @ symbol to represent that the box contains a *package* or a C symbol to represent that the box contains a class. Next to the symbol is the name of the package or class. Beneath that is a list of methods and fields with an icon to the left of each line. The key to the icons is shown in Table 6-1.

Table 6-1. Key for the icons used in this chapter's UML diagrams

Field	Method	Visibility
□	■	Private
○	●	Public

The status code constants are declared on each chaincode for static error codes according to the error, as seen in Example 6-1. They help to determine the nature of the error occurring within the blockchain server.

Example 6-1. Status code constants

```
const (
    // OK constant - status code less than 400, endorser will endorse it.
    // OK means init or invoke successfully.
    OK = 200

    // BAD_REQUEST constant - error specifically for use when request params do not
    // meet the requirement
    BAD_REQUEST = 400

    // NOT_FOUND constant - error when requested resource could not be found but may
    // be available in the future
    NOT_FOUND = 404

    // INTERNAL_SERVER_ERROR constant - a generic error message, given when an
    // unexpected condition was encountered and no more specific message is suitable
    INTERNAL_SERVER_ERROR = 500

    // CONFLICT constant - error when the request could not be processed because of
    // conflict in the current state of the resource
    CONFLICT = 409
)
```

A diagram showing how the chaincodes and their classes relate to one another is shown in Figure 6-4, and lines showing the connections are marked *Many* where there are many calls. The chaincodes' model review and project version are not shown because they stand alone.

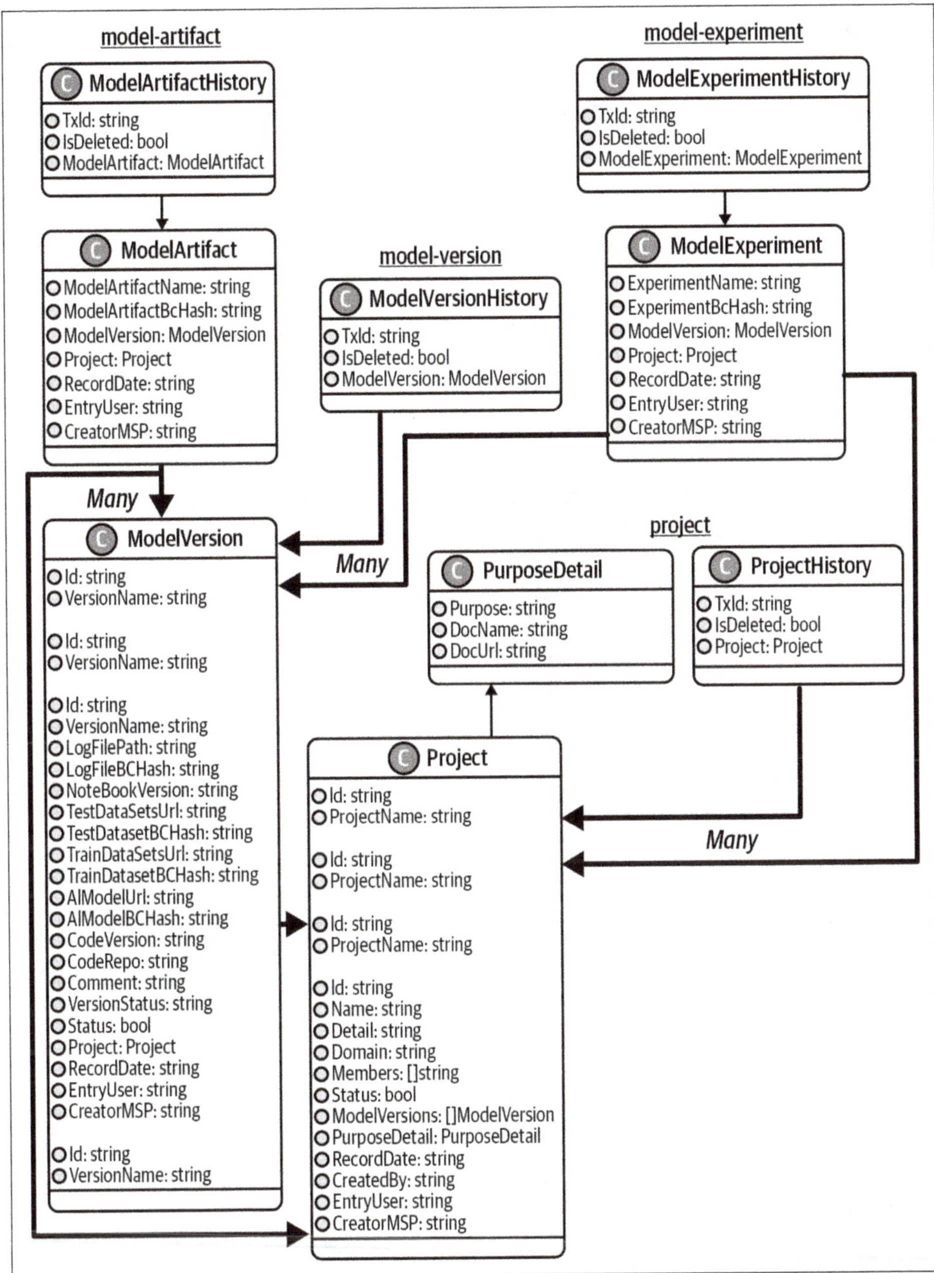

Figure 6-4. Diagram showing how the chaincode classes call one another

Understanding Response Struct

The response format that is created on each chaincode for sending every success and error response is seen in Example 6-2.

Example 6-2. Chaincode response

```
// Response Struct
type Response struct {
   StatusCode int32       `json:"statusCode,omitempty"`
   Message    string      `json:"message,omitempty"`
   Result     interface{} `json:"result,omitempty" metadata:",optional"`
}
```

Using GetTxDateTime

The `GetTxDateTimeString` function, as seen in Example 6-3, converts a transaction timestamp into a human-readable format as a date time string—for example, 2022-07-12T13:00:46Z.

Example 6-3. `GetTxDateTimeString` function

```
// GetTxDateTimeString function gets transaction timestamp and converts into UTC
// date time string
func GetTxDateTimeString(ctx contractapi.TransactionContextInterface)
   (string, error) {
   log := NewLogger("GetTxDateTimeString")
   currentDateTime, err := ctx.GetStub().GetTxTimestamp()
   if err != nil {
       log.Error(errors.Wrap(err, "Failed to get transaction time stamp"))
       return "", err
   }
   unixTimeUTC := time.Unix(currentDateTime.Seconds, 0) //gives unix timestamp in utc
   return unixTimeUTC.Format(time.RFC3339), nil
}
```

Project (project)

UML class diagrams for *project* and *project-version* are shown in Figures 6-5 and 6-6. These include certain functions commonly used within different modules in blockchain.

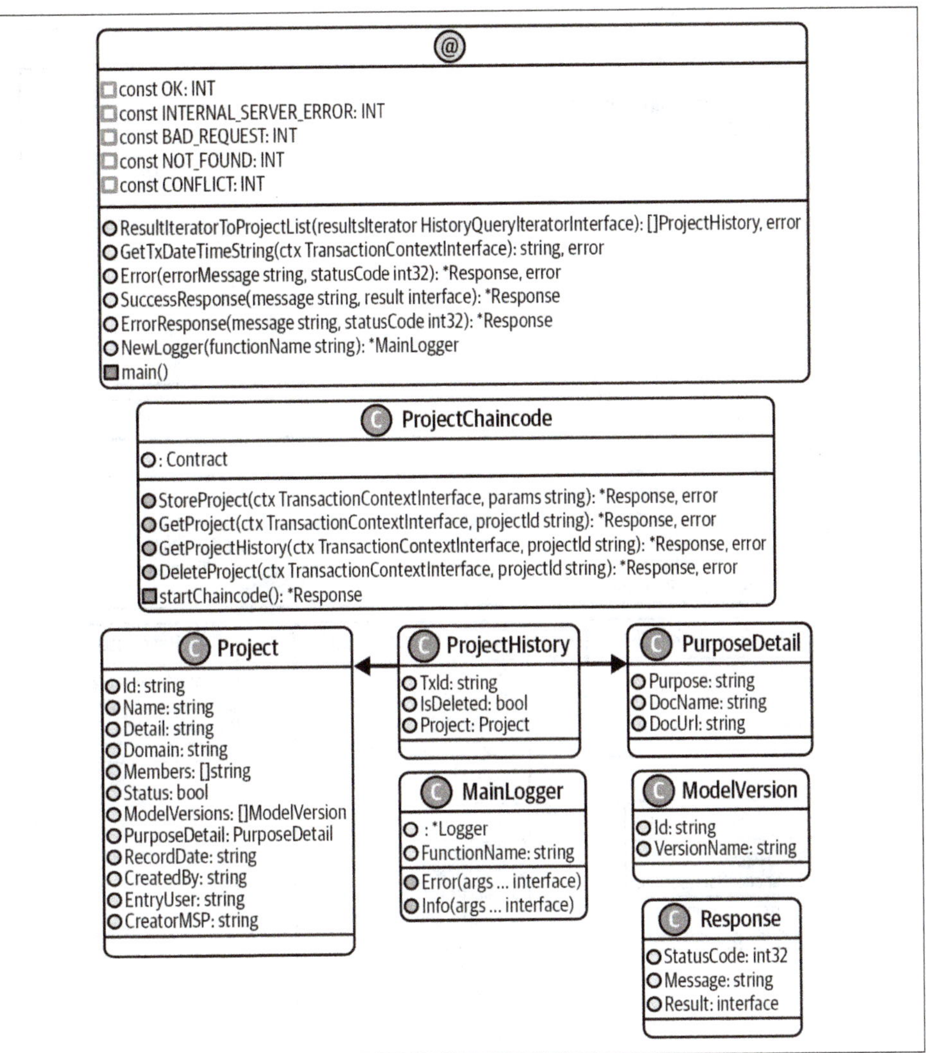

Figure 6-5. UML diagram of the project.go chaincode and its classes

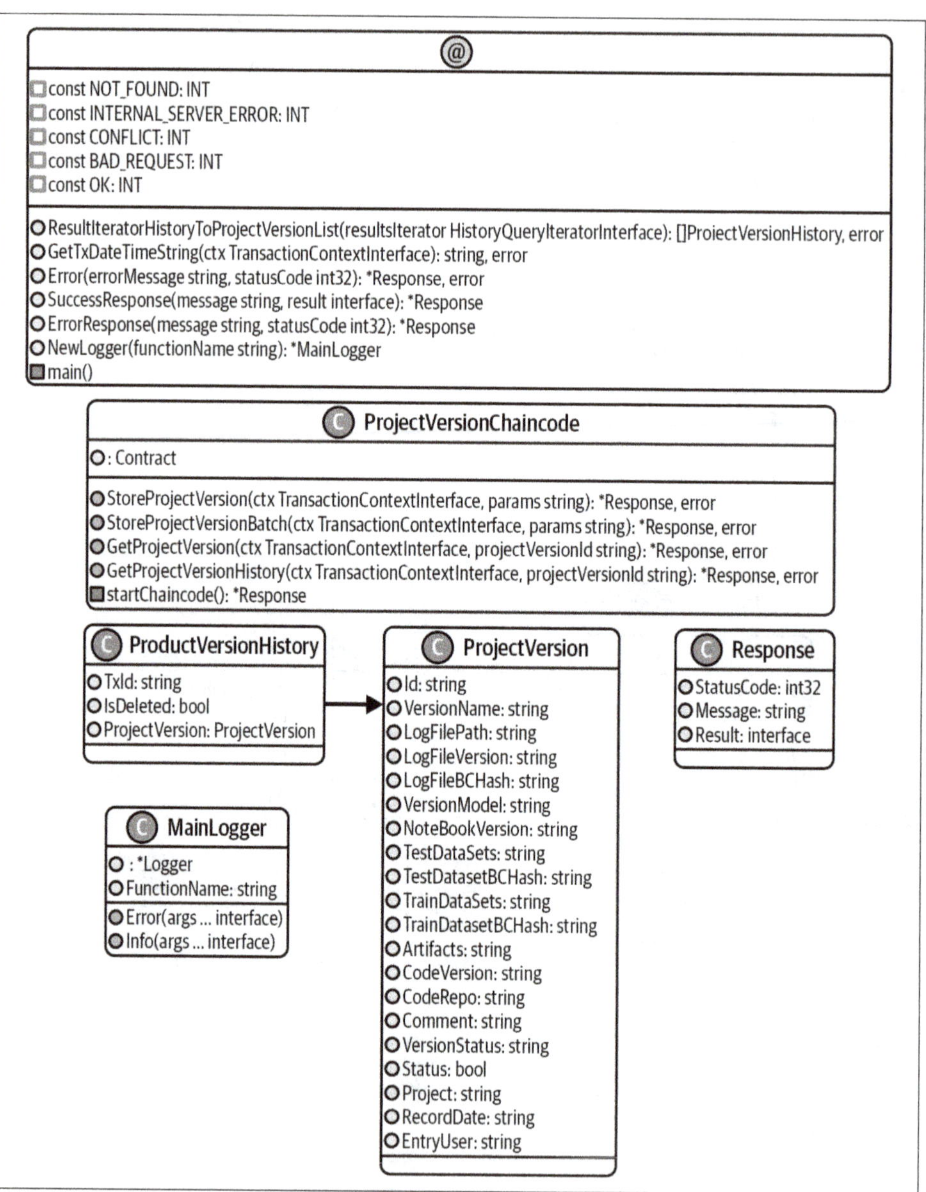

Figure 6-6. UML class diagram of the project-version.go chaincode and its classes

The chaincode *project* is installed on the organization admin, stakeholder, MLOps engineer, and AI engineer organizations, on channel *c1-channel* of every member because the data should be accessed by all the members. The following script installs chaincode to the peers of those participants:

```
$ ./installChaincode.sh project
```

After installation is completed, the following will display:

```
----------------------------------------------------
Successfully installed and deployed project chaincode
----------------------------------------------------
```

Hyperledger Fabric calls these scripts chaincodes instead of *smart contracts*, which is a term used broadly to describe the logic driving the function of the blockchain system.

Model Version (model-version)

The chaincode model-version is installed on the organization admin, stakeholder, AI engineer, and MLOps engineer organizations. The model-version chaincode is installed on two channels. The first channel on which the chaincode is installed by every member (organization) is channel *c1-channel*, because the data of model-version should be accessed by every organization after the model version is submitted. The second channel that the chaincode is installed on by the AI engineer organization is channel *o5-ai-engineer-channel*. This is because the model version is created by the AI engineer on their private channel until the model version is submitted. The UML diagram for model-version is shown in Figure 6-7.

Run the following command to install chaincode for model-version:

```
$ ./installChaincode.sh model-version
```

After installation is completed, you will see this message:

```
----------------------------------------------------------
Successfully installed and deployed model-version chaincode
----------------------------------------------------------
```

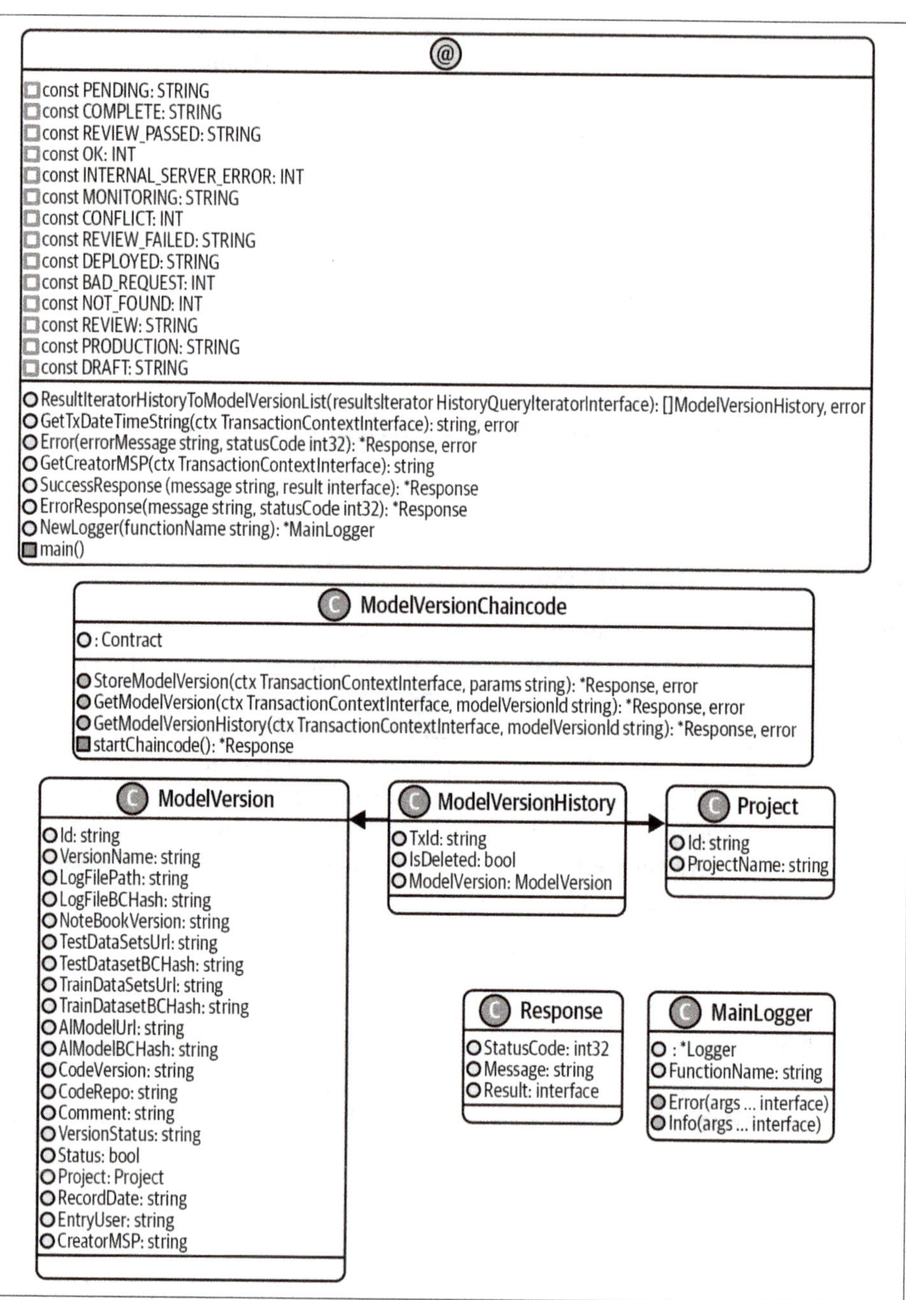

Figure 6-7. UML diagram of the model-version.go chaincode and its classes

The `ModelVersion` struct, as seen in Example 6-4, is created to store all the information about the model version in the defined format.

Example 6-4. `ModelVersion` format

```
// ModelVersion struct is defined for storing model version data on following format
type ModelVersion struct {
    Id                  string  `json:"id"`
    VersionName         string  `json:"versionName"`
    LogFilePath         string  `json:"logFilePath"`
    LogFileBCHash       string  `json:"logFileBCHash"`
    NoteBookVersion     string  `json:"noteBookVersion"`
    TestDataSetsUrl     string  `json:"testDataSetsUrl"`
    TestDatasetBCHash   string  `json:"testDatasetBCHash"`
    TrainDataSetsUrl    string  `json:"trainDataSetsUrl"`
    TrainDatasetBCHash  string  `json:"trainDatasetBCHash"`
    AIModelUrl          string  `json:"aiModelUrl"`
    AIModelBcHash       string  `json:"aiModelBcHash"`
    CodeVersion         string  `json:"codeVersion"`
    CodeRepo            string  `json:"codeRepo"`
    Comment             string  `json:"comment"`
    VersionStatus       string  `json:"versionStatus"`
    Status              bool    `json:"status"`
    Project             Project `json:"project"`
    RecordDate          string  `json:"recordDate"`
    EntryUser           string  `json:"entryUser"`
    CreatorMSP          string  `json:"creatorMSP"`
}
```

Model Review (model-review)

The chaincode model-review is installed on the company admin, stakeholder, MLOps engineer, and AI engineer organization. The model-review chaincode is installed on channel *c1-channel* of every member (organization) because the model reviews should be accessed by all the members inside the company. A UML diagram for model-review is shown in Figure 6-8.

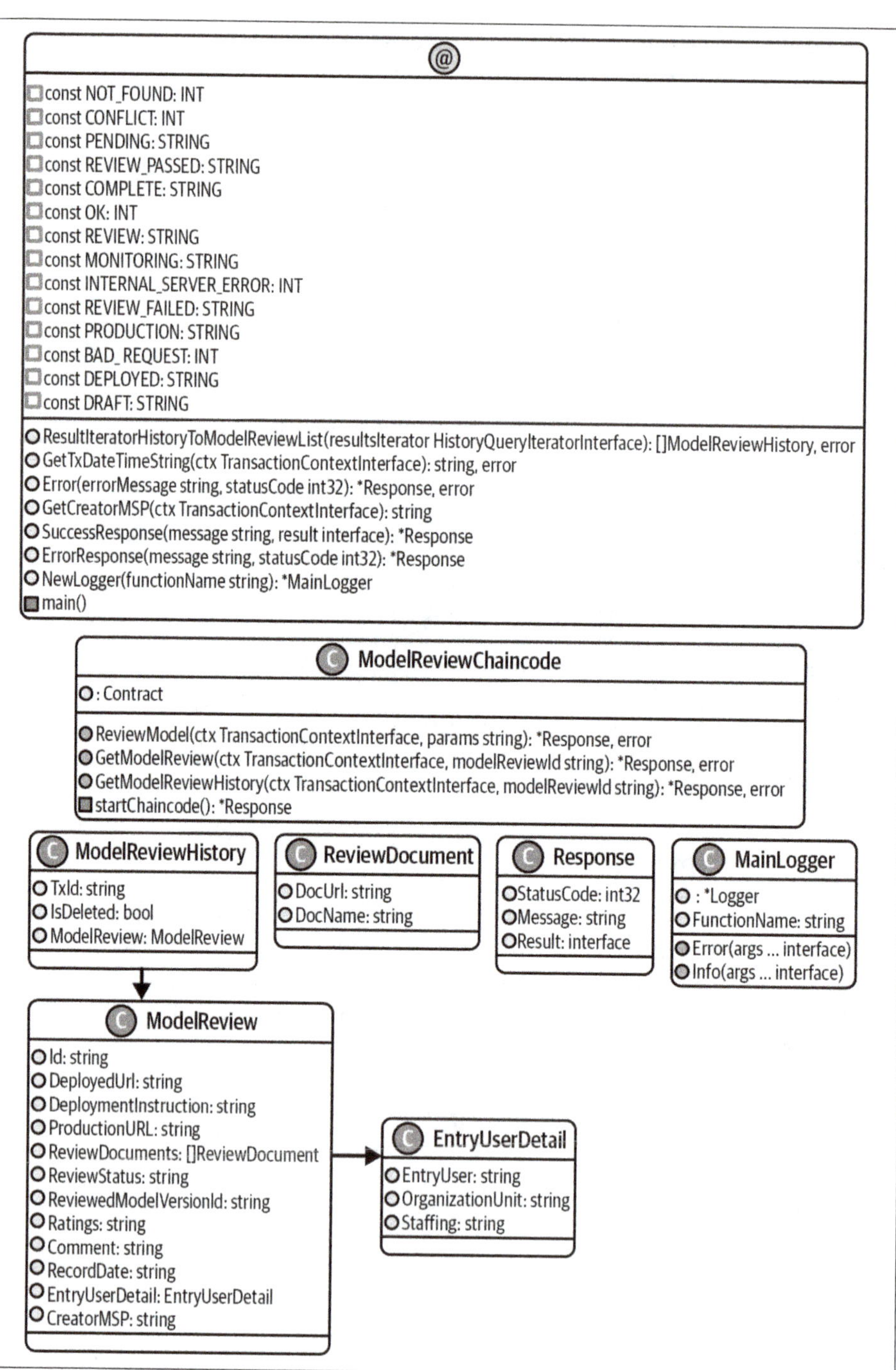

Figure 6-8. UML diagram of the model-review.go package and its classes

The script to install model-review chaincode on every organization is located at */script/installChaincode.sh*. Run the following command to install chaincode for model-reviews:

```
$ ./installChaincode.sh model-review
```

After installation is completed, you will see the following:

```
-----------------------------------------------------------
Successfully installed and deployed model-review chaincode
-----------------------------------------------------------
```

Using modelReview struct

The `ModelReview` struct, as seen in Example 6-5, is created to store all the information about the model review done by each user in the defined format.

Example 6-5. `ModelReview` format generated by each user

```
// ModelReview struct is defined for storing model review data on following format
type ModelReview struct {
   Id                      string           `json:"id"`
   DeployedUrl             string           `json:"deployedUrl,omitempty"`
   DeploymentInstruction   string           `json:"deploymentInstruction,omitempty"`
   ProductionURL           string           `json:"productionURL,omitempty"`
   ReviewDocuments         []ReviewDocument `json:"reviewDocuments,omitempty"`
   ReviewStatus            string           `json:"reviewStatus"`
   ReviewedModelVersionId  string           `json:"reviewedModelVersionId,omitempty"`
   Ratings                 string           `json:"ratings,omitempty"`
   Comment                 string           `json:"comment,omitempty"`
   RecordDate              string           `json:"recordDate"`
   EntryUserDetail         EntryUserDetail  `json:"entryUserDetail"`
   CreatorMSP              string           `json:"creatorMSP"`
}
```

Using GetModelReviewHistory

The `GetModelReviewHistory` function, as seen in Example 6-6, fetches all the history associated with the model review key from the blockchain state DB.

Example 6-6. `GetModelReviewHistory` function

```
// Get AI Model History By Id Key
   resultsIterator, err := ctx.GetStub().GetHistoryForKey(modelReviewId)
   if err != nil {
       log.Error(errors.Wrap(err, "Error fetching blockchain history: "))
       return Error("Error fetching blockchain history", INTERNAL_SERVER_ERROR)
   }
   defer resultsIterator.Close()
```

Using ModelReviewHistory struct

`ModelReviewHistory` struct, as seen in Example 6-7, is the response format that the chaincode returns while calling the History Fetch function.

Example 6-7. `ModelReviewHistory` format

```
// ModelReviewHistory struct defined for returning the model review history
response // on the following format
type ModelReviewHistory struct {
   TxId         string       `json:"txId,omitempty"`
   IsDeleted    bool         `json:"isDeleted"`
   ModelReview ModelReview `json:"modelReview,omitempty"`
}
```

Using storeModelReview

The `storeModelReview` function, as seen in Example 6-8, stores model reviews in the blockchain state, using the key as the ID of the model review.

Example 6-8. `storeModelReview` function

```
// Store modelReview state on ledger
   err = ctx.GetStub().PutState(modelReview.Id, modelReviewAsBytes)
   if err != nil {
       log.Error(errors.Wrap(err, "Failed to Store ModelReview"))
       return Error("Failed to Store ModelReview", INTERNAL_SERVER_ERROR)
   }
```

Model Artifact (model-artifact)

The chaincode model-artifact is installed on the organization admin, stakeholder, MLOps engineer, and AI engineer organization nodes. The model-artifact chaincode is installed on channel *c1-channel* of every organization because the model artifacts should be accessed by all the members inside the company. The UML diagram for model-artifact is shown in Figure 6-9.

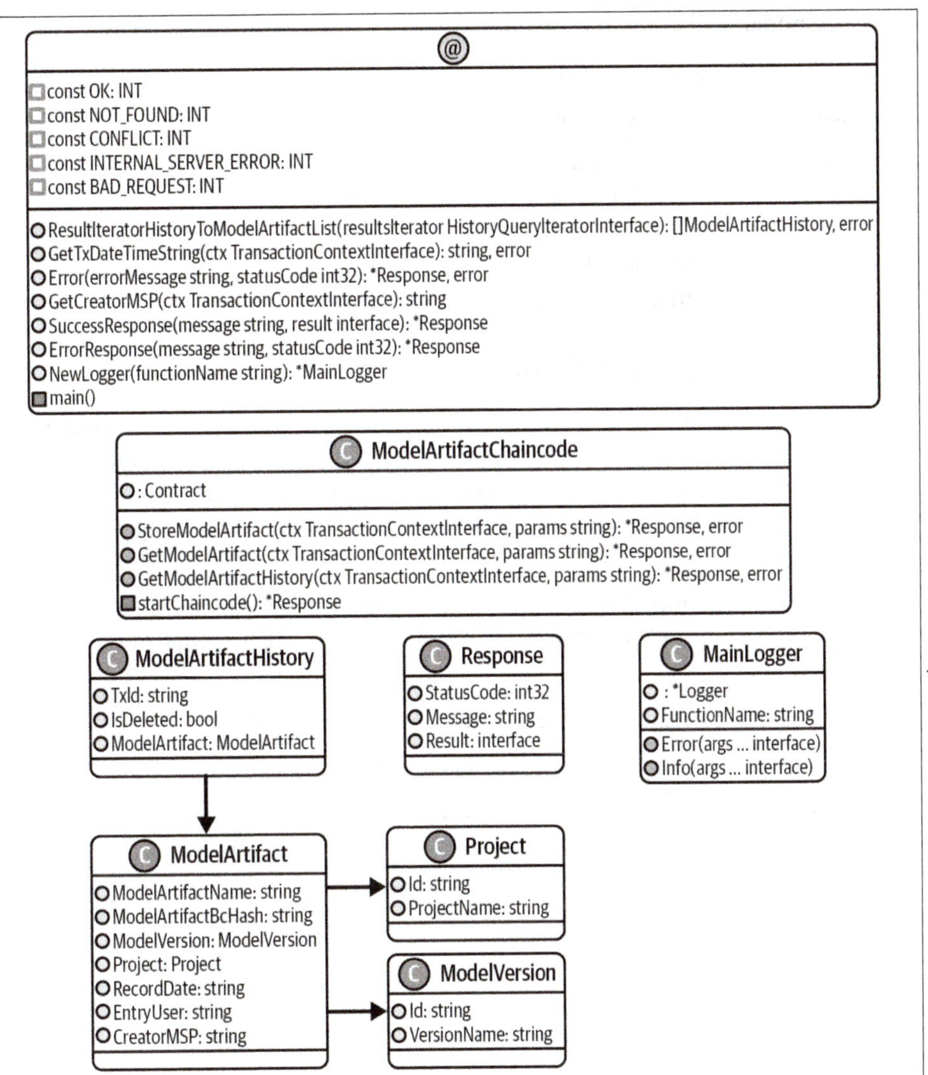

Figure 6-9. UML diagram of the model-artifact.go chaincode and its classes

To install model-artifact chaincode on every organization, run the following script:

```
$ ./installChaincode.sh model-artifact
```

After installation is completed, you will see this message:

```
---------------------------------------------------------
Successfully installed and deployed model-artifact chaincode
---------------------------------------------------------
```

In the next section, the sample code reflects how AI models are constructed in the blockchain section and also shows some of its important attributes.

Model Experiment (model-experiment)

The chaincode model-experiment is installed on the company admin, stakeholder, MLOps engineer, and AI engineer organizations. The model-experiment chaincode is installed on channel *c1-channel* of every member (organization) because the model experiment should be accessed by all the members inside the company. A UML diagram for model-experiment is shown in Figure 6-10.

The script to install model-experiment chaincode on every organization is located at */script/installChaincode.sh*. Run the following command to install the chaincode model-experiment:

```
$ ./installChaincode.sh model-experiment
```

After installation is completed, the following output is shown:

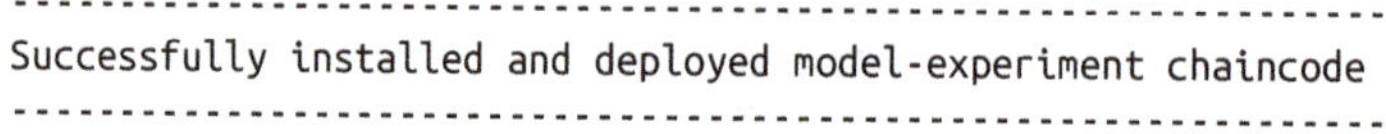

```
-----------------------------------------------------------
Successfully installed and deployed model-experiment chaincode
-----------------------------------------------------------
```

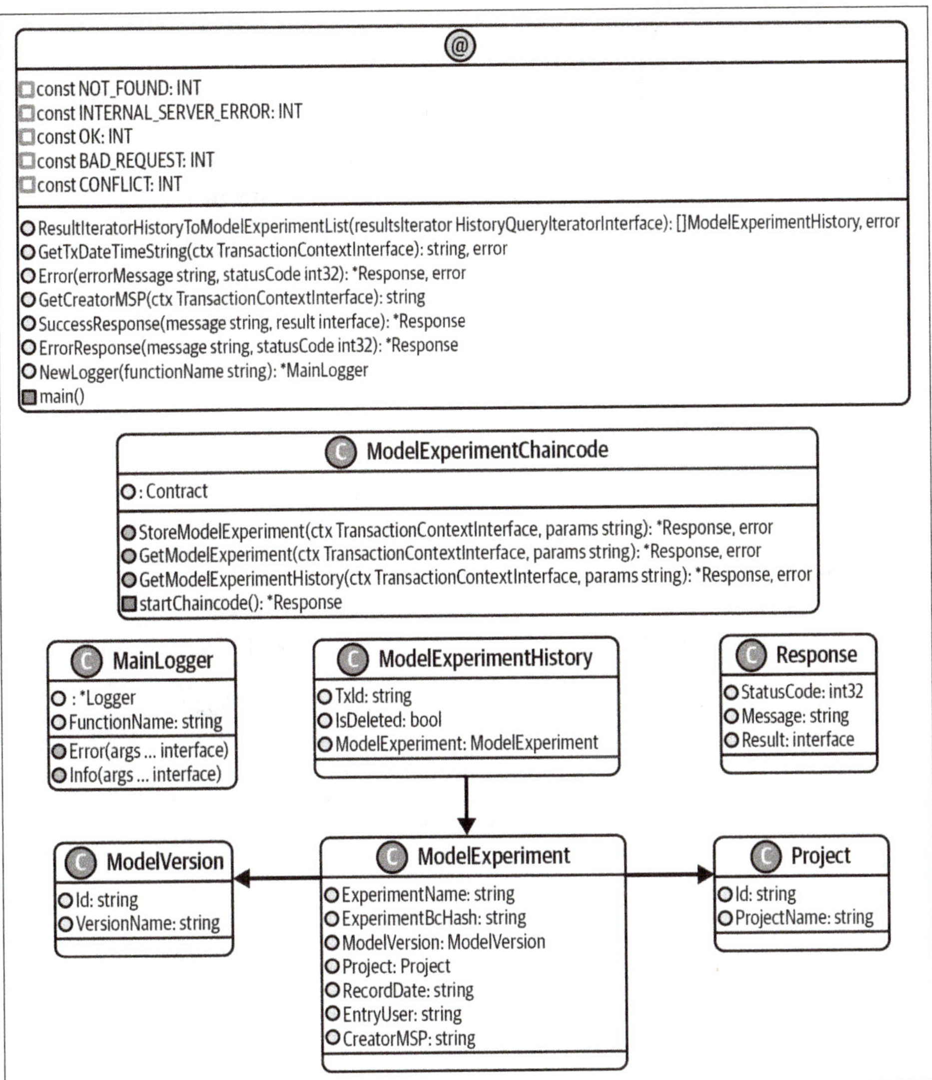

Figure 6-10. UML class diagram of the model-experiment package and its classes

Setting Up the Blockchain Connector

To set up nodes in the BTA web interface, you need to use a *blockchain connector*. This code connects the backend of the BTA web application with the blockchain network. Since your blockchain environment is installed and instantiated, you can run a script that configures the blockchain connector, so when you use your BTA web application, it is connected with your blockchain network.

The blockchain connectors that will install when you run the script are built using NestJS (a Node.js framework).

The number of blockchain connectors you need corresponds to the number of organizations that you have created on blockchain. For the BTA, you need to have five blockchain connectors: one each for super admin, organization admin, stakeholder, MLOps engineer, and AI engineer.

Each user's blockchain private and public key will be stored safely within their own organization in the wallet folder where the blockchain connector is deployed. For example, if any stakeholder wants their private and public key safe with them only, they can run their blockchain node and blockchain connector on their own virtual machine and then perform any transactions through their own virtual machine. In order for a blockchain connector to connect with the blockchain network, you need to set up the connection profiles.

The blockchain connector for each node will be deployed on the node's virtual machine.

You will clone the *bc-connector* repo, but you will run the next script from the *bta-blockchain/script* folder.

Run the following script to set up the blockchain connector for all of your organizations:

```
$ git clone https://github.com/kilroyblockchain/bc-connector.git
$ cd bta-blockchain/script
$ ./setupAndRunBlockchainConnector.sh
```

This will copy the *blockchain-connector* file to create your five blockchain connectors, create the *env* files, and run the blockchain connector on the Docker container. After you run the blockchain connector, you will see the following message:

```
----------------------------------------------
Successfully deployed all the blockchain connectors
----------------------------------------------
```

Blockchain connector node connections data is saved in the folder *bc-connector-node-info*. After the installation is completed, in the */bta-blockchain/bta-bc-connector* folder you can see a new folder called *bc-connector-node-info*. Inside the folder you will see that the files in Example 6-9 have been created.

Example 6-9. Files created after bc-connector-node installation

```
Peer01SuperAdminBtaKilroy.md
Peer03ShBtaKilroy.md
Peer05AIEngineerBtaKilroy.md
Peer02AdminBtaKilroy.md
Peer04MLOpsBtaKilroy.md
```

Example 6-10 shows the contents of the *Peer01SuperAdminBtaKilroy.md* file. These were automatically generated by the script for each organization. The file contains the organization name, bc-connector-node URL, and authorization token.

Example 6-10. Sample data inside the bc-connector-node-info folder

```
ORG_NAME=Peer01SuperAdminBtaKilroy
BC_CONNECTOR_NODE_URL=http://10.10.11.01:5007
AUTHORIZATION_TOKEN=aWNhLW8xLXN1cGVyLWFkbWluLWJ0YS1raWxyb3k6SWNhLU8xLVN1cGVyLUFk...
```

Creating Multiple Blockchain Connectors

Multiple folders for the blockchain connectors—one for each type of user—are created using the script. These include *connection-profile*, *crypto-files*, and an *env* file:

Connection profile setup
: The connection profile is the JSON file (located at */src/blockchain-files/connection-profile*) that contains all the node URLs and certificates to connect to the blockchain nodes. The connection profiles for five organizations are provided static on the folder located at */src/blockchain-files/connection-profile*. The script will replace the IP on the connection profile with the virtual machine private IP.

Certificate file transfer
: The certificates of peers, orderers, and intermediate CAs are necessary for blockchain connectors to connect to the blockchain network. The script copies those certificates from the blockchain network that you configured in Chapter 5

and pastes them to */src/blockchain-files/crypto-files* for use by the blockchain connector.

Configuring /bta-bc-connector/.env

The environment files are used for passing the static data to the blockchain connector application. The environment files are also modified by the script and add the blockchain organization information. Example 6-11 shows the *.env* file for the super admin's connector.

If you can't find your *.env* file, it might be because you are looking for it using a method that hides files that begin with a dot.

Example 6-11. Contents of /bta-bc-connector/bta-bc-connector-01-super-admin/.env file

```
CONNECTION_FILE_PATH=src/blockchain-files/connection-profile/
ICA_CONTAINER_NAME=ica.o1-super-admin.bta.kilroy
CA_ADMIN_ID=ica-o1-super-admin-bta-kilroy
CA_ADMIN_PWD=Ica-01-Super-Admin-Bta-Kilroy
CA_MSP_ID=Peer01SuperAdminBtaKilroyMSP
ORG_NAME=Peer01SuperAdminBtaKilroy
CERTIFICATE_TYPE=X.509
PEER_NAMES=["peer0.o1-super-admin.bta.kilroy"]
APP_PORT=5004
AUTHORIZATION_TOKEN=aWNhLW8xLXN1cGVyLWFkbWluLWJ0YS1raWxyb3k6SWNhLU8xLV...
ADMIN_ID=08db14a1076cd3dd43e99220f53a62635ba0502e3a7d1f89b4e90316ab558330

BTA_BC_CONNECTOR_NAME=bta_bc_connector_o1_super_admin
BTA_BC_CONNECTOR_IMAGE=bta-bc-connector-o1-super-admin
```

Whenever you want to restart the entire BTA and supporting systems—like if you stop work on this book's exercises and resume later—just restart the containers using Docker.

Setting Up the Oracle Connector

Oracle Connector is used for connecting backend applications with OCI. Here you will set up the Oracle Connector so OCI can interact with your blockchain.

To clone the Oracle Connector:

```
$ git clone https://github.com/kilroyblockchain/oracle-connector.git
```

After you clone the repo, look at the *README.md* file for any updated notes on installation.

You have to create a unique *env* file for your Oracle Connector, as explained in this section, to correspond to the resources you set up in Chapter 5 when you configured the Oracle Cloud. The sample *env* file, which is called *.env-sample* in the root of your *oracle-connector* folder, is shown in Example 6-12.

Example 6-12. Sample Oracle Connector env file, .env-sample, before copying it to .env and customizing it with your OCI configuration

```
OBC_ADMIN_HOST=https://idcs-a0e66701f946d0232218c29754daa988.identity.oraclecloud.com
AUTHORIZATION_TOKEN=Uhx0el9iKHwyMJv6NUJ90dZq3pqAH1HDY2KII9CkX!LH3bia3nFYlVIJ3oRx...
OBC_ADMIN_USERNAME=abc
OBC_ADMIN_PASSWORD=abc
OBC_ADMIN_SCOPE=urn:opc:idm:__myscopes__
#REDIS_HOST=localhost
#REDIS_PORT=5003
REDIS_HOST=obc-redis-cache
REDIS_PORT=6379
APP_PORT=3000
PORT=5818
API_AUTHORIZATION_TOKEN=b3JhY2xlLWJjLWNvbm5lY3Rvci1hcGktdGVzdGluZzo3NThlZXEyYWMt...
```

Make a copy of the sample and call it *.env*, as follows:

```
$ cd oracle-connector
$ cp .env-sample .env
```

Now, open the new *.env* with a code editor and follow the instructions on setting the environment variables to provide the information needed to connect your BTA to OCI.

Using Vim

As an alternative to a graphical code editor or an integrated development environment (IDE) with all the bells and whistles, you can use Vim or some other command-line editor to quickly make configuration file changes. Knowing how to use a command-line editor can save you lots of time in the long run, and get you out of trouble when your graphical interfaces won't load. Also, using a command-line editor prevents long lines of code and keys that can break if you mistakenly use a rich-text editor.

Errors caused by special characters inserted into rich-text editor–wrapped keys are extremely hard to find and can be really discouraging if you have done everything correctly and it just isn't working. Sometimes when things aren't working and there are no other answers, a good thing to try is copying a key from its original source and then pasting it back into the configuration file.

There is a wide variety of simple plain-text editors to choose from. While plain-text command-line editors have been around a very long time and are definitely archaic, you really only need to remember a few keystrokes to do the things you need in order to change configuration files. Here is how to use Vim:

```
$ vim .env
```

Simply type an `i` to put Vim into Insert mode. To delete to the end of a line, move your cursor to the first character you want to delete, press the Esc key, then press Shift+D. Type an `i` to return to Insert mode.

To paste text into the file, make sure you are in insert mode and then paste normally, using the menus or Ctrl+v.

After you are done making changes, press your Esc key then type **:** to bring up the Vim command line.

If you want to discard your changes instead of saving them, bring up the command line and then type **q** to quit and **!** to force Vim to quit without saving, and press Enter:

```
:q!
```

If you want to save your changes, then bring up the command line and type **w** for write to save the file, and **q** to quit Vim:

```
:wq
```

After you press Enter, your file will be saved and you will be back at the command prompt. To double-check it, use `type .env` to display the saved file's contents.

Also, if you use command-line editing for your normal work and you fix a configuration file with the command line directly on a server, you will need to remember to commit the file and push it to your repo; otherwise, the next time someone pulls the files, they could accidentally lose your fixes.

Configuring Your env File with Your OCI Variables

Log in to your OCI account and click Identity > Federation. Then, click the federation service available, OracleIdentityCloudService, as you did in Chapter 5 when you set up the buckets and connected the model to them. This brings up the Oracle IdentityCloudService window, as shown in Figure 6-11.

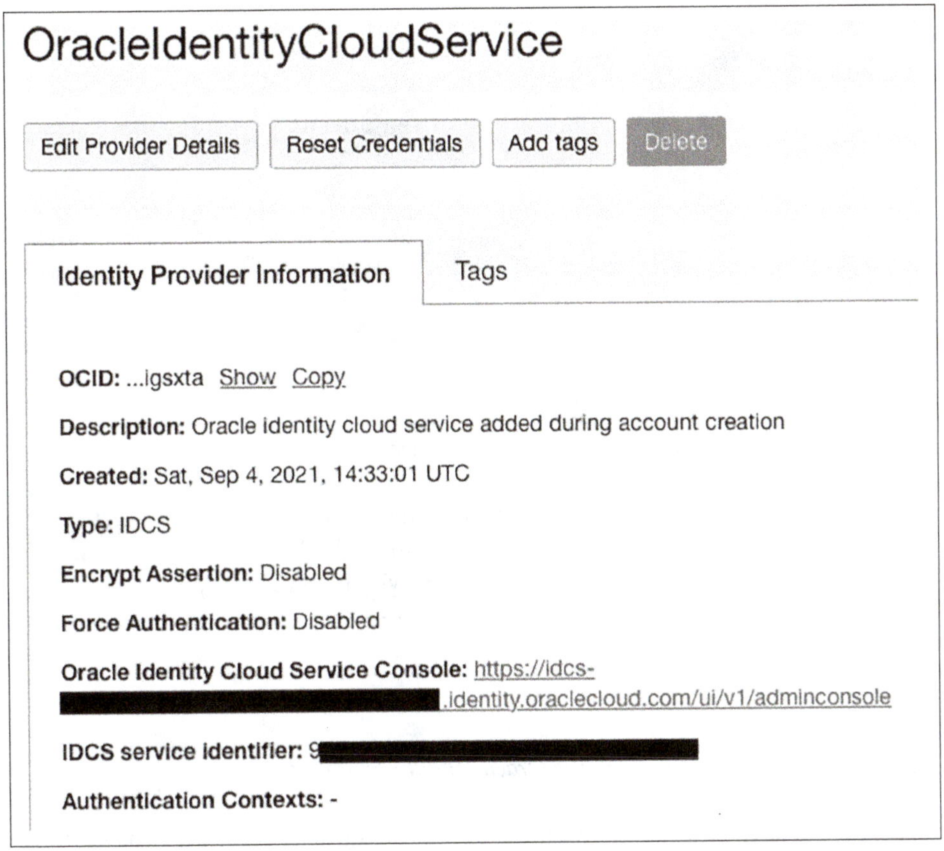

OracleIdentityCloudService

Edit Provider Details | Reset Credentials | Add tags | Delete

Identity Provider Information | Tags

OCID: ...igsxta Show Copy

Description: Oracle identity cloud service added during account creation

Created: Sat, Sep 4, 2021, 14:33:01 UTC

Type: IDCS

Encrypt Assertion: Disabled

Force Authentication: Disabled

Oracle Identity Cloud Service Console: https://idcs-█████.identity.oraclecloud.com/ui/v1/adminconsole

IDCS service identifier: 9█████

Authentication Contexts: -

Figure 6-11. The OracleIdentityCloudService console

Also use your text editor to open the *.env* file that is in the root of the *oracle-connector* folder, so you can copy and paste the values into the file as you find them in OCI.

OBC_ADMIN_HOST

You must copy the URL of your Oracle Identity Cloud Service Console, only up to and including the text *oraclecloud.com*. Paste it into your *env* file as the value for the variable `OBC_ADMIN_HOST`. The full URL will look something like this: *https://idcs-e2f496a4xxxxxxxxxe90dac0af081.identity.oraclecloud.com*.

AUTHORIZATION_TOKEN

Now click the Oracle Identity Cloud Service Console link found on the Identity Provider tab. This is the same link you copied for `OBC_ADMIN_HOST`. Clicking the link will open a new tab on your browser, as shown in Figure 6-12.

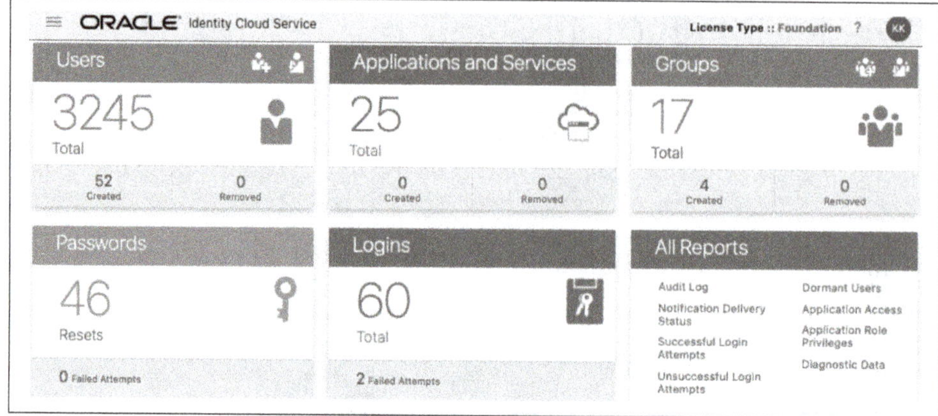

Figure 6-12. Accessing Oracle Identity Cloud Services

From the dashboard, click the menu in the upper-left corner, then select Oracle Cloud Services. As shown in Figure 6-13, you need the "oraclebc-..." cloud service. You must add a new Oracle Cloud Blockchain Service if you do not have any.

Figure 6-13. oraclebc-... shown in the Oracle Cloud Service list

After it is open, click the Configuration tab next to Details. Now, copy the client ID and client secret from the General Information section. Click the Show Secret button, as seen in Figure 6-14, to copy the client secret.

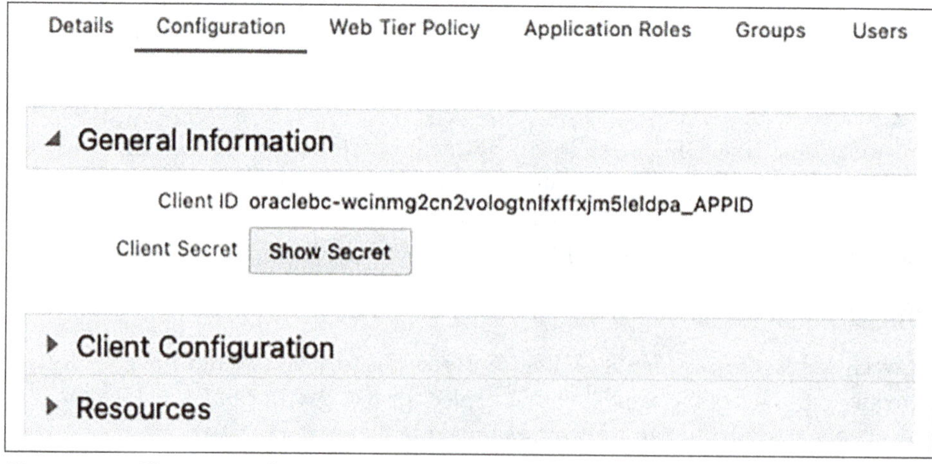

Figure 6-14. Show Secret button in the Oracle Cloud Service configuration

After copying the client ID and client secret, you have to encode it to a Base64 string. One way is to visit *base64encode.org*. Here, you copy the client ID and client secret in the format *<client_id>:<client_secret>*. Then you can click on the ENCODE button to get the encoded Base64 string.

Copy the encoded Base64 string and paste it into the *env* file as the value for the variable `AUTHORIZATION_TOKEN`.

OBC_ADMIN_USERNAME and OBC_ADMIN_PASSWORD

`OBC_ADMIN_USERNAME` is the variable that stores the username of your OCI user, which is the same one you use to log in.

`OBC_ADMIN_PASSWORD` stores the password of the OCI user.

OBC_ADMIN_SCOPE

`OBC_ADMIN_SCOPE` is required for accessing the Oracle cloud APIs. Complete this value as shown in Example 6-13.

Example 6-13. Value for `OBC_ADMIN_SCOPE`

```
OBC_ADMIN_SCOPE=urn:opc:idm:__myscopes__
```

REDIS_HOST and REDIS_PORT

`REDIS_HOST` is the redis host URL, which will be the localhost in your case. Redis is used to store the access token when logged in to OCI via the Oracle Connector. The Redis container will run when you run the script for running the Oracle Connector. The access token then will be used on every other operation including create user, get group list, and assign user to Oracle group.

`REDIS_PORT` is the redis deployed port number. You can leave it as the default port mentioned on the environment file, as shown in Example 6-14.

Example 6-14. Redis configuration

```
REDIS_HOST=obc-redis-cache
REDIS_PORT=6379
```

APP_PORT

`APP_PORT` is the port of the Oracle Connector to be listened to. `APP_PORT` can be left at the default value of `APP_PORT=3000`, so long as the port is not being used by any other application.

API_AUTHORIZATION_TOKEN

`API_AUTHORIZATION_TOKEN` is the unique token generated for a backend application to connect to our Oracle Connector. The authorization token will be used later on the backend application environment file. You need to set the `API_AUTHORIZATION_TOKEN` on the backend application environment file so it is the same as the current token.

After you have completed the values, close and save your file.

Starting the Oracle Connector

Next, start the Oracle Connector by running the following command:

```
$ ./setupAndRunOracleConnector.sh
```

After successful completion, this script returns the following output:

```
--------------------------------------------------
Oracle connector is up and running on port 5818
--------------------------------------------------
```

This was the last shell script needed for setup of the Oracle Connector. You have now completed this book's third major exercise.

More About Integrating Blockchain and the Application Layer

The application layer of the BTA, which you will set up in Chapter 7, faces the users and facilitates their ability to create projects, submit trained and tested AI models, and review them, binding with blockchain.

It is the frontend layer of the application based on the MEAN stack where NestJs is used as a backend, exposing APIs to the required calls. The BTA API is used to add a new model version in blockchain and MongoDB.

NestJS represents its files with a *.ts* extension, which stands for TypeScript. The BTA's blockchain code uses *.ts* files to integrate blockchain with the BTA application layer to generate functions such as `addNewVersion` and `invoke`, as explained here.

This chapter's UML class diagrams for NestJS/TypeScript (*.ts*) files were generated through the PlantUML plug-in for the UML Generator in JetBrains IntelliJ IDEA.

While the NestJS files included in the *bta-api* folder are too numerous to explain here, you can see in Figure 6-15 that they center around modules that contain one controller and two service files. The controller is used to handle the incoming requests and hand them to the program's logic, then return the outputs. This is the same pattern used for everything in the *manage-project* folder, including *ai-model*, *model-reviews*, *monitoring-report*, *project*, and *project-version*.

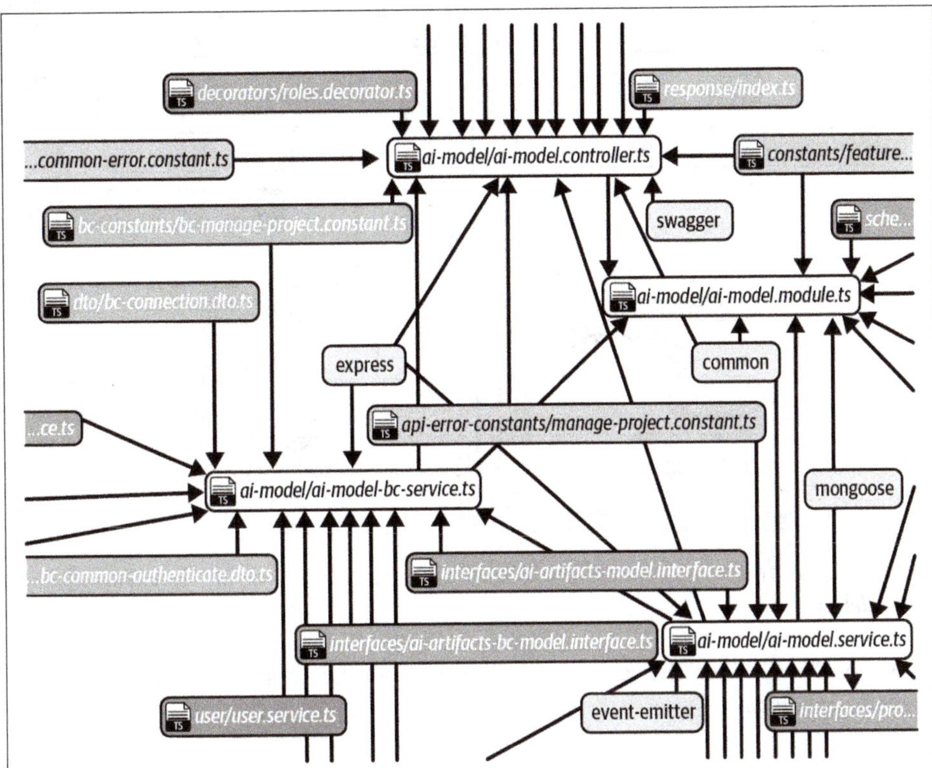

Figure 6-15. Key NestJS files from the bta-api folder are shown in white, with arrows indicating how they interrelate

The figures in this section illustrate one of these types, the controller and services for *ai-model*. Drilling down deeper in Figure 6-16, a look at the controller for the AI model, *ai-model-controller.ts*, shows the relationships between the module's controller and other NestJS files.

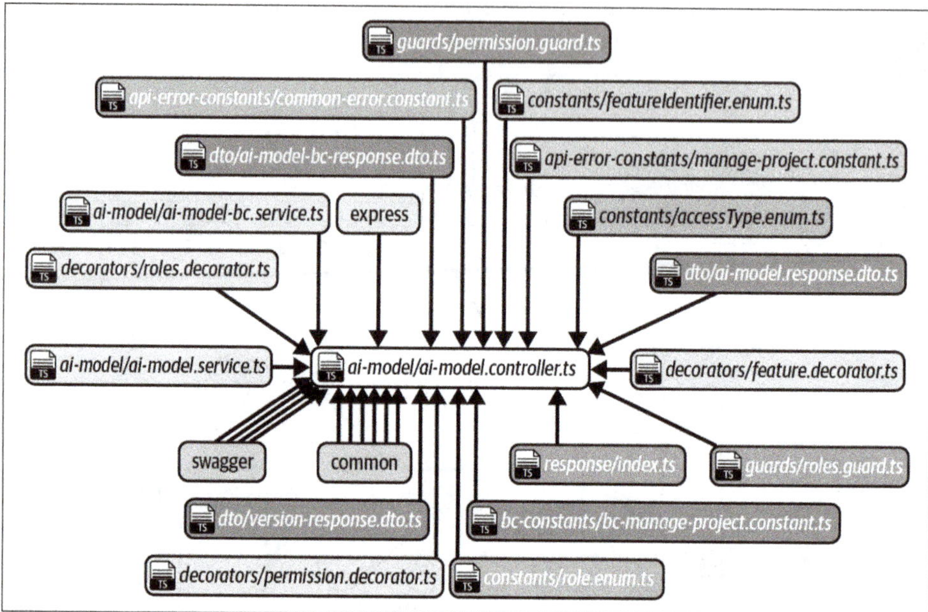

Figure 6-16. A deeper look into ai-model-controller.ts, showing the dependencies of the ai-model module

Figure 6-17 examines the values stored as well as the chaincode dependencies of *ai-model-module.ts*.

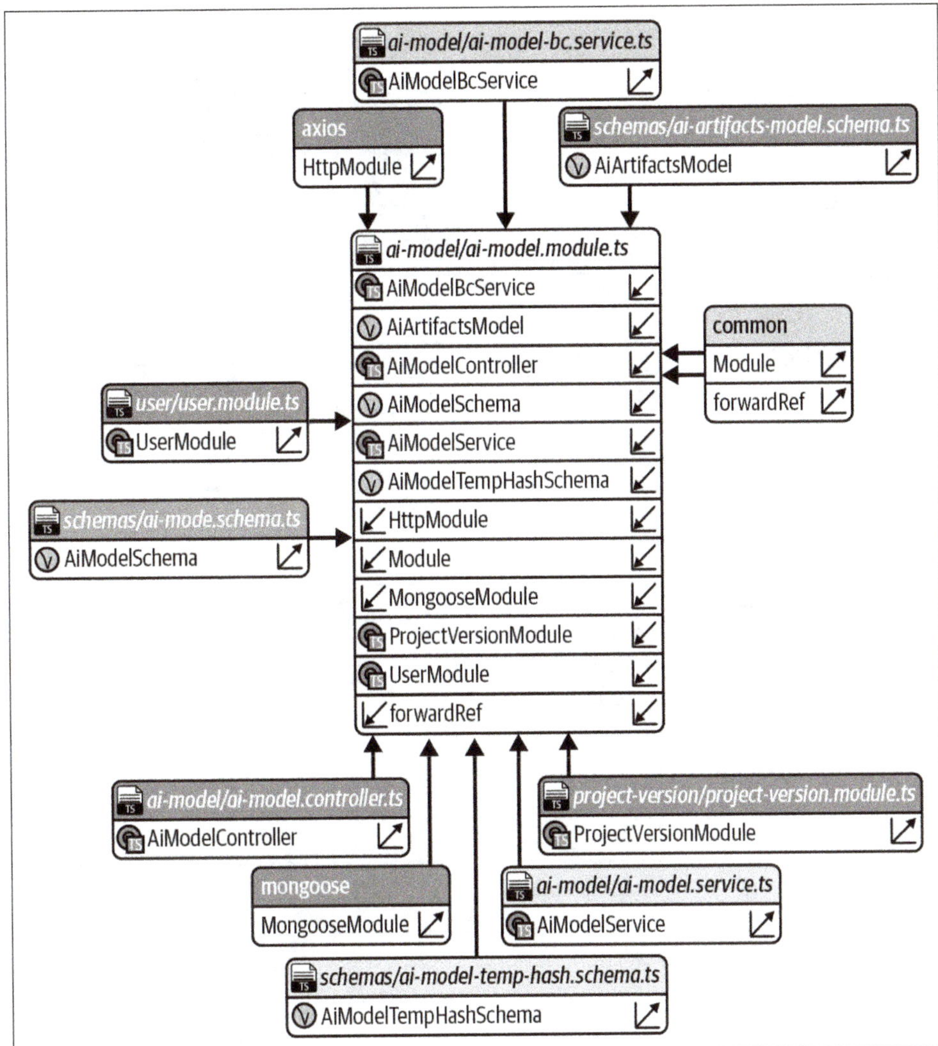

Figure 6-17. A look at the values and chaincode dependencies for ai-model-module.ts

Figure 6-18 shows dependencies for the AI model service.

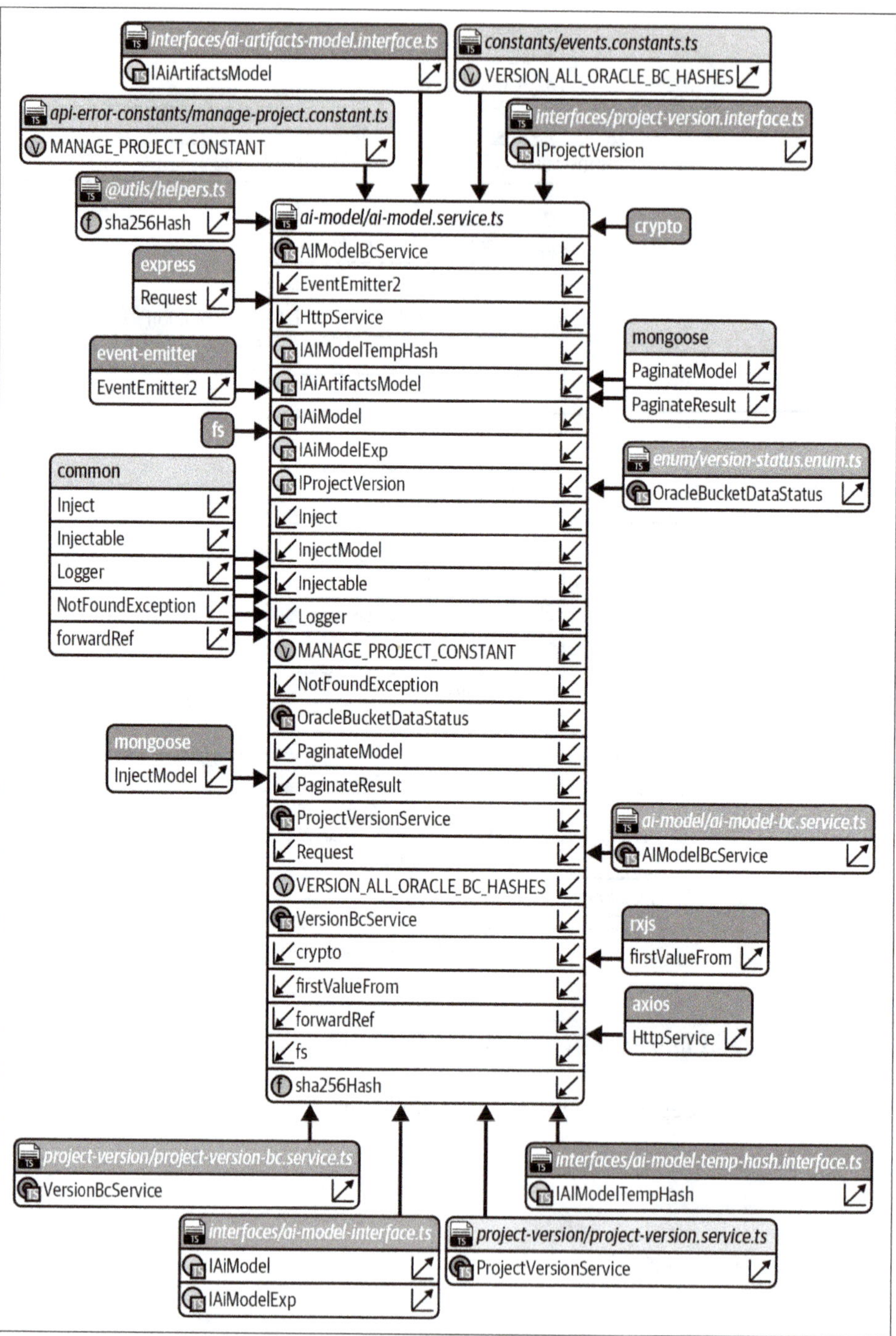

Figure 6-18. A look at the dependencies for the AI model service

Figure 6-19 shows the dependencies for the AI model blockchain service.

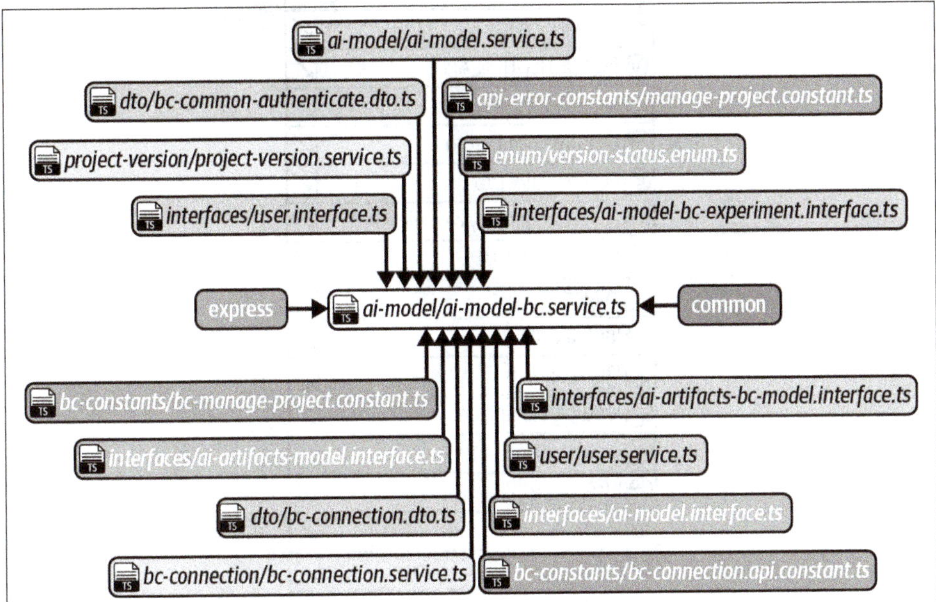

Figure 6-19. A look at the dependencies for the AI model blockchain service

Figure 6-20 shows the values stored in *ai-model-bc.service.ts*.

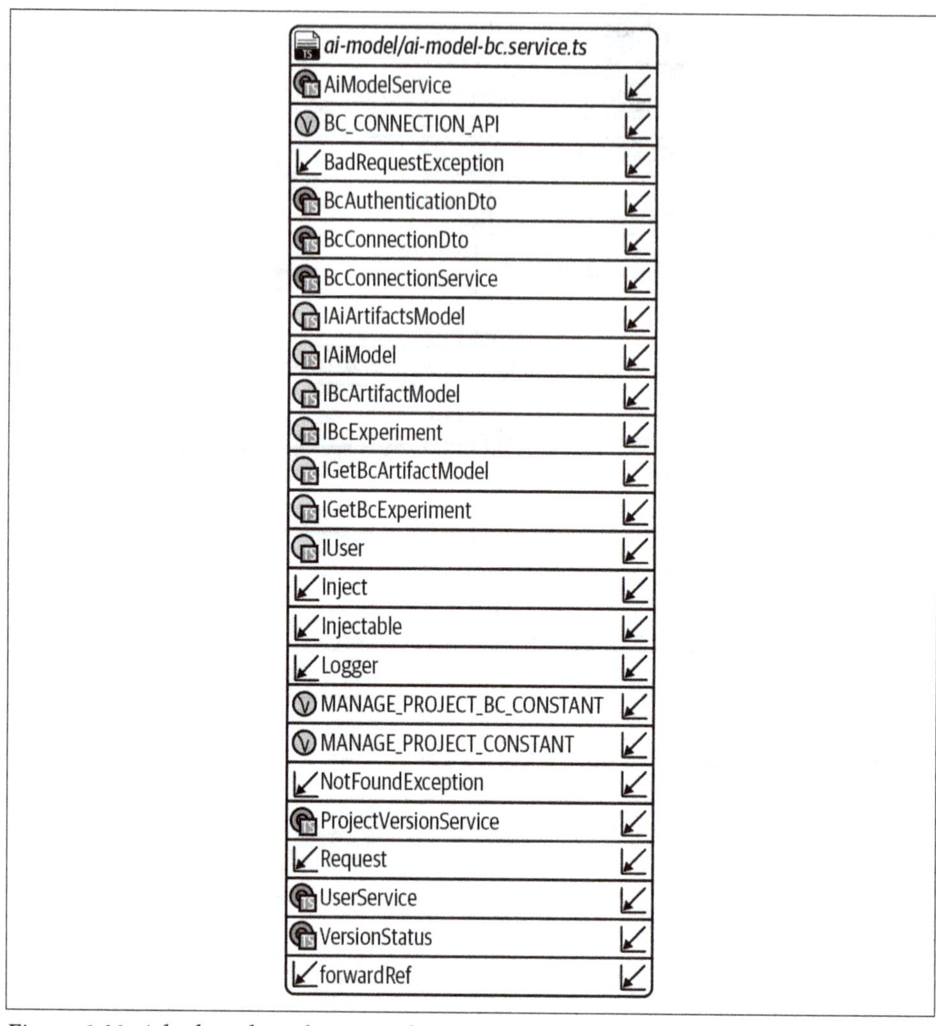

Figure 6-20. A look at the values stored in ai-model-bc.service.ts

Blockchain Connector

Several code functions are important in connecting the application to the blockchain, as shown in Figure 6-21. The functions are `query`, `registerUser`, `getAllGroupList`, and `addUserToGroup`.

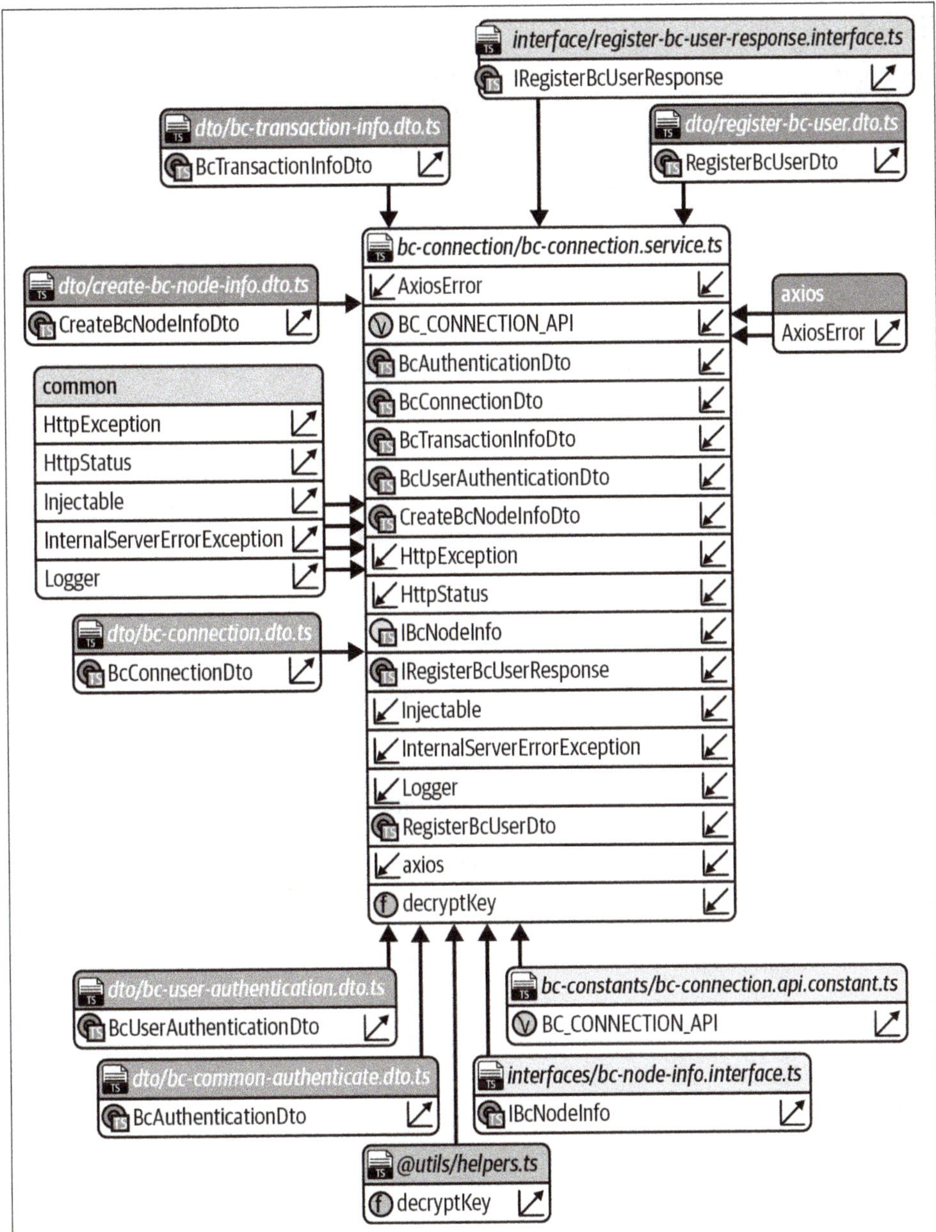

Figure 6-21. UML class diagram showing blockchain connection services

query

The `query` function, as shown in Example 6-15, calls the query API through the blockchain connector which reads the data from the blockchain state. It receives a parameter `bcAuthenticateDto`, containing data for authentication of the blockchain connection.

Example 6-15. The `query` function

```
async query(bcAuthenticateDto: BcAuthenticationDto): Promise<BcConnectionDto> {
            try {
          const response = await axios.get(bcAuthenticateDto.nodeUrl +
bcAuthenticateDto.bcConnectionApi, {
              headers: {
                  'Content-Type': 'application/json',
                  // authorization token for blockchain node
                  authorization: 'Basic ' + bcAuthenticateDto.basicAuthorization,
                  // organization name of blockchain node
                  org_name: bcAuthenticateDto.organizationName,
                  // name of blockchain channel
                  channel_name: bcAuthenticateDto.channelName,
                  // decrypting blockchain key
                  key: await decryptKey(bcAuthenticateDto.bcKey),
                  // salt for compare blockchain key
                  salt: bcAuthenticateDto.salt
              }
          });
          return new BcConnectionDto(response.data.data);

        // Handling the errors of get request
       } catch (error) {
          const err = error as AxiosError;
           logger.error(err.response ? JSON.stringify(err.response.data) : err);
           throw err;
       }
   }
```

In this function, the Axios package is used to communicate with the blockchain connector. Here, you call the get request of the Axios by sending the URL of the blockchain node, and headers for authentication of the request. After completing the `get` request, it returns a response of the `BcConnectionDto` type.

OC User Service

The OC user service supports user registration and management. Classes and dependencies for *oc-user.service.ts* are shown in Figure 6-22.

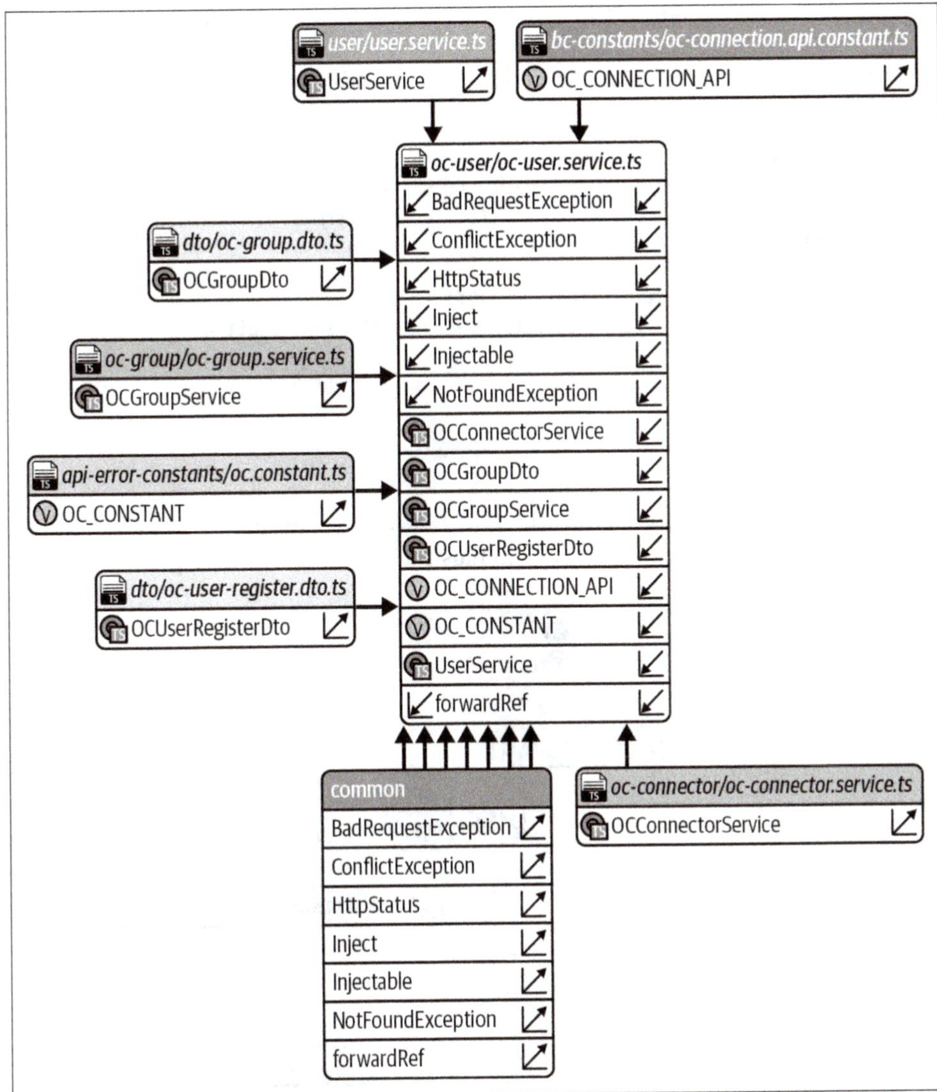

Figure 6-22. Classes and dependencies for oc-user.service.ts

The `registerUser` function, shown in Example 6-16, calls the Oracle Cloud connector function, which creates user accounts in the Oracle Cloud with their email addresses. If the given email is already registered in the cloud, it throws an error with the message "User with the same email already exists."

Example 6-16. `registerUser` function

```
async registerUser(ocUserRegisterDto: OCUserRegisterDto): Promise<void> {
   try {
      // default password for Oracle Cloud
       ocUserRegisterDto.password = 'Test@1234';
      // this function sends the post request for registering on Oracle Cloud
       await this.ocConnectorService.post(ocUserRegisterDto,
       OC_CONNECTION_API.REGISTER_USER);
   } catch (err) {
       if (err.status == HttpStatus.CONFLICT) {
           throw new ConflictException(['User with the same email already exists']);
       }
   }
}
```

OC Group

The application needs to get all of the Oracle Cloud group list so that they can be properly assigned to the user. Figure 6-23 illustrates the Oracle Cloud group.

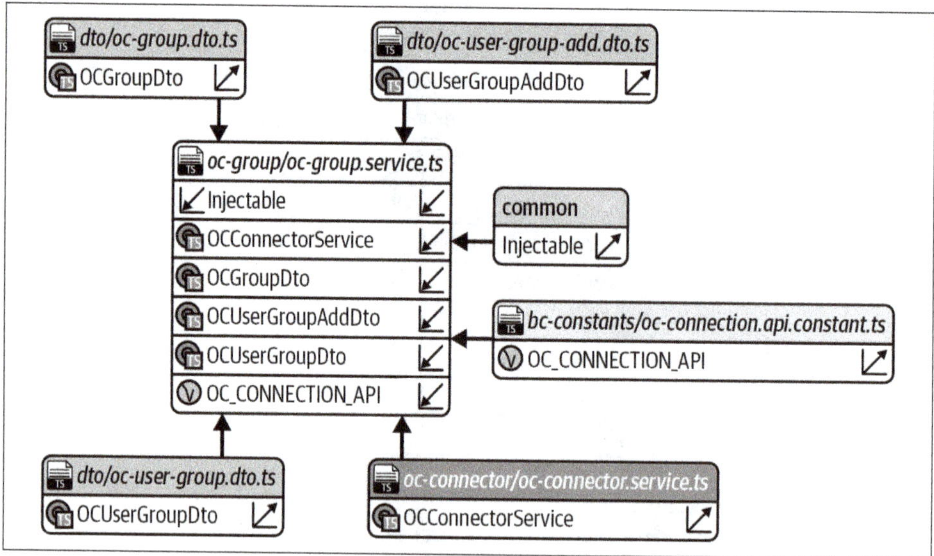

Figure 6-23. UML class diagram showing classes in oc-group-service.ts

The `getAllGroupList` function, shown in Example 6-17, lists all the groups of the Oracle Cloud.

Example 6-17. `getAllGroupList` function

```
async getAllGroupList(): Promise<OCGroupDto[]> {

   // this function sends the get request for getting all group of oracle cloud
   const ocConnectionResponse = await this.ocConnectorService.get(
                                OC_CONNECTION_API.GROUP_LIST);

   const ocGroupDtoList: OCGroupDto[] = [];
       for (const data of ocConnectionResponse.data) {
           const ocGroupDto = new OCGroupDto();
           ocGroupDto.id = data.id;
           ocGroupDto.displayName = data.displayName;
           ocGroupDtoList.push(ocGroupDto);
       }
       // returns all group of oracle cloud
       return ocGroupDtoList;
}
```

The `addUserToGroup` function, shown in Example 6-18, adds user groups in Oracle. These Oracle groups hold the policies (permissions) of the Oracle Cloud buckets.

Example 6-18. `addUserToGroup` function

```
async addUserToGroup(ocUserGroupAddDto: OCUserGroupAddDto): Promise<void> {
    const ocUserGroupDto = new OCUserGroupDto();

    // add the user in group by group id
    ocUserGroupDto.groupId = ocUserGroupAddDto.groupId;
    // add user in group by user email as username
    ocUserGroupDto.userName = ocUserGroupAddDto.email;

    // this function sends the post request to Oracle Cloud
    // for adding user in Oracle group
    await this.ocConnectorService.post(ocUserGroupDto,
    OC_CONNECTION_API.ADD_USER_TO_GROUP);
}
```

Extract, Transform, and Load

Enterprise blockchain platforms and blockchain business analytics usually provide a security model with capabilities such as user and organization identity, permissioning, data access control, and various privacy features, such as channels or private data collections in Hyperledger Fabric. However, it may be undesirable to externally extract data because blockchain applications may have stringent extract, transform, and load (ETL) (*https://oreil.ly/G84Js*) policies due to security, performance, or replication concerns.

ETL is a three-step data integration process used by organizations to combine and synthesize raw data from multiple data sources into a data warehouse, data lake, unified data repository, relational database, or any other application. Data migrations and cloud data integrations are common use cases for ETL. Initially, organizations wrote their own ETL code, but now there are a number of open source tools and cloud servers available from major companies like IBM, Google, and Microsoft. The tools collect the data and hold it in temporary storage during the *extraction* phase, process the data so the values and structures are consistent and specific to the use case during the *transformation* phase, and transfer the data into on-prem or cloud target data storage during the *load* phase.

Current ledger implementations in many blockchain platforms are not particularly well suited for analytics queries as that is not their primary design goal. To address this limitation, it is best to use a platform that stores the latest snapshot of the data in a secondary database. For example, Oracle offers a rich history database (*https://oreil.ly/Ajo0I*) that runs alongside the Oracle Blockchain (*https://oreil.ly/adhRw*) implementation of Hyperledger Fabric, keeping a record of transactions on channels that you select. The rich history data can be used to produce analytics reports and visualizations.

It is also a good idea to use a platform that supports CouchDB. CouchDB supports storage and retrieval of JSON data and provides richer query capability that resonates with solution designers. The requirement for the analytics capability is that the data in the key-value pairs is recorded in the JSON format.

Summary

Your blockchain network is up and running, and ready to connect to the bucket containing your model. In the next chapters you will bring up your BTA web application and connect it to the blockchain and the bucket. Then you will use the system to simulate the activities of an AI engineering team to conduct trackable, traceable AI experiments that can be audited through blockchain.

CHAPTER 7

Preparing Your BTA

In the previous exercises, you set up everything you need in order to create a blockchain tethered AI. In this chapter, "Exercise: Installing and Launching Your BTA" details the last step of installation: setting up the frontend and backend of the BTA and configuring it so it is integrated with the blockchain, the model, and the bucket. Then, you will go on to "Exercise: Creating Users and Permissions" on page 207, where you will create your BTA's users and permissions.

Exercise: Installing and Launching Your BTA

Your BTA has a backend and a frontend system. You have already set up the blockchain and the buckets, and configured the connections so your resources will all communicate once your BTA is up. The installation instructions for each development environment follow.

Installing the BTA Backend

To set up the backend of the BTA application (the BTA server), change directories to your project folder, then clone the *bta-backend* repository as follows:

```
$ git clone https://github.com/kilroyblockchain/bta-backend.git
$ cd bta-backend
```

After you check the *README.md* file for any new installation notes, run the script to set up and run the backend of the BTA:

```
$ ./setupAndRunBTABackend.sh
```

The files in the *bta-backend* folder are primarily related to migrating the blockchain code to the MongoDB database. The backend *env* file is located here, as described in the following section.

Understanding Your BTA Backend's env File

In */bta-backend* you have a file called *.env* that contains all the necessary environment variables used by `docker-compose`. This file was automatically copied and configured for each organization when you ran the *setupAndRunBlockchainConnector.sh* script and installed the blockchain connector in Chapter 6.

The first section of the file, dealing with general settings, is shown in Example 7-1.

Example 7-1. Ports that are set in the env file

```
COMPOSE_PROJECT_NAME=kilroy
NODE_ENV=development
ENVIRONMENT=local
APP_NAME=BTA
PORT=3000
APP_PORT=3340
APP_DEBUG_PORT=9230
MONGO_EXPRESS_UI_PORT=3341
MAILCATCHER_PORT=3342
DB_PORT=27034
```

The default *env* file database settings that impact MongoDB are shown in Example 7-2.

Example 7-2. Database and container settings for which you can accept all defaults

```
MONGO_URI=mongodb://bta-db:27017
MONGO_HOST=bta-db
MONGO_USERNAME=btaapi
MONGO_PASSWORD=a458CsBsaosf3KYhiNxrdF
DATABASE_NAME=kilroy-bta-api
MONGO_DEBUG=true

APP_CONTAINER_NAME=bta_api_local
MONGODB_CONTAINER_NAME=bta-db
MONGO_EXPRESS_UI_CONTAINER_NAME=mongoExpressNest
MONGODB_CONTAINER_NAME=bta-db
MONGO_EXPRESS_UI_CONTAINER_NAME=mongoExpressBta
MAILCATCHER_CONTAINER_NAME=mailcatcherBta

DATABASE_VOLUME_MOUNT=./psvolumes/bta-db

# Use bta_nodemodules if you want to use Docker volume instead of bind mount
LOCAL_NODE_MODULES_VOLUME_MOUNT=./node_modules
```

The MailCatcher container, port, email host, and email port are configured in the lines shown in Example 7-3.

Example 7-3. Additional MailCatcher variables in the env file

```
EMAIL_HOST=mailcatcherBta
EMAIL_PORT=1025
```

The next lines, in Example 7-4, configure the *JSON Web Tokens* (JWTs) included with Node.js. JWTs are used in your BTA for securely transmitting JSON-formatted information between the BTA web application and the other parts of the BTA. You do not have to generate your own JWT in order to demo the BTA, so you can accept the defaults for this part of the *env* file.

Example 7-4. You can accept these env file defaults for the demo

```
JWT_SECRET=YTS!QtTA69uP6nk*WG*pM6b
ENCRYPT_JWT_SECRET=oxRynN220cpFBiFURvtj8kz
JWT_EXPIRATION=30m # 30 minutes
RESET_PASSWORD_SECRET=dYsyq9K4x9TCcRh5Cfgaberc?2yTSS@3&eM
SIGNUP_LIMIT=100
PAGE_VISIT_LIMIT=1000
RESET_WRONG_PASSWORD_BLOCK_TOKEN=dYsyq9K4x9TCcRh5CN3r@yTSS@3@eME
```

As we go down the *env* file, the next section we come to impacts a login challenge provided by Google reCAPTCHA. Since this is a demo, Google reCAPTCHA has been disabled by default. If you want to enable Google reCAPTCHA in your BTA, visit the Google reCAPTCHA page (*https://oreil.ly/7mfQr*) and register a new site. After completing the registration, Google reCAPTCHA provides your secret key and reCAPTCHA site key. If you were enabling this, the reCAPTCHA secret key would be used in this env file and the reCAPTCHA site key would be used in your *environments.ts* file. Since reCAPTCHA is disabled by default for the demo, you are not required to change the lines shown in Example 7-5.

Example 7-5. reCAPTCHA status and secret key

```
RE_CAPTCHA_STATUS=DISABLED
RE_CAPTCHA_SECRET=xxxxxxxxxxxxxxxxxxxxxxxxxxxxx
```

The next variables impact the blockchain connector. Example 7-6 shows defaults that you can accept for your demo.

Example 7-6. Demo defaults

```
REFRESH_TOKEN_EXPIRATION_MIN=10080 #7 Days
```

The `CLIENT_APP_URL` variable, as seen in Example 7-7, shows the URL of the BTA application web user interface. Like all of the settings in the *env* file, the defaults will work for the demo.

Example 7-7. Address of the BTA user interface

```
CLIENT_APP_URL=http://localhost:4200
```

The next part of the *env* file, as shown in Example 7-8, impacts the application log.

Example 7-8. Application log env settings that configure how log files are transported

```
# Application log transported to file settings
NO_APP_LOG_T_FILE= # Add any string to disable application log
APP_LOG_ZIPPED_ARCHIVE=false # Pass true | false value
APP_LOG_DATE_PATTERN=YYYY-MM-DD
APP_LOG_MAX_SIZE=20m
APP_LOG_MAX_FILES=14d

# Application log transported to file settings
NO_APP_LOG_T_FILE= # Add any string to disable application log
APP_LOG_ZIPPED_ARCHIVE=false # Pass true | false value
APP_LOG_DATE_PATTERN=YYYY-MM-DD
APP_LOG_MAX_SIZE=20m
APP_LOG_MAX_FILES=14d
```

The next section of the *env* file is for configuring the blockchain nodes used by the super admin. Since the super admin is the first user, this has to be done during installation, before the BTA is fully up and running. First, here is an explanation of the variables in this section:

`BC_NODE_ORG_NAME`
: This is the blockchain organization name for the super admin, and should be the same as the blockchain organization name you used when you created the blockchain node for the super admin.

`BC_NODE_LABEL`
: This can be any unique label to distinguish one peer from another. You can leave the default of `Peer0`.

`BC_NODE_URL`
: This is the address of the super admin's blockchain connector. You can leave this at the default value.

`BC_NODE_AUTHORIZATION`
: This is the key that enables the backend application to authenticate with the super admin blockchain connector APIs.

`BC_SUPER_ADMIN_REGISTRATION_TOKEN`
: This is the key used to access the backend API for registering the super admin from the migration script. This token can be any unique key that will be used to register a super admin user.

Example 7-9 shows how the configuration for the super admin blockchain node looks in the env file.

Example 7-9. Super admin's blockchain nodes as configured in the env file

```
BC_NODE_ORG_NAME=Peer01SuperAdminBtaKilroy
BC_NODE_LABEL=Peer01SuperAdmin
BC_NODE_URL=http://bta_bc_connector_o1_super_admin:3000
BC_NODE_URL=http://localhost:5004
BC_NODE_AUTHORIZATION=aWNhLW8xLXN1cGVyLWFkbWluLWJ0YS1raWxyb3k6SWNhLU8xLVN1cGVyLU...

BC_NODE_ORG_NAME=Peer01SuperAdminBtaKilroy
BC_NODE_LABEL=Peer01SuperAdmin
BC_NODE_URL=http://192.168.1.7:5004
BC_NODE_AUTHORIZATION=aWNhLW8xLXN1cGVyLWFkbWluLWJ0YS1raWxyb3k6SWNhLU8xLVN1cGVyLU...

BC_SUPER_ADMIN_REGISTRATION_TOKEN=c3VwZItYWRtaW4tdGVzdDpzdBlci1hZG1pbi10ZN0LWtleQ==
BC_CONNECTOR_ADMIN_ID=08db14a176cd3dd43e9220f53a62635ba0502e3a7d1f894e90316ab558330
```

Oracle Connector API authentication is set in the `OC_AUTHORIZATION_TOKEN`, as shown in Example 7-10. This is the same Base64 value that you computed for `AUTHORIZATION_TOKEN` in "Setting Up the Oracle Connector" on page 182.

Example 7-10. Update the `OC_AUTHORIZATION_TOKEN` in the env file

```
OC_CONNECTION_HOST=http://oc_connector:3000

OC_AUTHORIZATION_TOKEN=XXXXXXXXXXXXXXXXXXXXXXXXXXXXXXXXXXXXXXXXXXXXXXXXXXXXXXXXXXXXXXX
```

In Example 7-11, super admin's credentials are set in the *env* file, since this is the BTA's first user. This port is only accessible from inside Docker, and is not exposed to your localhost.

Example 7-11. Default super admin credentials in the env file, used to register the BTA's first user

```
REGISTER_SUPER_ADMIN_BC=http://localhost:3000/api/v1/user/register-super-admin-bc

SUPER_ADMIN_EMAIL=btasuperadmin@mailinator.com
```

You can leave this address in here and just make a note of it. You don't need a real email address because you will be using MailCatcher.

Understanding Your environment.ts File

The frontend of the BTA application has environment variables that are written in the environment file. This file, */bta-app/bta-web/source/environment.ts*, contains the project's required environment variables, and they are configured for you automatically. The configuration is shown in Example 7-12.

Example 7-12. Contents of /bta-app/bta-web/source/environments.ts

```
export const environment = {
    project: 'bta',
    apiURL: 'http://localhost:3340/api/v1',
    hostURL: 'http://localhost:4200/#/',
    disableCaptcha: true,
    recaptchaSiteKey: 'xxxxxxxxxxxxxxxxxxxxxxx'
};
```

More information on these variables follows:

`project`
: The `project` variable stores the name of the project. Unless you chose a different name for your project, it is `bta`.

`apiURL`
: The `apiURL` is the address of the BTA web application backend. You can get the URL after running the backend application, but it is most likely `http://localhost:3340/api/v1`.

`hostURL`
: The `hostURL` is the address of the frontend, and you will use this in your browser to use the BTA: `http://localhost:4200/#/`.

Launching the BTA Frontend

To set up the frontend of the BTA application, clone the *bta-frontend* repository into your project folder as follows, making sure to read the *README.md* for any last-minute changes:

```
$ git clone https://github.com/kilroyblockchain/bta-frontend.git
$ cd bta-frontend
$ ./setupAndRunBTAFrontend.sh
```

```
----------------------------------------------------
BTA frontend has been successfully started
Subscribe using http://localhost:4200/#/auth/register
Log in as super admin to approve new subscription.
----------------------------------------------------
```

The backend will be listening for requests from your web browser. Check *http://localhost:4200/#/auth/register* to start working with your BTA!

Exercise: Creating Users and Permissions

With your BTA all up and running, you are now ready to create users and permissions. This exercise helps you set up the super admin ID, use that ID to approve a new organization, use the organization admin ID to create organization units and staffings, and finally create users who have permissions set by organization units and staffings.

Using MailCatcher

MailCatcher (*https://mailcatcher.me*) is a free utility that catches routed mail and lets you see it in a web browser. For testing this type of multiuser environment, using a tool like MailCatcher is easier than checking multiple email accounts. MailCatcher was installed as part of your BTA backend.

Since the IDs you create will receive emails, including your super admin ID, you'll want to open and use MailCatcher in another browser tab so you can easily check those emails. When you are selecting email addresses for testing, you do not have to use real addresses since all of your email routed by the BTA will show up in MailCatcher when you open it at *http://localhost:3342*.

Configuring the Super Admin

To set up the super admin, go to your BTA registration page and click Login, which brings up the login screen shown in Figure 7-1. Log in using your super admin credentials, which can be found in the first welcome email you received in MailCatcher.

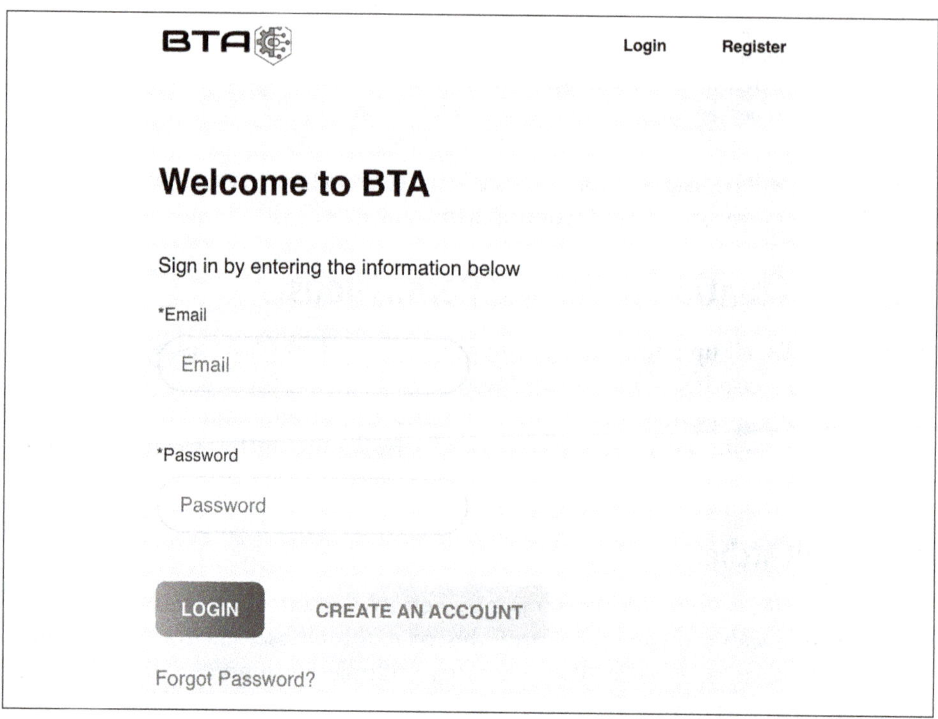

Figure 7-1. Login screen for your BTA

Once you have logged in as super admin, you will be asked to verify your blockchain key, as shown in Figure 7-2.

After the blockchain verification step, since it is your first login, you will be required to change your password. Next you will see the super admin's dashboard. It displays a summary of logins, as shown in Figure 7-3.

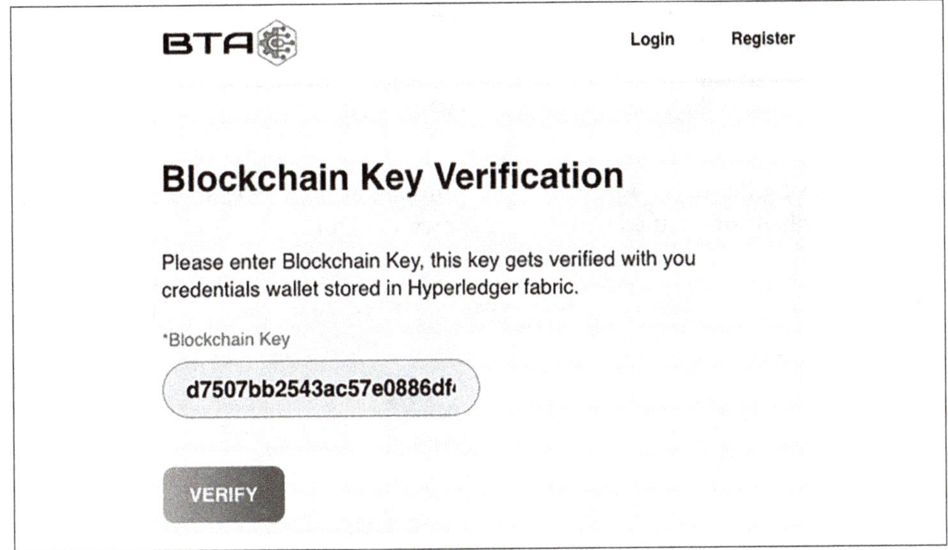

Figure 7-2. Blockchain verification for your super admin

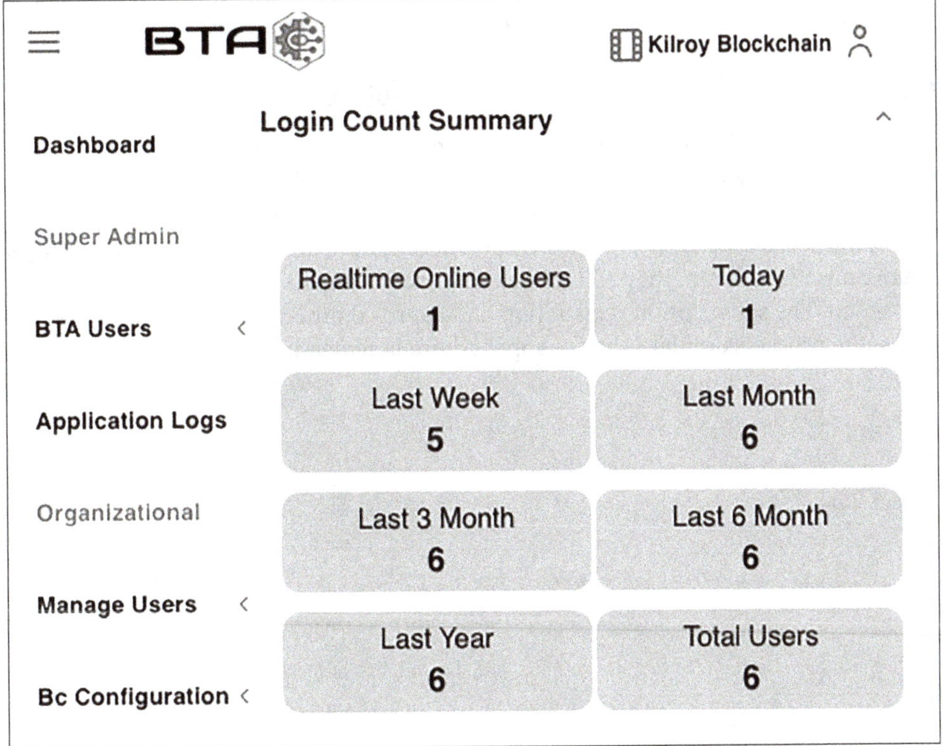

Figure 7-3. Super admin's dashboard showing login counts

Super admin login credentials are used from the *env* file and created as a super admin user by the migration script of the backend application. Verification emails will go to email addresses listed under the variable name `SUPER-ADMIN-EMAIL`.

While still using the super admin ID, you can look at the blockchain configuration you created when you verified your key, as shown in Figure 7-4.

Organization Name	Label	Node URL	Authorization Token	Created By	Created At	Status	Updated At	Actions
Peer02Admin	Peer02Admin	http://129.146.	aWNhLW8yLV	Super Admin	2022-10-13	Enabled	2022-10-13	
Peer01Super	Peer01Super	http://129.146.	aWNhLW8xL>	Super Admin	2022-10-13	Enabled	2022-10-13	

Figure 7-4. List of all blockchain nodes, showing the super admin's node

Creating a New Subscription Account in Your BTA

Now that your BTA is up and running, the next step is to create an account. Because the BTA is multitenant, any number of organizations could be using the same BTA. It is designed to segment the information and the users by organization. A new organization is created by registering for a new subscription, and the person registering is the organization admin; they will take care of everything inside the organization once it is set up. The subscription registration and approval process is shown in Figure 7-5. The setup process completed by the super admin is shown in detail in Figure 7-6.

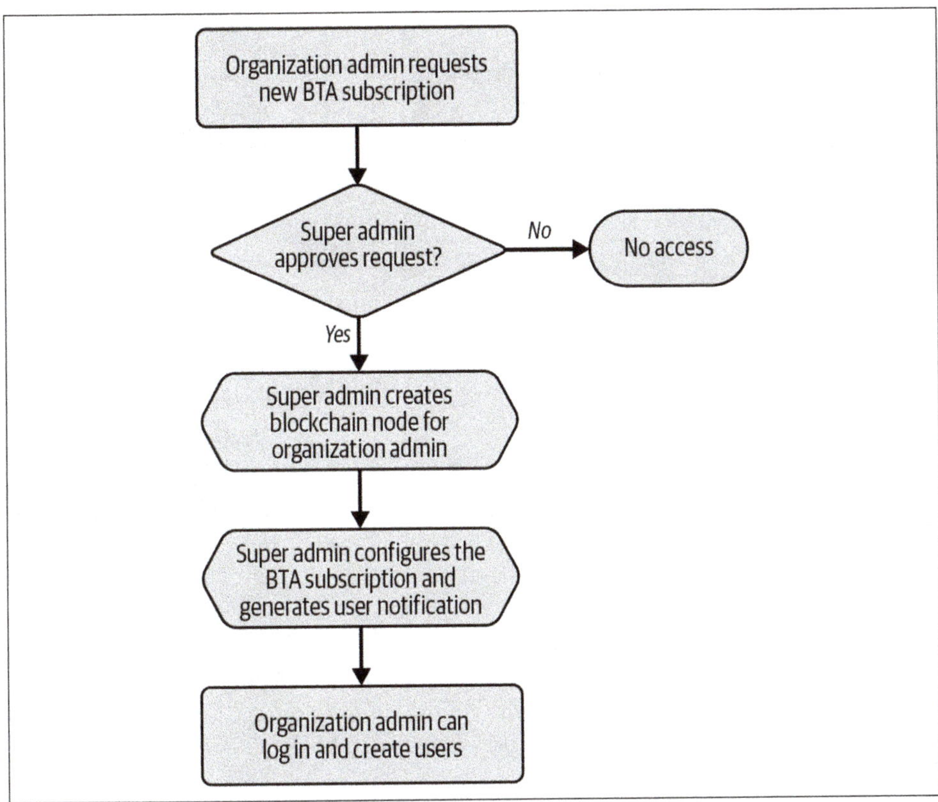

Figure 7-5. Subscription approval and creation of users

To create a new subscription account, fill in your BTA's "Start Registration for Your Account" page (*http://localhost.com:3000/#/auth/register*), choose Staff for Subscription Type, complete the rest of the fields, and click the Register button to submit the new account form.

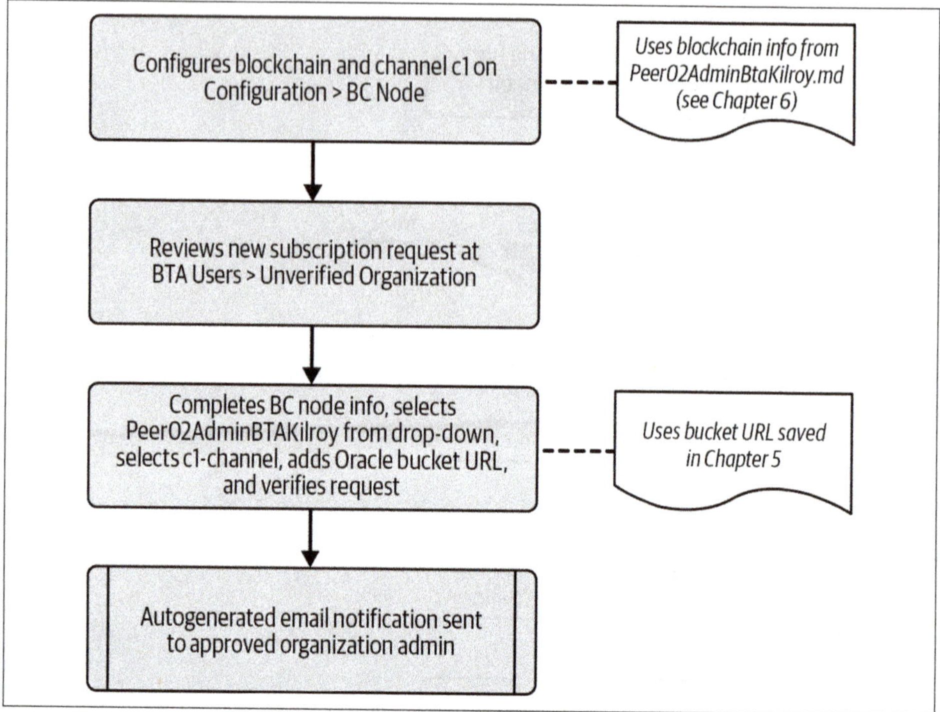

Figure 7-6. Super admin configures new subscription

Configuring Organization Admin's Node

As super admin, you will approve the new organization admin, but first you will need to add the node info for them. To do this, click BC Configuration and then BC Node. Click the ADD BC NODE button. This brings up the New Bc Node Info screen, which allows you to add the blockchain nodes that you created in Chapter 6, as follows:

- *Organization Name:* Peer02AdminBtaKilroy
- *Node URL:* http://192.168.1.7:5005
- *Authorization Token:* aWNhLW8yLWFkbWluLWJ0YS1raWxyb3k6SWNhLU8yLUFkbWluLUJ0YS1LaWxyb3k=
- *Label:* AI_Test_Organization

For this demo, you can get the blockchain node info that you are assigning to the organization admin from your */bta-blockchain/bta-bc-connector/bc-connector-node-info/Peer02AdminBtaKilroy.md* file.

Click SAVE to create the blockchain node for the organization admin. You will see a pop-up confirmation that the node information has been saved. Now you will see the Bc Node Info in the list of nodes.

Configuring Organization Admin's Channel

You need to create only one channel, which is the *c1-channel* created in "Exercise: Setting Up Hyperledger Fabric" on page 155. Click Bc Configuration > Channel Details, then choose the ADD NEW CHANNEL button.

Fields to be entered while creating each channel are as follows:

- *Channel Name:* c1-channel
- *Label:* AI engineer channel

Click the SAVE button to save the channel. You will see a pop-up confirmation that the channel has been saved successfully. Now you will see the new channel in the list of channels.

Verifying the Subscription

Click BTA Users > Unverified Organizations, and you should see the organization name that you registered. Next to the name, find and click the icon labeled Verify in the Actions column. This opens up a pop-up, as seen in Figure 7-7.

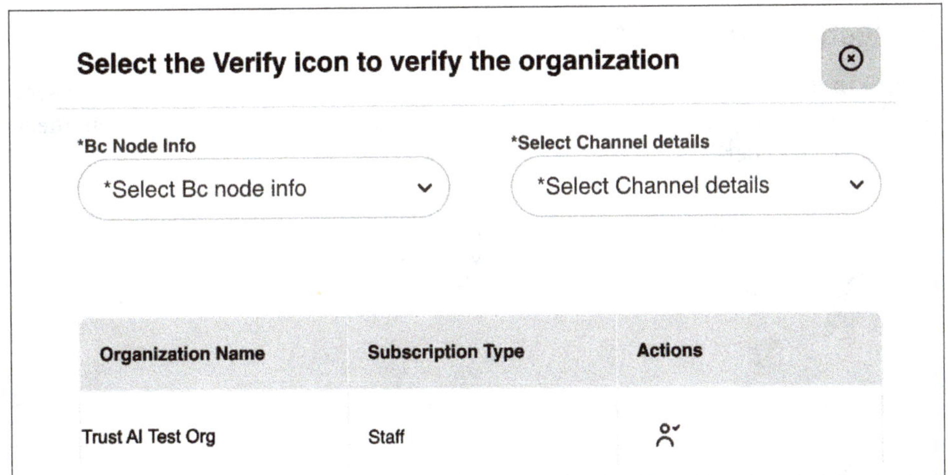

Figure 7-7. Approving a new subscription

Complete the screen as follows:

- *BC Node Info:* Select Peer02AdminBTAKilroy from the drop-down.
- *Select Channel:* Select c1-channel from the drop-down.

After you have made the selections, click the human silhouette icon beneath the Actions column to verify the configuration. You will see a system confirmation that you have successfully verified the user.

Now the organization admin has their own blockchain node and bucket to store the logs and artifacts. Once the organization admin logs in, their BTA account will be active.

Activating Your Organization Admin

Next, check MailCatcher for an email for the new organization admin, containing the organization admin's login credentials and blockchain key. Visit *https://localhost:4200* in your browser, and choose Login to sign in using the new credentials.

If you forget to add the rest of the required team members and then try to add a project, you'll see a reminder that you have to add at least one user in each role first.

Configuring Access for Your AI Team

Logged in as the organization admin, you can set up access and create other users. For the exercises, your AI team consists of one AI engineer, one MLOps engineer, and one stakeholder.

The organization admin needs to configure blockchain nodes and channels for all of the users who will be building, reviewing, and finalizing the AI model, and does this using the BTA interface.

To set up the users, as organization admin you will add their blockchain nodes to the BTA, add channels, create organization units and staffings for access control, and create login credentials. This process is shown in Figure 7-8.

First user?

No

Yes

All users communicate across this channel

Configures blockchain node
o5-ai-engineer-channel
Configuration > BC Node

Creates organization unit AI Organization
Manage Users > Organization Unit

Uses blockchain node and channel configuration details from this chapter

Creates ai-engineer-staffing and adds URL for bucket
Manage Users > Organization Unit > Action Column > +

Uses configuration details from this chapter and bucket URL saved in Chapter 5

Creates AI engineer user
Manage Users > User > Add User

Select AI Organization as organization unit and ai-engineer-staffing as staffing

Repeat for MLOps engineer and stakeholder

New users get credentials and activation link via automated email
MailCatcher

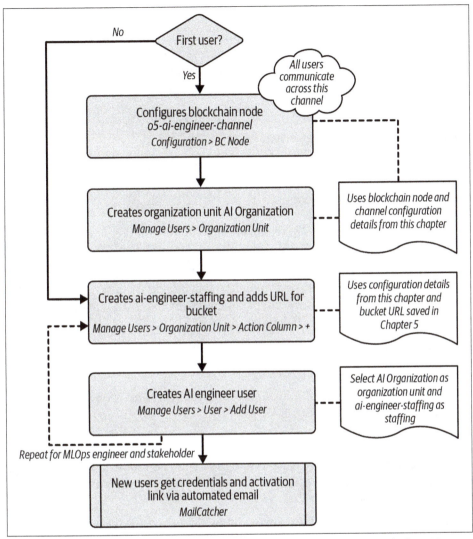

Figure 7-8. Organization admin configuring access for a new AI team including AI engineer, MLOps engineer, and stakeholder users

Important! Copying Authorization Keys

It might drive you crazy if you try to copy your authorization keys from a rich text document into the BTA. To properly copy your keys, you need to make sure you are copying them from plain text, such as using *type /bta-blockchain/bta-bc-connector/bc-connector-node-info/Peer05AIEngineerBtaKilroy.md* to copy the key inside so you can paste it into the BTA Bc Node Info.

Configuring user nodes

First, you will configure nodes for each user. To do so, click Bc Configuration > Bc Node Info. Click ADD BC NODE and complete the info as follows for the AI engineer's blockchain node (same configuration as */bta-blockchain/bta-bc-connector/bc-connector-node-info/Peer05AIEngineerBtaKilroy.md*):

- *Organization Name:* Peer05AIEngineerBtaKilroy
- *Node URL:* http://192.168.1.7:5008
- *Authorization Token:* aWNhLW8yLWFkbWluLWJ0YS1raWxyb3k6SWNhLU8yLUFkbWluLUJ0YS1LaWxyb3k=
- *Label:* AI engineer

Click SAVE to return to the Bc Node Info screen. You will see a pop-up message saying your Bc Node Info was added successfully, and you'll see your new Bc Node for the AI engineer in the list.

Next, click ADD BC NODE and complete the info as follows for the MLOps engineer's blockchain node (same configuration as */bta-blockchain/bta-bc-connector/bc-connector-node-info/Peer04MLOpsBtaKilroy.md*):

- *Organization Name:* Peer04MLOpsBtaKilroy
- *Node URL:* http://192.168.1.7:5007
- *Authorization Token:* aWNhLW80LW1sb3BzLWJ0YS1raWxyb3k6SWNhLU80LU1MT3BzLUJ0YS1LaWxyb3k=
- *Label:* MLOps engineer

Click SAVE to return to the Bc Node Info screen, and you will see a pop-up message saying your Bc Node Info was added successfully, and your new Bc Node for the MLOps engineer will be in the list.

Finally, click ADD BC NODE and complete the info as follows for the stakeholder's blockchain node (same configuration as */bta-blockchain/bta-bc-connector/bc-connector-node-info/Peer03ShBtaKilroy.md*):

- *Organization Name:* Peer03ShBtaKilroy
- *Node URL:* http://192.168.1.7:5006
- *Authorization Token:* aWNhLW8yLWFkbWluLWJ0YS1raWxyb3k6SWNhLU8yLUFkbWluLUJ0YS1LaWxyb3k=
- *Label:* stakeholder

Click SAVE to return to the Bc Node Info screen, and you will see your new Bc Node for the stakeholder in the list.

Configuring a channel for users

Now, you can configure one channel for all users to communicate across. To do so, click BC Configuration > Channel Details. Create a channel called *o5-ai-engineer-channel*, with a label of "o5 channel." You only have to do this once. Click SAVE to see your new channel in the list.

Creating an organization unit

Next, you will set up access control in the form of one *organization unit* that impacts the entire organization, and staffings within it for each type of user (AI engineer, MLOps engineer, and stakeholder). The organization unit controls the features that the assigned users can see. (Staffings, which we create next, are children of the organization unit.)

If this were more than a demo, you could use multiple organization units to provide a more granular level of access control.

To create your organization unit, click Manage Users > Organization Unit. Click the ADD ORGANIZATION UNIT button, as shown in Figure 7-9. This opens up a pop-up that gathers details about the organization unit.

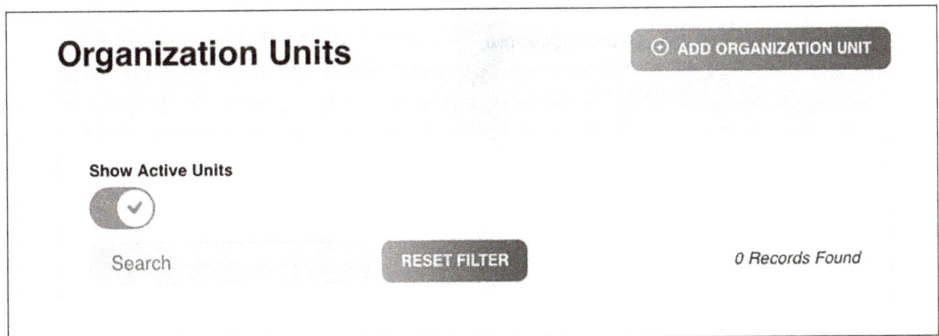

Figure 7-9. Organization units; later on in this exercise you will be able to see the staffings you create by clicking the twistie next to the unit name

Complete the fields using the following sample unit name and description, or make up your own:

- *Unit Name:* AI Organization
- *Description:* Test organization unit

Since the organization unit is where you determine how features are delegated to users, complete the Features section of the form by selecting the following choices: Personal Detail, Organization Detail, Project, Project Purpose, Model Version, Model Review, and Model Monitoring, as seen in Figures 7-10 through 7-12, and then click SAVE.

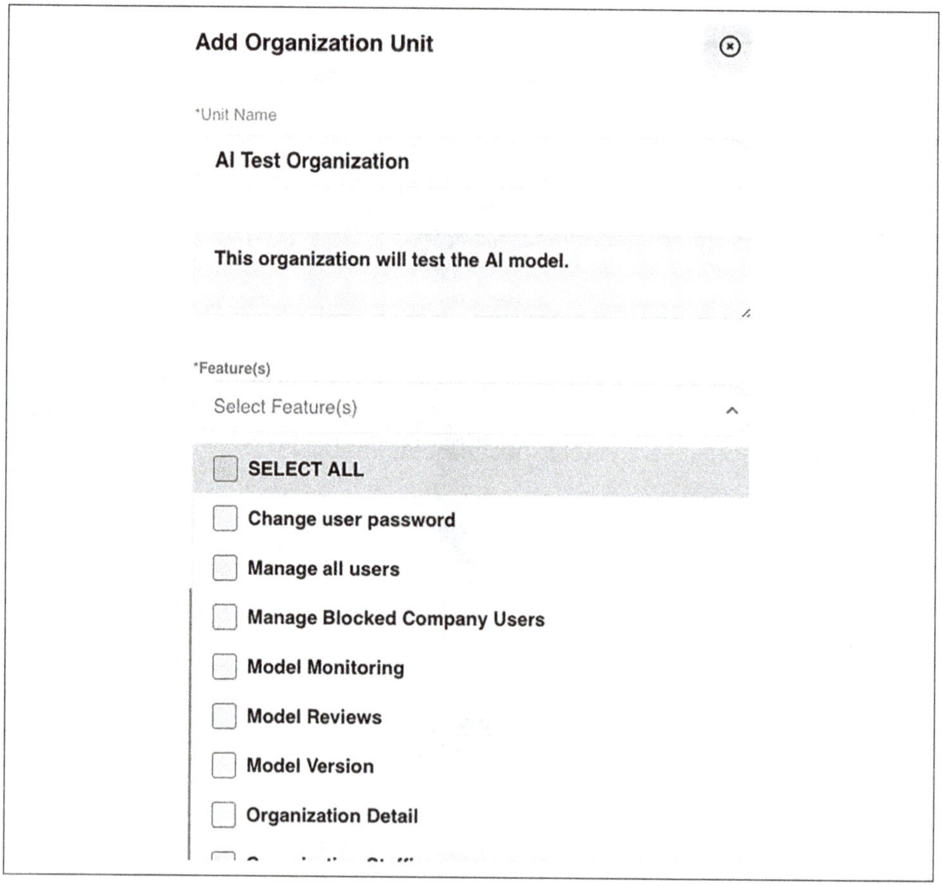

Figure 7-10. Organization unit features

Add Organization Unit

*Unit Name

AI Test Organization

This organization will test the AI model.

*Feature(s)

Model Monitoring, Model Reviews, Model Version, Or...

- [ ] SELECT ALL
- [ ] Change user password
- [ ] Manage all users
- [ ] Manage Blocked Company Users
- [x] Model Monitoring
- [x] Model Reviews
- [x] Model Version
- [x] Organization Detail

Figure 7-11. Selecting organization unit features

Organization units filter staffings that are beneath them, so if you don't select a feature here, you won't be able to assign create-read-write privileges for that feature in the staffings.

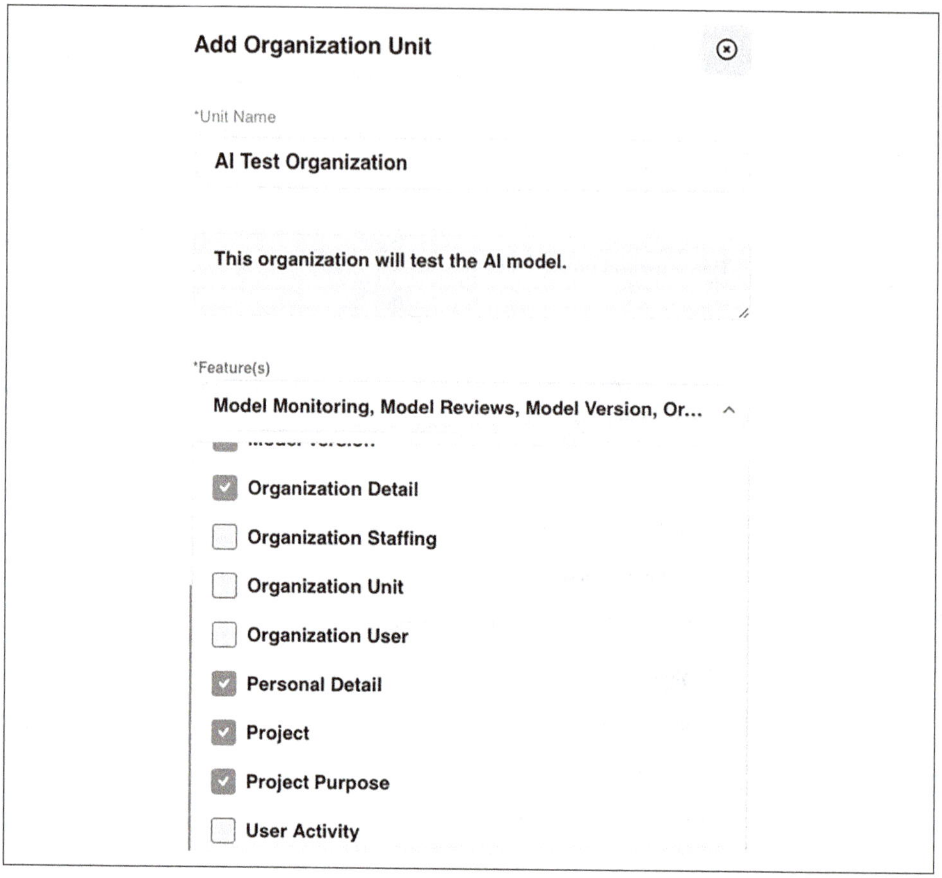

Figure 7-12. Selecting more organization unit features

After you complete these steps and save your organization, you can see it in the list.

Once you configure your users to use the new organization unit, when they log in they will see only the features you selected when you created it. But before you can assign your organization unit to your users, you must create staffings within it.

Creating staffings

After the organization unit is created, as organization admin you will need to create three staffings for the three kinds of participants we have discussed: AI engineer, MLOps engineer, and stakeholder. There is a "+" under the Action column that brings up the Add Organization staffing box for the organization unit you created in the previous step, which looks like Figure 7-13. Use Table 7-1 to find the information for each of the staffings.

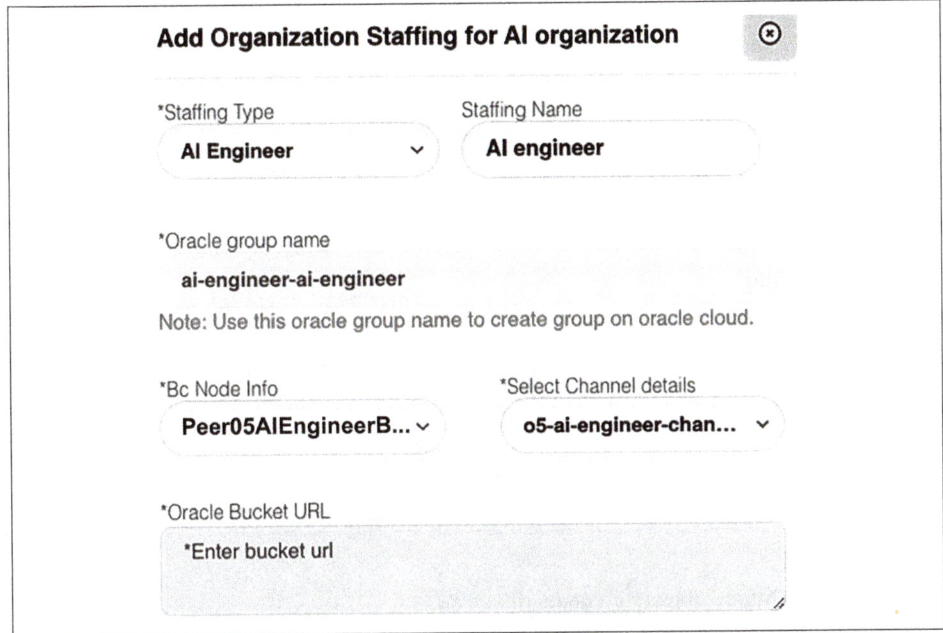

Figure 7-13. Add AI engineer staffing for the AI organization's organization unit

Table 7-1. Staffing attributes for each participant role

Attributes	AI engineer	MLOps engineer	Stakeholder
Staffing Type	AI engineer	MLOps engineer	Stakeholder
Staffing Name	AI engineer name	MLOps engineer name	Stakeholder's name
Oracle group name	ai-engineer-1	mlops-engineer-1	stakeholder-1
BC Node Info	Peer05AIEngineerBtaKilroy	Peer04MLOPsBtaKilroy	Peer03ShBtaKilroy
Oracle Bucket URL	User's OCI bucket	User's OCI bucket	User's OCI bucket
Project	R W U	R	R
Project Purpose	R	R	R W U
Model Version	R W U	R	R
Model Reviews	R W	R W	R W
Model Monitoring	R W	R W	R W
Personal Detail	R U	R U	R U
Organizational Detail	R	R	R

Adding a bucket URL

To assign a bucket to a BTA staffing, add the URL for the bucket to the staffing. Copy the pre-authenticated request that you saved earlier in "Creating a Pre-authenticated Request" on page 136 and paste it in the Oracle Bucket URL, as shown in Figure 7-14.

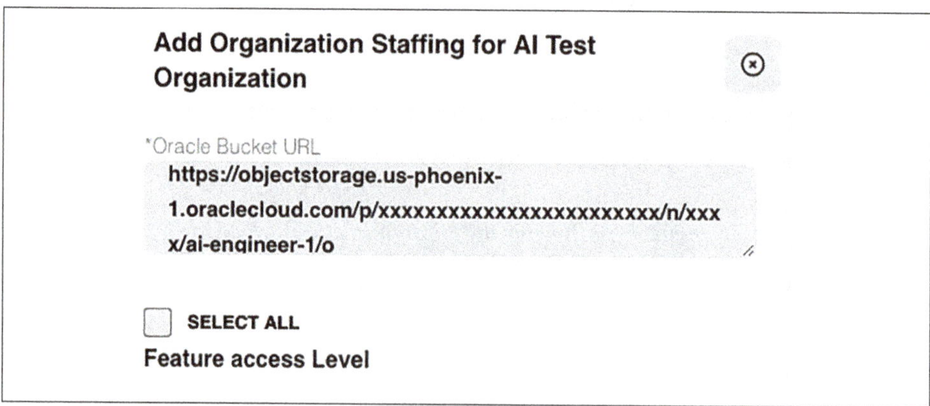

Figure 7-14. Assigning a bucket to a BTA staffing

Now the created staffing can be saved, and the user for the particular staffing can be created. After you complete the Staffing Type, Staffing Name, Oracle group name, Bc Node Info, Select Channel details, and Oracle Bucket URL fields, scroll down to set the feature access level, as shown in Figure 7-15.

Depending on the feature, you will see an R, W, and U to the right of the feature name. Those stand for Read, Write, and Update, and control the users' data access level that corresponds to each feature. Selecting Read lets the user display the feature's data but not change it, Write lets the user create new records using the feature, and Update lets the user change the contents of an existing record that was generated by the feature. As a shortcut, you can choose SELECT ALL and then deselect certain checkboxes to remove those permissions.

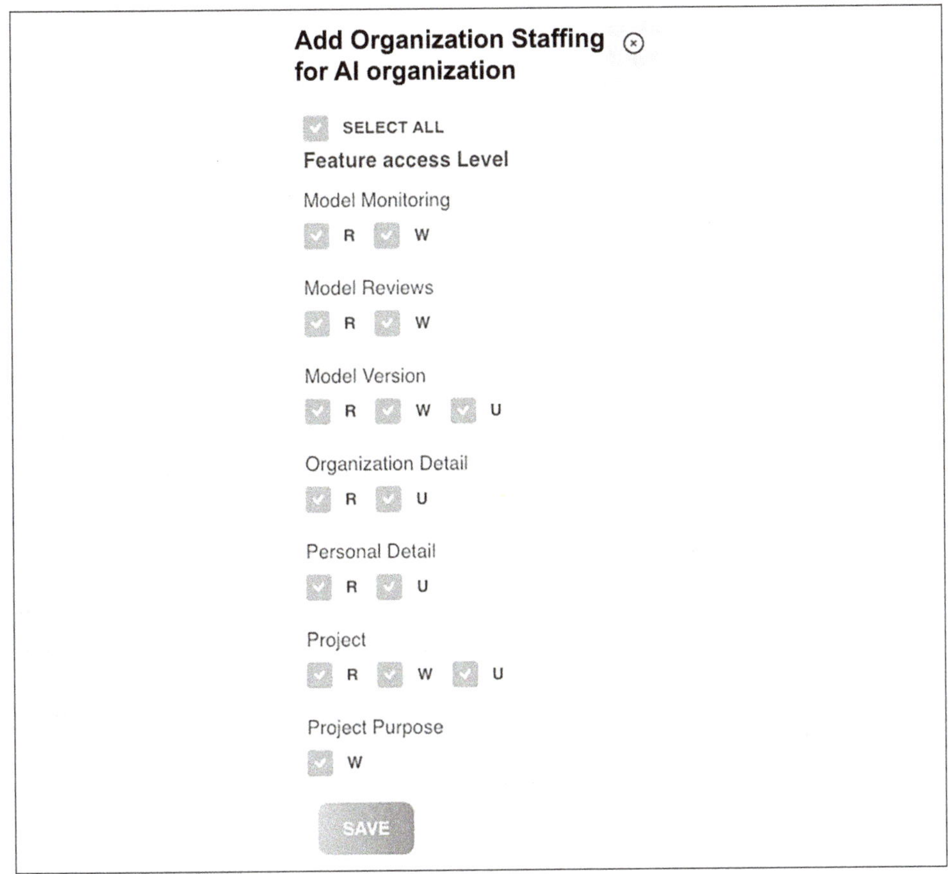

Figure 7-15. Add AI engineer staffing for AI organization's organization unit, scrolled down to set feature access levels

Repeat this process of creating staffings for the MLOps engineer and stakeholder. When you are finished, your list of staffings will look similar to those shown in Figure 7-16.

Unit Name	Description	Created Date	Status
⌄ AI Organization	test organization unit	2022-11-30	Enabled
AI Engineer-AI engineer	-	2022-11-30	Enabled
MLOps Engineer-MLOps engineer	-	2022-11-30	Enabled
Stakeholder-Stakeholder	-	2022-11-30	Enabled

Figure 7-16. Organization units list with staffings expanded, showing the staffings you just created for the AI engineer, MLOps engineer, and stakeholder

Creating users

Now that your organization unit and staffings are set up, you can create users. As you have learned, you need an AI engineer, an MLOps engineer, and a stakeholder to simulate the process of testing, reviewing, and approving a model using your BTA. This section walks through creating the AI engineer; repeat the steps here to create your MLOps engineer and stakeholder using the corresponding staffings that you set up in the previous section.

Still logged in as the organization admin, select Manage Users > Users. This brings up a pop-up where you can enter the new user's email address. Add the email address of your AI engineer first (something like *karen+aie@kilroyblockchain.com*), and click NEXT to open a pop-up window where you have to add their personal details. Remember to select your organization unit, AI Organization, from the drop-down.

Each user in your BTA has a blockchain key that they have to enter at the time of login. This demonstrates how blockchain can be used to provide an additional layer of user security, since no user would be admitted without providing this key.

To create a user, choose Manage Users > Users and click the Add User button, then complete the information, as shown in Figures 7-17 and 7-18.

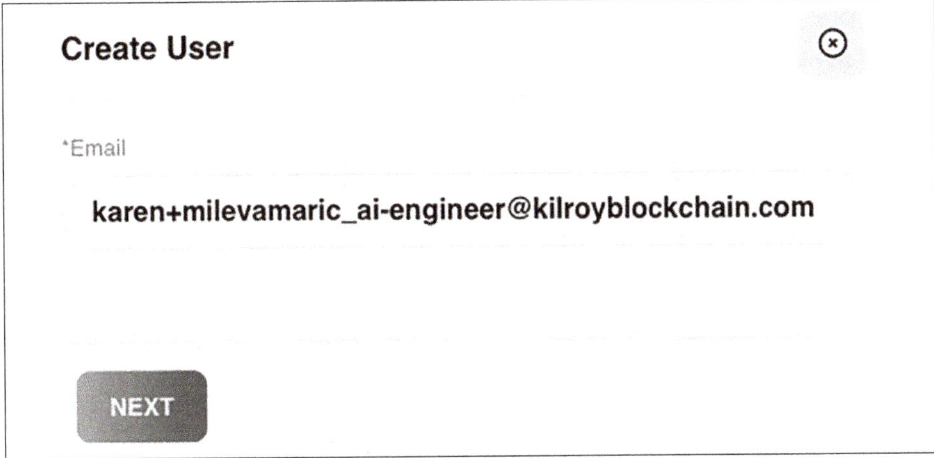

Figure 7-17. The first step in creating a user is to add their email address

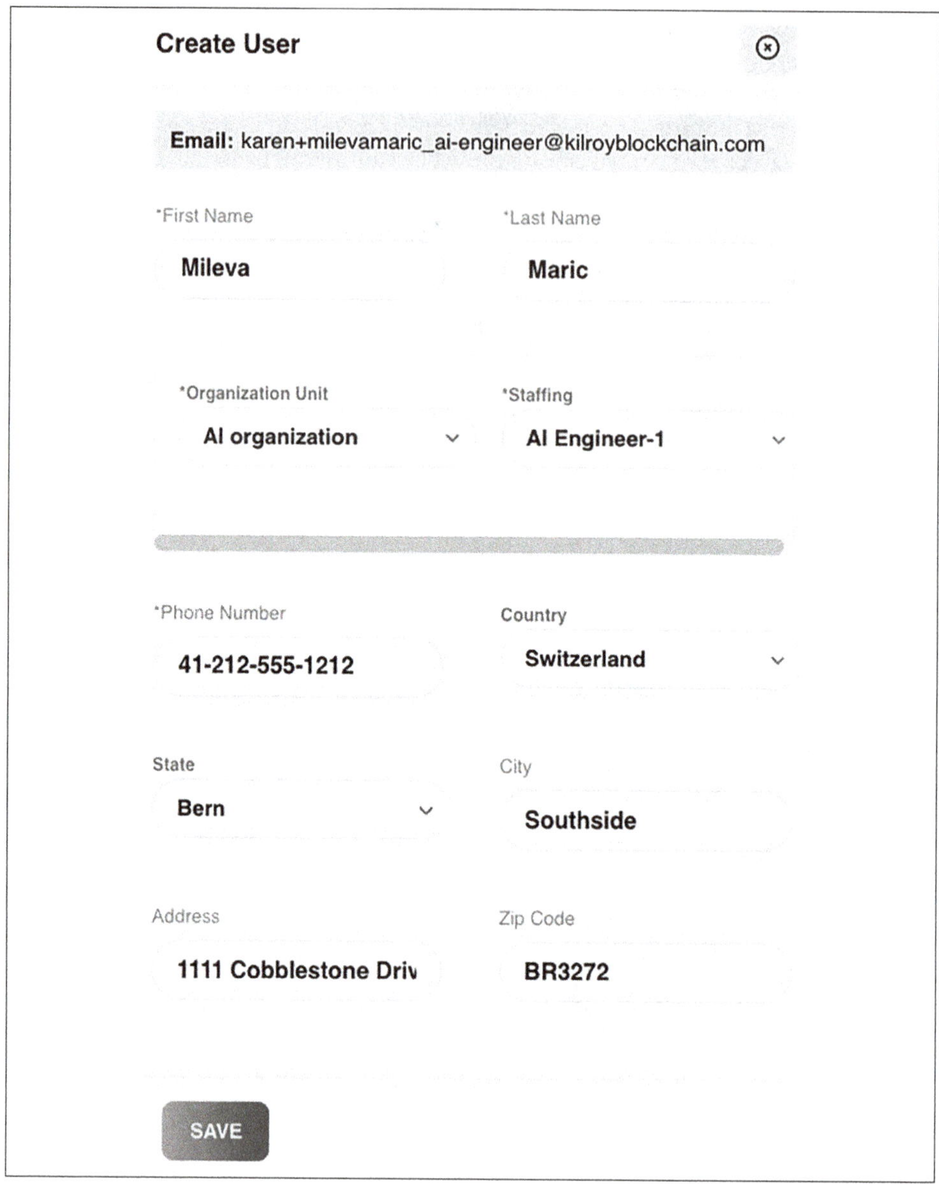

Figure 7-18. Filling in details needed to create the new AI engineer user

Simplifying BTA Testing with Email Subaddressing

You do not have to use this method, since you are using MailCatcher and nothing will route beyond your localhost. However, tagging the email address with the role still helps you to be able to remember which user is supposed to do which job.

That said, each BTA user must have a unique email address. To make testing and demonstration easier, the BTA allows you to register multiple unique users from one email address, through the use of *subaddresses*.

Subaddresses, or *tag addresses*, are created dynamically, simply by using them. They are indicated in an email address by *tag*, or unique text string, by adding a + and a tag immediately before the @ in an email address, like this: *email+tag@yourdomain.com*.

To apply this, you can use unique descriptive tags (*+aiengineer*, *+mlopsengineer*, and *+stakeholder*) that all route to one actual email account (like *milevamaric 1875@gmail.com*).

Email addresses with meaningful tags include:

- *milevamaric1875@gmail.com*
- *milevamaric1875+aiengineer@gmail.com*
- *milevamaric1875+mlopsengineer@gmail.com*
- *milevamaric1875+stakeholder@gmail.com*

Keeping the tags meaningful will help you to easily identify which type of user is doing what when you are testing your workflow.

As you create each user, they will get two welcome emails: one from the BTA and one from Oracle. For this demo, check your email for both messages. The welcome email from the BTA looks like the one you received when you subscribed, confirming an email address, password, and blockchain key, as shown in Figure 7-19.

Welcome to BTA!

We are excited for having you in the BTA project. Please use following credentials and instructions to login into BTA web application

Subscription

Staff

Email

karen+mileviamaric_ai-engineer@kilroyblockchain.com

Password

1qdq06vg

Blockchain Key

77956b7b8c25fb7f7f1744af428bd6
2183c337fc5e3c528936ccdd288a94388d

Log In

Figure 7-19. BTA welcome email for AI engineer user

If this system were intended for production, it would offer a more secure method for communicating credentials, or would require a password reset on the first login. You could also integrate SecurID or other third-party authenticator to increase the security.

You will also receive a confirmation from Oracle Cloud that your bucket was created. That email looks like the one in Figure 7-20.

Clicking the Activate Your Account button in the email from Oracle will prompt you to reset your password. Follow the prompts to reset the Oracle password for the new user, and make a note of it. This completes the user setup for the AI engineer.

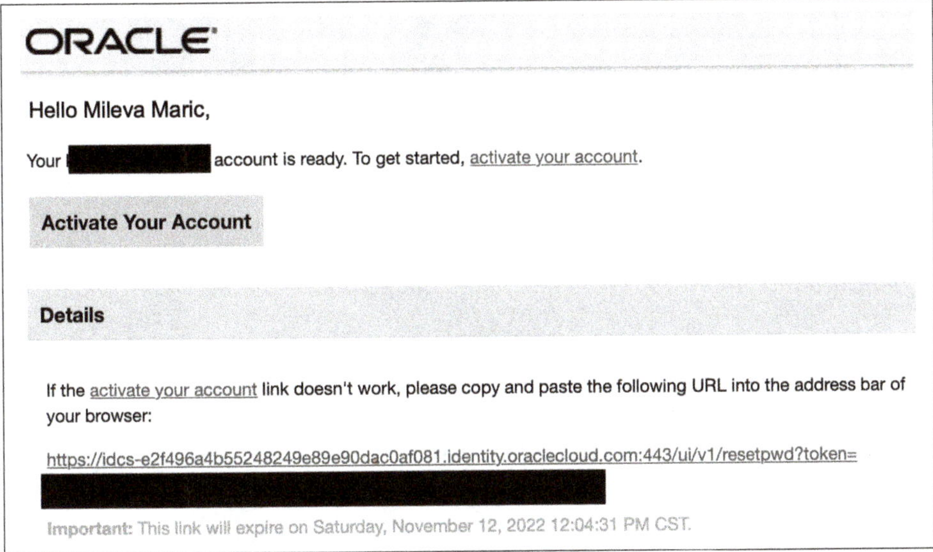

Figure 7-20. Oracle account activation email

After you complete the AI engineer setup, follow the same steps to create the MLOps engineer and the stakeholder before moving on. When you are finished, you should have all the credentials you need in order to test your BTA.

At this point, you have set up blockchain nodes, channels, organization units, staffings, and users, and are prepared to start building, reviewing, and finalizing AI models using your BTA.

After you have each of your users set up, move on to Chapter 8, where the next exercise guides you through logging in with each user to introduce, review, and approve a model.

Summary

In this chapter, you installed and launched your BTA and created your first subscription. You logged in as super admin, approved your new subscription, and configured your organization administrator. Next, you logged in as your new organization administrator, configured your nodes and channels, and added your first users, one for each persona.

You are very close to being one of the first people in the world to achieve blockchain tethered AI. The next chapter, your final one, helps you test your BTA's workflow using each of the user personas.

CHAPTER 8

Using Your BTA

By the time you have finished this chapter, you will have tried your BTA as super admin, organization admin, AI engineer, MLOps engineer, and stakeholder. You will register a fictitious organization as a brand new organization admin, and then as super admin you will approve the new subscription. As organization admin, you will create IDs for an AI engineer, MLOps engineer, and a stakeholder. Then, as the AI engineer, you will run a training event on your model which gets reviewed and approved by the MLOps engineer and stakeholder.

This chapter—and the book—concludes with a discussion on how this audit trail might be used to reverse the training of the model.

Exercise: Recording Critical AI Touchpoints to Blockchain

You created your users in the previous exercise, which are organization admin, AI engineer, MLOps engineer, and stakeholder. This exercise guides you through using the BTA as each user, taking part in a process where a model is created, its original intent is specified, and the model is processed through the users, with each critical step being recorded to blockchain. This blockchain audit trail is used here in this exercise to check the steps used to create and train the model.

Adding a New Project

To get started, choose Manage Projects > Projects to see a list of all projects. Here is where you can choose Add Project to establish the parameters of the model creation and review process, as shown in Figure 8-1.

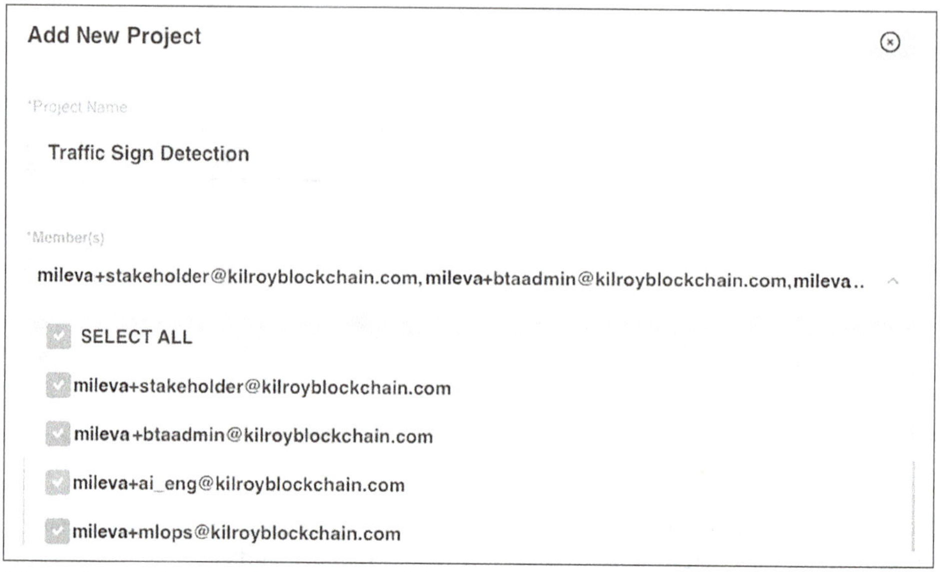

Add New Project

*Project Name

Traffic Sign Detection

*Member(s)

mileva+stakeholder@kilroyblockchain.com, mileva+btaadmin@kilroyblockchain.com,mileva..

SELECT ALL

mileva+stakeholder@kilroyblockchain.com

mileva+btaadmin@kilroyblockchain.com

mileva+ai_eng@kilroyblockchain.com

mileva+mlops@kilroyblockchain.com

Figure 8-1. Add project begins the model creation and sharing process

Fill in a name for your project, such as Traffic Signs Detection. In the Member(s) field, include all the users you created by checking SELECT ALL. Click to a blank part of the box, and you will see each member's name show up in the Member(s) field. When you have completed the form, click Save, and your project should now appear in your All Projects list.

To see what you added, in the All Projects list click the three dots to the right of the project name to bring up the Actions menu, and choose View Project. You will see the project info, a list of project members, and at the bottom, a section for model details which should indicate that no models have been added. Once you complete the next step to add a version, the model will show up here.

Adding a New Version

Next, still in the role as AI engineer, open the project's Actions menu again (the three dots next to the project name) and select Add Version.

This brings up the Add New Version box, shown in Figure 8-2. When you give the project a Version Name number, such as "1," this causes the Log File Path, Test Data Sets URL, Train Data Sets URL, and AI Model URL to all automatically complete. This is possible because these fields use a standard naming convention that adds the version to make the paths unique. For the purposes of this test, you can also enter a 1 in the Notebook Version, Code Repo, and Code Version fields, along with a comment, like "first version of BTA test project."

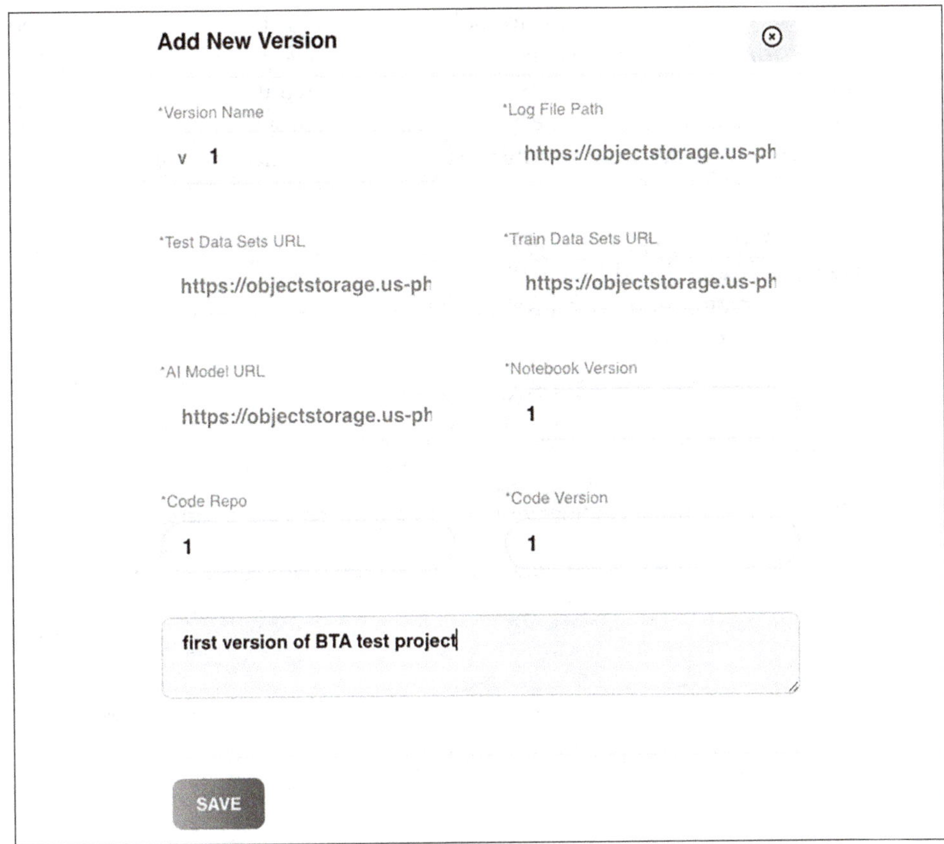

Figure 8-2. Adding a new version to your project

When you click SAVE, you will see a dialog box that tells you your model has been successfully saved, and that the system will process for an additional 30–40 seconds before the version is ready to use.

Now that you have created a version, you can take a look at what has been set up behind the scenes by choosing View Project from the project's Actions menu.

Now if you look at Model Details, instead of an empty section you will see the version name that you set up in this step, along with the paths that were automatically generated for you. When you are finished looking at Model Details, close the box.

Now use the version's Actions menu to look at the Version Details. As you can see in Figure 8-3, drilling down into Version Details reveals several errors indicating that blockchain hashes are missing (because they are not created until the corresponding information has been uploaded to the bucket). The BTA automates computing a hash of the uploaded information and storing it on blockchain, which is the key to making the data tamper evident.

Specifically, there is an error, shown in red type, for the Test Data Sets BC Hash, Train Data Sets BC Hash, and the AI Model BC Hash. This is because the AI engineer needs to load this information into the bucket before these hashes can be created, which is done in the following steps.

Project Name:	Traffic Sign Detection
Version Name:	v1
Log File Path:	https://objectstorage.us-phoenix-1....-1/o/Traffic Sign Detection/v1/logs
Test Data Sets URL:	https://objectstorage.us-phoenix-1....rtifacts/datasets/test_datasets.zip
Test Data Sets BC Hash:	The object 'Traffic Sign Detection/v1/artifacts/datasets/test_datasets.zip' was not found in the bucket 'ai-engineer-1'
Train Data Sets URL:	https://objectstorage.us-phoenix-1....tifacts/datasets/train_datasets.zip
Train Data Sets BC Hash:	The object 'Traffic Sign Detection/v1/artifacts/datasets/train_datasets.zip' was not found in the bucket 'ai-engineer-1'
AI Model URL:	https://objectstorage.us-phoenix-1....c Sign Detection/v1/artifacts/model
AI Model BC Hash:	The object 'Traffic Sign Detection/v1/artifacts/model/Traffic Sign Detection_model_0.pkl' was not found in the bucket 'ai-engineer-1'

Figure 8-3. Errors found on the Version Details screen indicating that blockchain hashes are missing

Understanding How Training and Testing Data Use Blockchain

The training data set and test data set are retrieved while adding the model version on the web application. The training data set and test data set links are autogenerated when the version name is added on the input field, as in Figure 8-4.

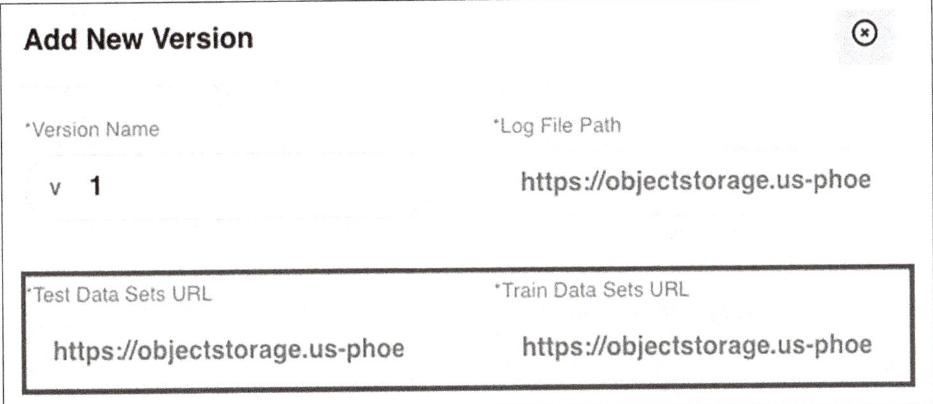

Figure 8-4. Adding the training data set and test data set to the bucket

The training data set and test data set are then fetched from the Oracle cloud on the basis of autogenerated URLs after users create the model version.

Understanding How Models and Algorithms Use Blockchain

The AI engineer used the BTA to add models and algorithms to the bucket. The models are inside the *artifact* folder, and the name of the algorithm used to train the AI model is stored as a part of the log in the *logs* folder.

The model is retrieved from the bucket when the AI engineer creates the model version. The AI model, data set, and log URLs are autogenerated when the version name is added. Once the model is uploaded into the BTA, a hash of the model is computed and stored on blockchain.

Understanding How Inputs and Outputs Use Blockchain

The experiments are written by an AI engineer on the notebook. The experiment inputs and outputs are stored in the *logs* folder on the bucket. In the BTA, inputs and outputs work the same as artifacts, meaning the data is retrieved from the bucket using the autogenerated URL when you complete the model version form, and a hash of that data is computed and stored on the blockchain. Hyperparameters, the number of epochs, learning rate, and batch size are included in the inputs, as shown in Example 8-1.

Example 8-1. Experiment data including hyperparameters to be stored on the blockchain

```
[
  {
    "exp": {
      "exp_no": "exp_1",
      "datetime": "08/02/2022, 03:52:05",
      "hyperparameters": {
        "data_dir": "./data",
        "algorithm_name": "Convolutional Neural Network",
        "hidden_size": 64.0,
        "total_epochs": 5.0,
        "batch_size": 64.0,
        "learning_rate": 2e-5
      },
    }
  }
]
```

The demo model used by this book's exercises, the Traffic Signs Detection model, has 43 classes. Each class represents a type of traffic sign like Stop, Go, School area, and so on. The project has around 50K images, almost equally divided among the classes. The images are stored in a bucket inside a particular model version in this folder structure: *V1/artifacts/dataset/Classes.*

Outputs include the number of classes used to train the model where MLOps engineers can verify the number of images from the bucket stored in each class of a particular model version in the *dataset* folder. Like artifacts, logs, and new models, when a revised model is submitted as a new version by an AI engineer, hashes of the inputs and outputs are computed and stored in the blockchain right after the version is submitted. This log file blockchain hash, as shown in Example 8-2, becomes part of the BTA's audit trail.

Example 8-2. Example log file blockchain hash

```
Log File BC Hash: 9275e1a764a87d19b5a9be57a7b87e79af1a724b9dd20dc97054a9b92289febd
```

Understanding How Performance Metrics Use Blockchain

The performance metrics are also included in the experiment log data. They measure how accurately the model is learning and are calculated when the model is trained. You can get info about the particular log file of an experiment and inspect the metrics, as shown in Example 8-3.

Example 8-3. Log file showing experiment performance metrics

```
[
  {
    "exp": {
      "exp_no": "exp_1",
      "datetime": "08/02/2022, 03:52:05",
      "test_metrics": {
        "test_accuracy": 0.8637999892,
        "test_f1_score": 0.8629577756,
        "test_loss": 0.6077153683000001,
        "test_precision": 0.8629577756,
        "test_recall": 0.8629577756
      },
    }
  }
]
```

The data of performance metrics is also included in the hash generated for the experiment logs.

Understanding How New Model Versions Use Blockchain

The model version and its related files are kept as a draft and stored on the AI engineer's blockchain ledger. Once the AI engineer submits the version, the model version will be distributed to the company's channel and stored in the respective nodes.

Understanding How the Uploads Work

Your notebook contains the Python script that uploads the models and algorithms, training and testing data sets, inputs and outputs, as well as logs and artifacts, to the bucket. The code shown in Examples 8-4 through 8-6 uploads the final log file, AI model, and data sets to the bucket, respectively. Figure 8-5 is the local file structure as seen in your Jupyter Notebook.

Example 8-4. Uploading the final log to the bucket

```
def upload_file_bucket(latest_version):
    # Creating experiment number from latest_version
    version_number = latest_version.split("_")
    testver = version_number[-1]
    testno = int(testver)

    json_path = f"finallogfile/{latest_version}/log_exp_{testno}.json"
    print(json_path)
```

```
    split_name = json_path.split("/")
    splited_text = split_name[-1]
    print(splited_text)

    # Upload a file to your OCI Bucket; first value is the path
    # of the directory, second value is bucket name, and third value
    # is filename with version folder name
    s3.meta.client.upload_file(json_path, BUCKET_NAME, PROJECT_NAME
    +'/'+VERSION_NO+'/logs/'+splited_text)
```

When run, the preceding code provides the log filename and path as output: e.g., `finallogfile/version_0/log_exp_0.json`.

Example 8-5. Uploading the final model to the bucket

```
def upload_model(latest_version):

    # creating experiment number from latest_version
    version_number = latest_version.split("_")
    testver = version_number[-1]
    testno = int(testver)
#       testno = int(testver) +1


    # save the model to local disk
    model_name = f'model/{latest_version}/{PROJECT_NAME}_model_{testno}.pkl'
    with open(model_name, 'wb') as files:
      pickle.dump(model, files)


    json_path = f"model/{latest_version}/{PROJECT_NAME}_model_{testno}.pkl"
    print(json_path)
    split_name = json_path.split("/")
    splited_text = split_name[-1]
    print(splited_text)


    # Upload a file to you OCI bucket, 1st value is the path of the directory,
    # 2nd value is bucket name, and 3rd value is file name with version foldername
    s3.meta.client.upload_file(json_path, BUCKET_NAME, PROJECT_NAME
    +'/'+VERSION_NO+'/artifacts/model/'+splited_text)

upload_model(latest_version)
```

When run, the preceding code provides the model file path as output: e.g., `model/version_0_MNIST_model_0.pkl`.

Example 8-6. Uploading data sets to the bucket

```
# Upload the zip data sets to Oracle Cloud artifacts buckets
data_zip_path = f'zipdatasets'
for parent_path, dirs, filenames in os.walk(data_zip_path):
    for f in filenames:
        json_path=os.path.join(parent_path, f)
        s3.meta.client.upload_file(json_path, BUCKET_NAME, PROJECT_NAME
        + '/'+VERSION_NO+'/artifacts/datasets/'+f)
print("Zip data sets upload completed")
```

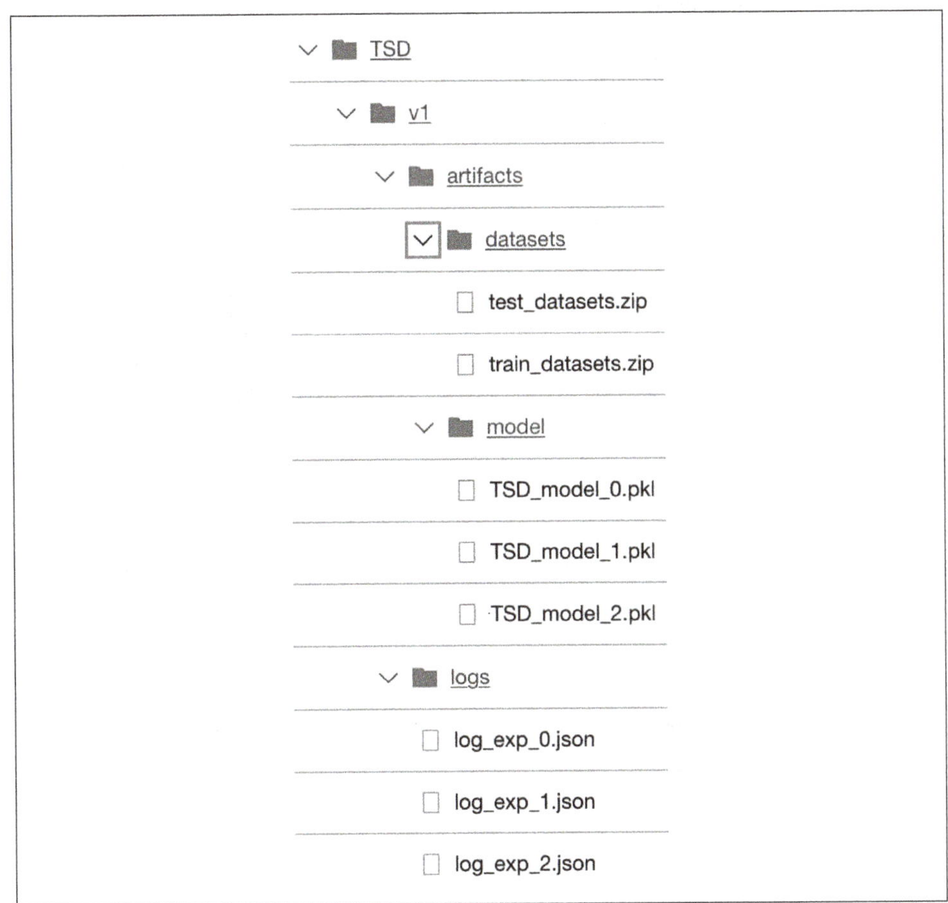

Figure 8-5. Bucket file structure showing training and testing data sets

Your BTA executes a Python script to refactor the PyTorch native log into the BTA format, another script to convert each data set into a ZIP file, and a third script to upload the logs and artifacts into a bucket.

Reviewing and Approving the Model

When using the BTA demo, your AI engineer, MLOps engineer, and stakeholder must each review and approve the model before it goes live.

To kick off the workflow in the BTA, log in as the AI engineer and perform a simple experiment. You don't have to actually change anything in the model to test the BTA, but you can if you like. Example 8-7 shows the Python code for your model.

Example 8-7. The code for your model

```
model = LitMNIST()

# Define the Lightning trainer
trainer = Trainer(
    gpus=AVAIL_GPUS,
    max epochs=5,
    progress_bar_refresh_rate=20, logger=logger,
)
trainer.tune (model)
trainer.fit(model)
```

When the preceding code is run, you'll see output as shown in Example 8-8 and status indicators in the notebook UI as files are downloaded and extracted.

Example 8-8. Training the model that you set up in a bucket in Chapter 6, using PyTorch

```
/opt/conda/lib/python3.7/site-packages/pytorch_lightning/trainer/connectors/...
    f"Setting `Trainer (progress_bar_refresh_rate=(progress_bar_refresh_rate...
GPU available: False, used: False
TPU available: False, using: 0 TPU cores
IPU available: False, using: 0 IPUs
Downloading http://yann.lecun.com/exdb/mnist/train-images-idx3-ubyte.gz
Downloading http://yann.lecun.com/exdb/mnist/train-images-idx3-ubyte.gz to ...
Extracting ./MNIST/raw/train-images-idx3-ubyte.gzto./MNIST/raw
Downloading http://yann.lecun.com/exdb/mnist/train-labels-idx1-ubyte.gz
Downloading http://yann.lecun.com/exdb/mnist/train-labels-idxl-ubyte.gz to ...
```

Next, add a new version of your model, as described earlier in "Adding a New Version" on page 232, to start the approval process.

Then log in as the MLOps engineer and use the BTA to deploy the model. This generates a Deployed Model URL to be used during the review process, as shown in Figure 8-6. Figure 8-7 shows a star rating that the MLOps engineer has given to the test version of the model.

Model Review

REVIEWS MODEL REVIEW

Deployed

*Deployed Model URL

http://█████.47/

This AI model was deployed and tested on web app by using flask framework

Review Supporting Documents

Choose Files file-sample_100kB.doc

1.Sample.Pdf X 2.File-Sample_100kB.Doc X

Figure 8-6. A model review

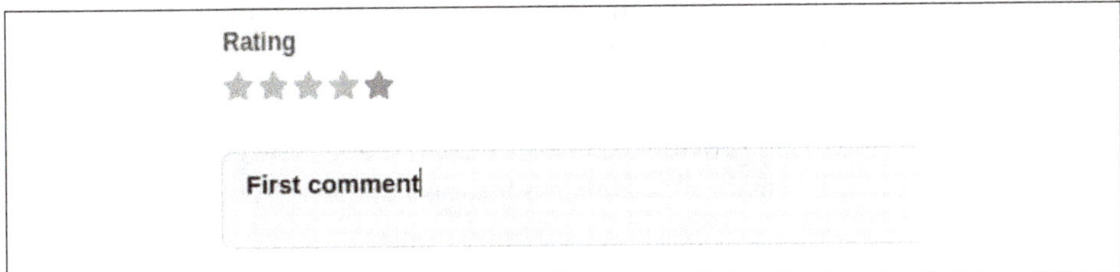

Figure 8-7. A model's rating (from review screen)

The Deployed checkbox will appear only for the MLOps engineer. When you click the SAVE button, it gives you another pop-up where you as the MLOps engineer should enter the details of the tests you have done against the submitted model, as shown in Figure 8-8.

If the model is not performing per expectation, then the MLOps engineer declines the model, which sends a rejection notification to the AI engineer. The AI engineer can retrain the model based on the reviewer's feedback by creating a new model version.

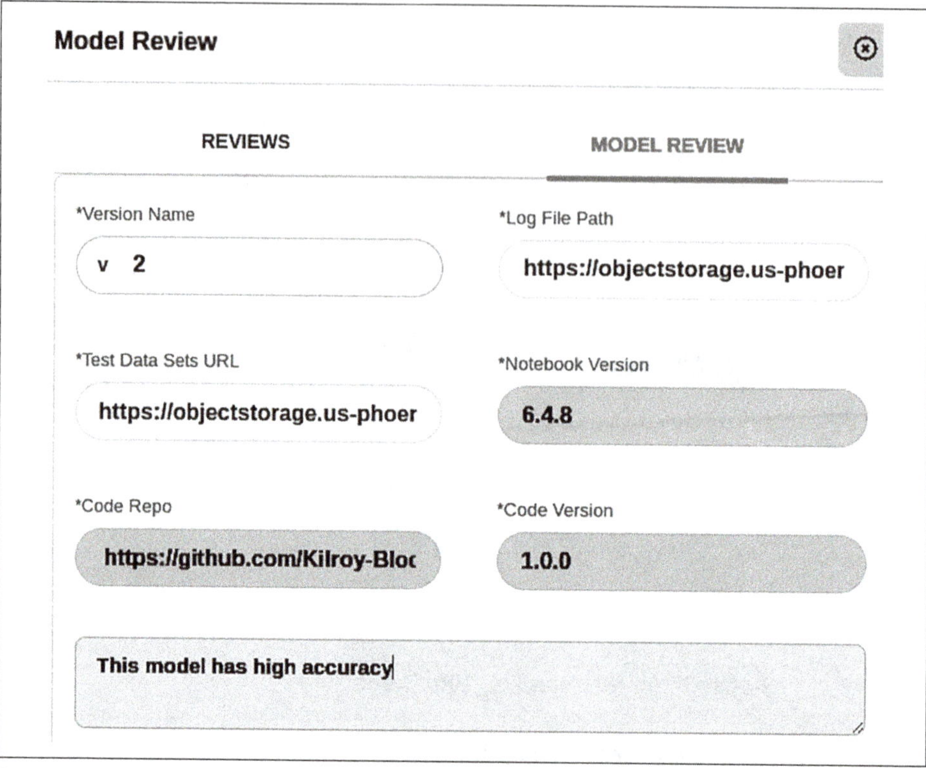

Figure 8-8. MLOps engineer entering the proof of the test done against the AI model

The MLOps engineer who is a reviewer of the model enters the model version and log file path (which has information on input, hyperparameters, output, and metrics). The engineer should also enter the path of the data set that is used during the review and the code repo.

All users test the model and provide feedback through the Review process, where the status of the model will remain QA. Figure 8-9 shows the stakeholder reviewing the deployed model.

If the feedback is good and the review by the engineer is also good, then, if this were not a demo, the model would be deployed to production.

The submitted model passes through several statuses by the actions of different users, as described in Table 8-1.

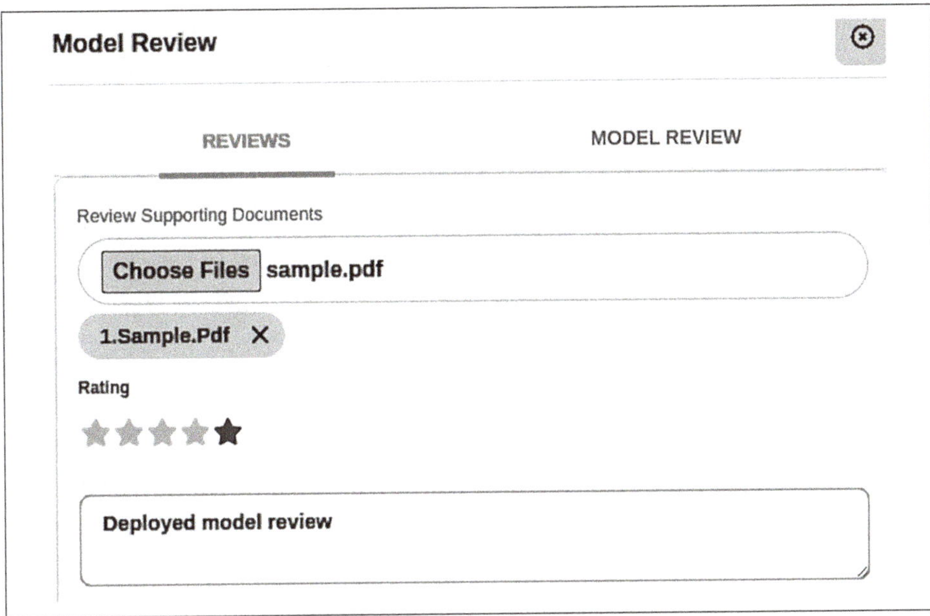

Figure 8-9. Stakeholder also adding a review of the deployed model

Table 8-1. A sample of BTA status indicators by user, and what they mean

User	Status	Detail
AI engineer	Draft	The AI engineer can keep model versions in draft status.
AI engineer	Pending	This is the status when the AI engineer submits the model for review by the MLOps engineer.
MLOps engineer	Review Passed/Failed	The MLOps engineer can review the model and change the status to Passed or Failed.
MLOps engineer	Deployed	This status means that the MLOps engineer has deployed the model as a web service so the other users can test it.
AI engineer, MLOps engineer, stakeholder	QA	The status while all users perform quality assurance testing on the model and give feedback.
MLOps engineer	Production	The status when the MLOps engineer launches the model to production.
AI engineer, MLOps engineer, stakeholder	Monitoring	The status when all users can monitor the launched model and give feedback.
Stakeholder	Complete/ Decline	The stakeholder can set the status to Complete or Decline, based on all reviews and testing from different users and themselves.

Once the model is launched, only the engineer can change the status of the model to Monitoring. *Monitoring* is the status given for the model launched into production. The AI engineer, MLOps engineer, and stakeholder can monitor the production-based model and report bugs or issues.

This monitoring report, which you can add and run as shown in Figures 8-10 and 8-11, will also be appended to the review information generated by the other members of the AI team that the BTA stores for the model.

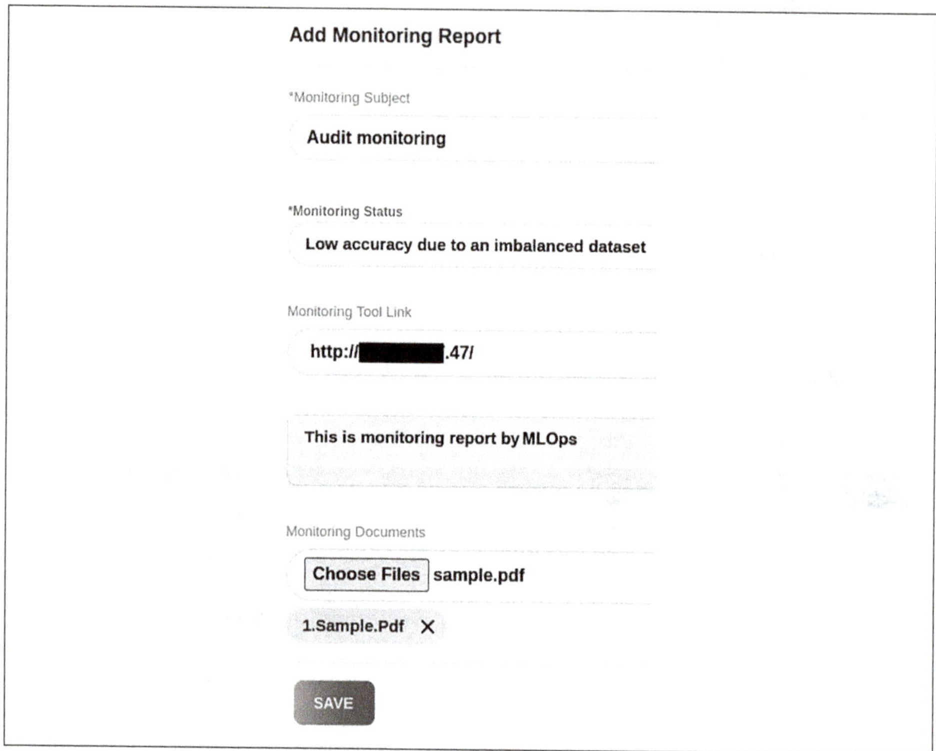

Figure 8-10. Adding a monitoring report

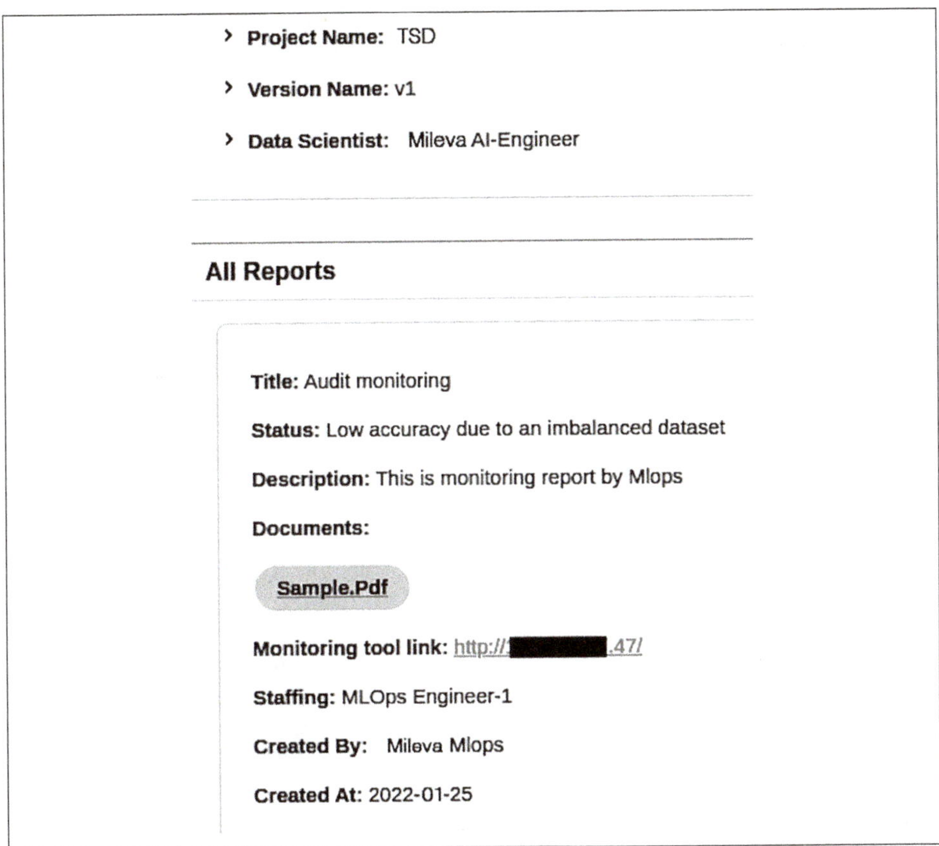

Project Name: TSD
Version Name: v1
Data Scientist: Mileva AI-Engineer
All Reports
Title: Audit monitoring
Status: Low accuracy due to an imbalanced dataset
Description: This is monitoring report by Mlops
Documents:
Sample.Pdf
Monitoring tool link: http://1 .47/
Staffing: MLOps Engineer-1
Created By: Mileva Mlops
Created At: 2022-01-25

Figure 8-11. Running the monitoring report

After everyone has approved the model, the MLOps engineer gets a notification to take the model live. Open the browser tab where you are logged in as the MLOps engineer and choose Manage Projects > Project. You will see a list of projects, as shown in Figure 8-12. Approve the submitted model version.

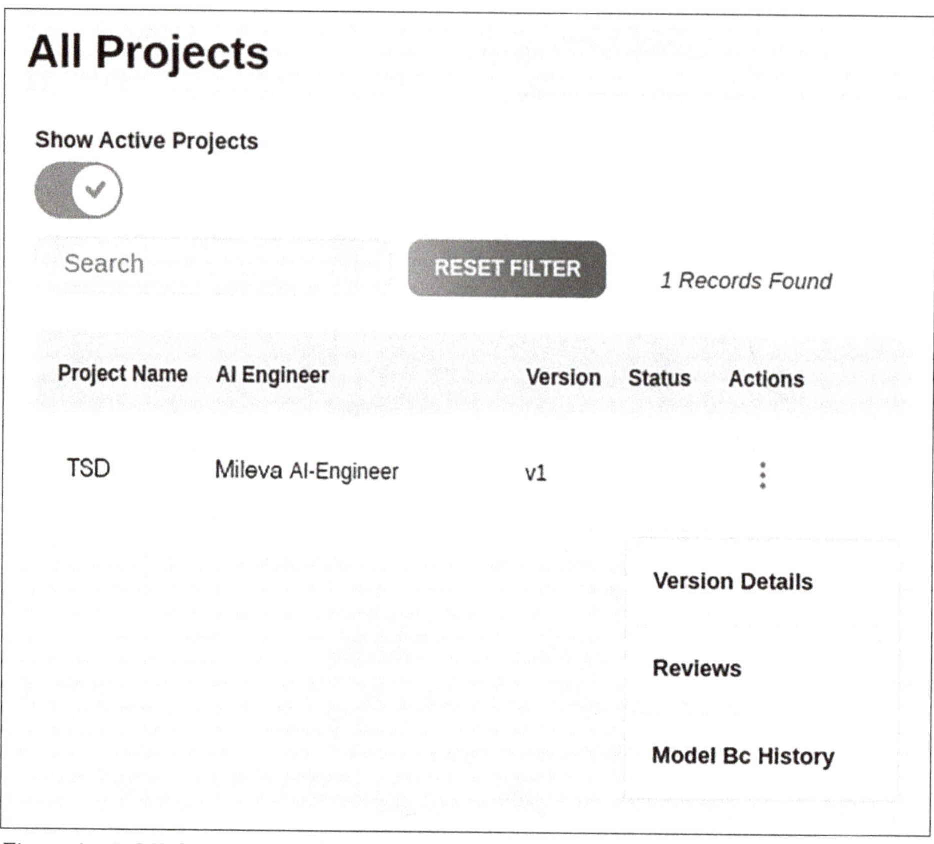

Figure 8-12. MLOps can see a list of projects, along with their status

Open the browser tab for stakeholder and repeat the process used for MLOps.

Adding AI's Purpose and Intended Domain

Since AI models can easily outlive their stakeholders, it may be important to the stakeholders to keep the AI true to its original intent (purpose and limitations) and domain (the environment in which it should be used).

Your BTA configuration allows only the stakeholder to record the model's purpose and intended domain (you could expand this permission to the AI engineer or MLOps engineer using your BTA's staffings and permissions).

To demonstrate adding a purpose for your project, log in to the BTA as the stakeholder user. Choose Project > Add Model Purpose, as shown in Figure 8-13. Like everything else to do with your model, when your Model Purpose is saved, hashes of the model purpose and its documentation are computed and then stored on blockchain.

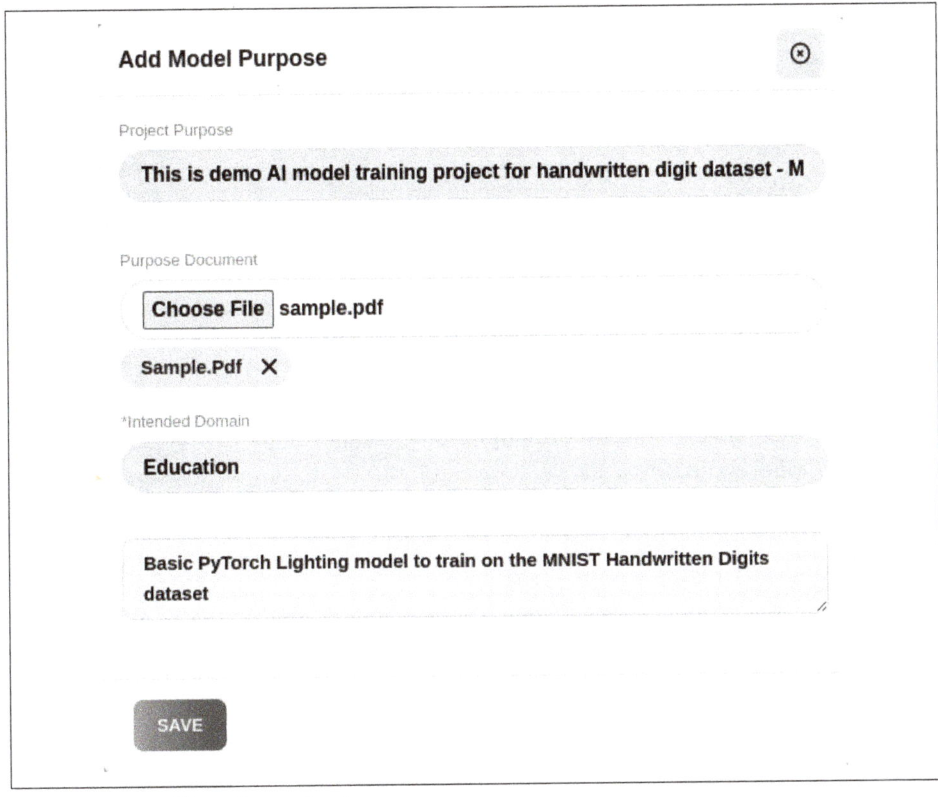

Figure 8-13. Adding the project's purpose

The audit trail of the addition is shown in Figures 8-14 and 8-15.

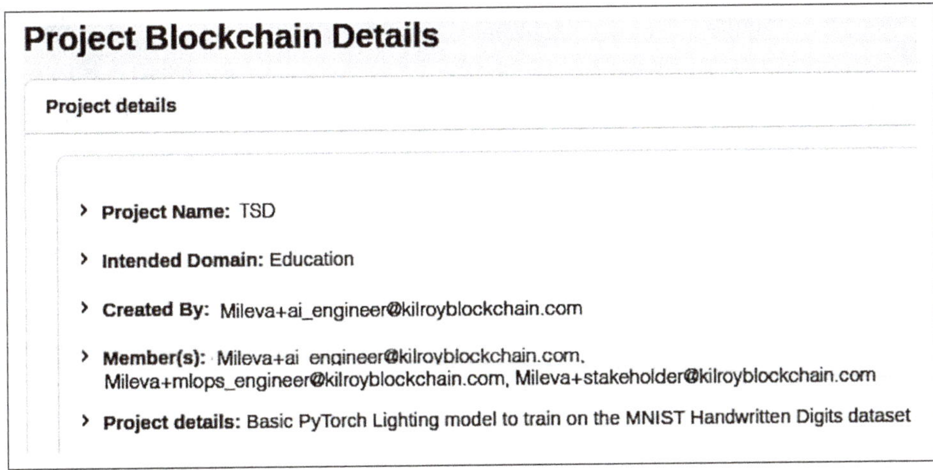

Figure 8-14. Project info retrieved from the blockchain, reflecting the intended domain

Tx Id	Tx DateTime	Created By	Intended Domain	Model Version	Project Purpose
5e8c894...5317a4f	2022-08-31T09:36:41Z	Mileva+stakeholder@	Education	- v1	This is demo AI model training project for handwritten digit dataset - MNIST

Figure 8-15. Project blockchain history, showing timestamps and transaction IDs associated with creating a tamper-evident record of the project's purpose

The blockchain project history shows an audit trail containing evidence of the user who has created the AI model development project, along with evidence of the stakeholder who has defined its purpose, and corresponding transaction IDs and timestamps.

Exercise: Auditing Your BTA

This exercise, the book's final one, provides an opportunity for you to reflect on the avenues you have to explore when questions come up regarding the integrity of your model and its components, including training and test data sets, inputs and outputs, performance metrics and model development, and how to identify tampering.

Tracking Your Model's Training and Test Data Sets

As you have learned, when a model is created, its training and testing data are uploaded to buckets and hashes put on blockchain, and are always traceable for each version of the model, as Figure 8-16 shows.

When you need to look back at your previous data sets, you can check the *dataset :model* folder for each version, so you have a trail of what data sets have been used for each training event.

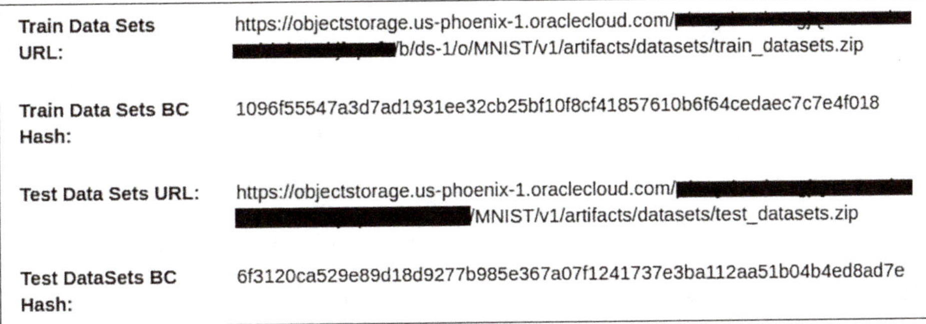

Train Data Sets URL:	https://objectstorage.us-phoenix-1.oraclecloud.com/[redacted]/b/ds-1/o/MNIST/v1/artifacts/datasets/train_datasets.zip
Train Data Sets BC Hash:	1096f55547a3d7ad1931ee32cb25bf10f8cf41857610b6f64cedaec7c7e4f018
Test Data Sets URL:	https://objectstorage.us-phoenix-1.oraclecloud.com/[redacted]/MNIST/v1/artifacts/datasets/test_datasets.zip
Test DataSets BC Hash:	6f3120ca529e89d18d9277b985e367a07f1241737e3ba112aa51b04b4ed8ad7e

Figure 8-16. Training data set hashes stored on blockchain

Tracing Your Inputs and Outputs

As mentioned in the previous exercise, all of the required input fields are stored in the log, and the hash of the log is stored in blockchain as follows. This log file contains proof of the epochs and experiments conducted, and the inputs and outputs surrounding them:

```
Log file path: https://objectstorage.us-phoenix-1.../b/ds-1/o/MNIST/v1/logs
```

The number of experiments conducted within the model version is shown in Figure 8-17. You can see the Log File BC Hash and the contents of the log file, including a directory of experiments and epochs. In this figure, you can find the number of the experiments conducted to build, train, and test the model.

Log Hash: 59a19d1c89892c78a6feee353b311e055c1f5cc17f840324cae93d5392aef7b2

Experiment ID	Date	Actions
exp_0	2022-08-29	👁
exp_1	2022-08-29	👁

Figure 8-17. Log file data

You can even find out how many epochs there were in an experiment by clicking the experiment name—in Figure 8-18, it's *exp_0*. You can also see the details of each epoch within the experiment by clicking the epoch name.

Epoch	train_acc	train_f1_score	train_loss	train_precision	train_recall	val_accuracy	val_loss
0	0.5535091162	0.5537427068	1.7227270603	0.5537427068	0.5537427068	0.790743649	1.0716173649
1	0.7799999714	0.7800992727	0.8703170419	0.7800992727	0.7800992727	0.85660600660	0.6212589145
2	0.8267272711	0.8267925978	0.6158729792(	0.8267925978	0.8267925978	0.8779667616	0.4854764342
3	0.8503272533	0.8504058123	0.5155982971	0.8504058123	0.8504058123	0.88686710600	0.4242433906
4	0.8653454781	0.8654130697	0.4578905404	0.8654130697	0.8654130697	0.8924050927	0.3884941339

Figure 8-18. Log showing epoch details

Verifying Performance Metrics

Performance metrics are stored in the log file of an experiment. In cases where an AI engineer has submitted multiple experiments under a version, and an MLOps engineer has reviewed the model, you can use your BTA to compare their accuracy metrics, as shown in Figure 8-19.

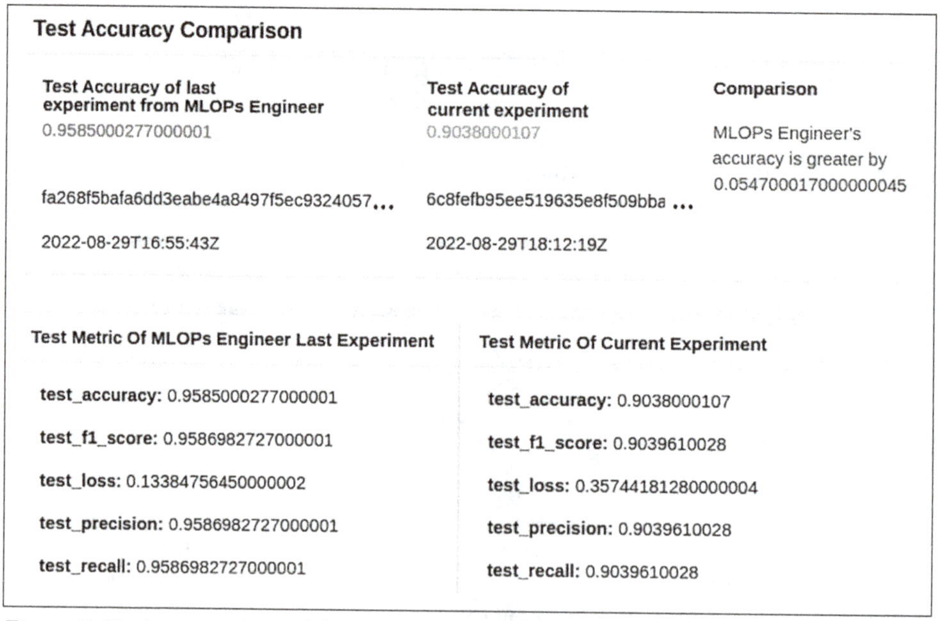

Test Accuracy Comparison

Test Accuracy of last experiment from MLOPs Engineer	Test Accuracy of current experiment	Comparison
0.9585000277000001	0.9038000107	MLOPs Engineer's accuracy is greater by 0.054700017000000045
fa268f5bafa6dd3eabe4a8497f5ec9324057...	6c8fefb95ee519635e8f509bba ...	
2022-08-29T16:55:43Z	2022-08-29T18:12:19Z	

Test Metric Of MLOPs Engineer Last Experiment	Test Metric Of Current Experiment
test_accuracy: 0.9585000277000001	**test_accuracy:** 0.9038000107
test_f1_score: 0.9586982727000001	**test_f1_score:** 0.9039610028
test_loss: 0.13384756450000002	**test_loss:** 0.35744181280000004
test_precision: 0.9586982727000001	**test_precision:** 0.9039610028
test_recall: 0.9586982727000001	**test_recall:** 0.9039610028

Figure 8-19. A comparison of the accuracy of current and previous experiments

This comparison will help you to know if the submitted model is optimal or has poor performance as well.

Tracing Identity of People and AI Systems

Your BTA is created in such a way that every record holds a traceable identity of the user who created it. You may notice the name of the person, organization, and staffing they belong to associated with each blockchain transaction. Additionally, it shows the name of the peer that the user owns. Without this information, audits are meaningless, because the actions would not be traceable to certain identities.

Tracking and Tracing Model Development

The aim of the BTA is to show all participants involved in the AI model development, deployment, and production retrieving their activities from blockchain nodes. Figure 8-20 shows that an AI engineer submitted the model ID, timestamp, and transaction ID created as a proof in blockchain storage, and that the MLOps engineer has passed the model in the review and decided to move forward.

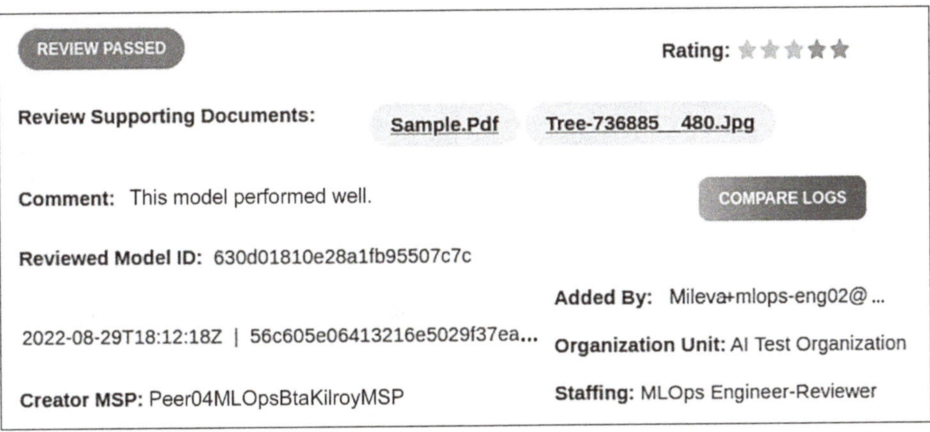

Figure 8-20. Model submitted by AI engineer and reviewed by MLOps engineer

The COMPARE LOGS button on the right compares the MLOps engineer's accuracy received from the testing with the AI engineer's accuracy, as shown in Figure 8-21.

The Comparison column shows by what value the MLOps engineer's accuracy is greater or lesser than the AI engineer's accuracy. Figure 8-22 shows that the MLOps engineer has deployed the submitted model and provided a deployed URL where QA can be performed. It also has fields for testing instructions.

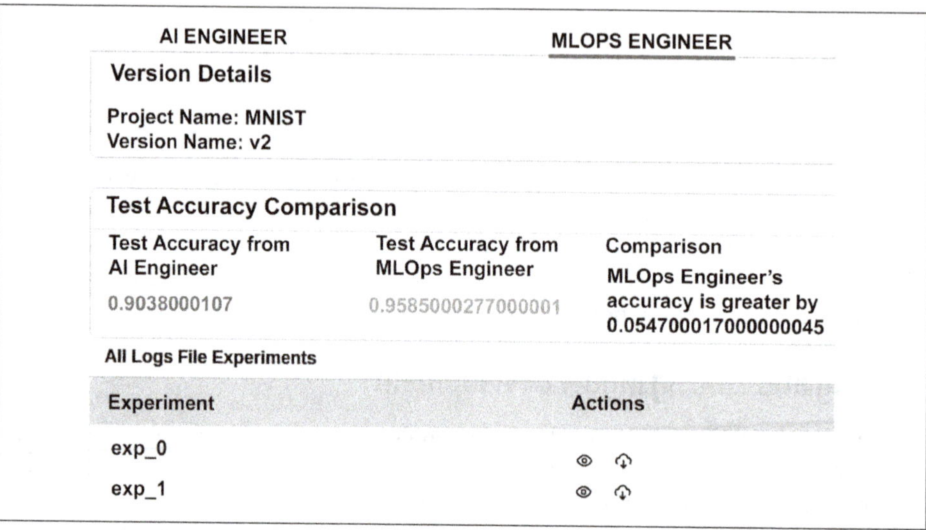

Figure 8-21. Comparing MLOps test accuracy with that of the AI engineer's last experiment

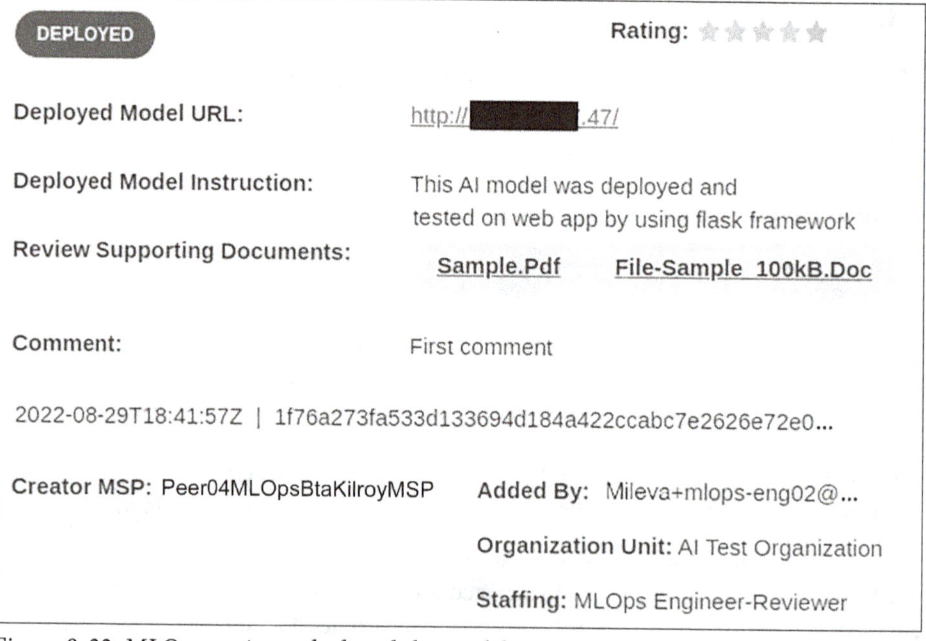

Figure 8-22. MLOps engineer deployed the model

Figure 8-23 shows that the model has undergone QA so that different participants, such as the stakeholder and MLOps engineer, could test it. They can provide their feedback in the Comment field. The stakeholder can also see the accuracy comparison feature.

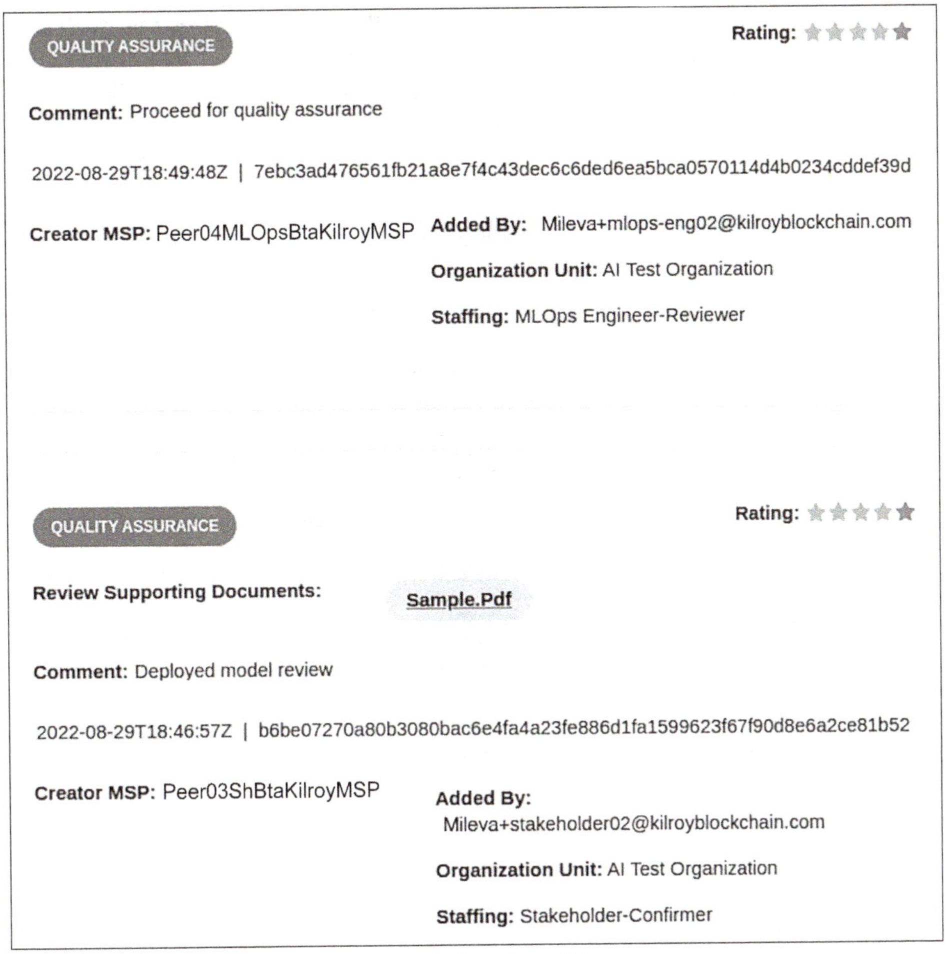

QUALITY ASSURANCE

Rating: ★★★★★

Comment: Proceed for quality assurance

2022-08-29T18:49:48Z | 7ebc3ad476561fb21a8e7f4c43dec6c6ded6ea5bca0570114d4b0234cddef39d

Creator MSP: Peer04MLOpsBtaKilroyMSP

Added By: Mileva+mlops-eng02@kilroyblockchain.com

Organization Unit: AI Test Organization

Staffing: MLOps Engineer-Reviewer

QUALITY ASSURANCE

Rating: ★★★★★

Review Supporting Documents: Sample.Pdf

Comment: Deployed model review

2022-08-29T18:46:57Z | b6be07270a80b3080bac6e4fa4a23fe886d1fa1599623f67f90d8e6a2ce81b52

Creator MSP: Peer03ShBtaKilroyMSP

Added By: Mileva+stakeholder02@kilroyblockchain.com

Organization Unit: AI Test Organization

Staffing: Stakeholder-Confirmer

Figure 8-23. Different users testing the deployed model

Figure 8-24 shows that the model is going through production and monitoring stages. The model status is changed from QA to Production, then from Production to Monitoring, by the MLOps engineer.

If this were a real scenario, the model would then be deployed to production, and the stakeholders would publish the production URL or web services that their end users could test. Post-production, in the BTA, the model goes to the Monitoring stage where all participants can monitor and provide feedback, as is done in the QA stage.

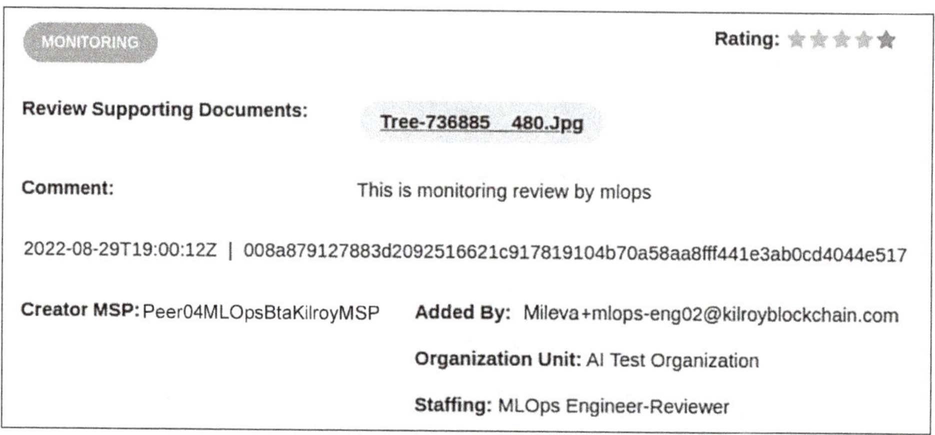

Figure 8-24. MLOps engineer changing the model status from Production to Monitoring

Figure 8-25 shows the production model reviews conducted by the MLOps engineer and the stakeholder prior to the model undergoing monitoring.

Figure 8-26 shows how the stakeholder, after reviewing all reviews and accuracy, changes the status of the model from Monitoring to Completed. Now the lifecycle of the model is complete.

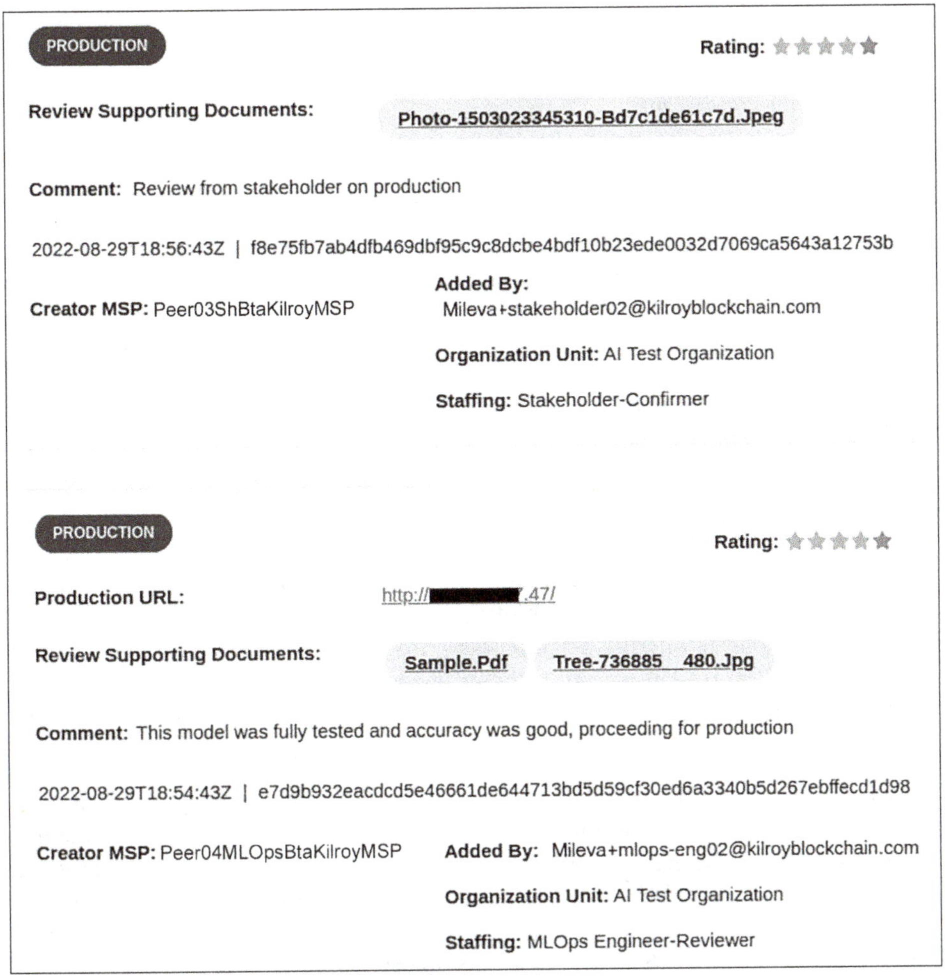

PRODUCTION

Rating: ★★★★★

Review Supporting Documents: Photo-1503023345310-Bd7c1de61c7d.Jpeg

Comment: Review from stakeholder on production

2022-08-29T18:56:43Z | f8e75fb7ab4dfb469dbf95c9c8dcbe4bdf10b23ede0032d7069ca5643a12753b

Creator MSP: Peer03ShBtaKilroyMSP

Added By: Mileva+stakeholder02@kilroyblockchain.com

Organization Unit: AI Test Organization

Staffing: Stakeholder-Confirmer

PRODUCTION

Rating: ★★★★★

Production URL: http://[redacted].47/

Review Supporting Documents: Sample.Pdf Tree-736885__480.Jpg

Comment: This model was fully tested and accuracy was good, proceeding for production

2022-08-29T18:54:43Z | e7d9b932eacdcd5e46661de644713bd5d59cf30ed6a3340b5d267ebffecd1d98

Creator MSP: Peer04MLOpsBtaKilroyMSP

Added By: Mileva+mlops-eng02@kilroyblockchain.com

Organization Unit: AI Test Organization

Staffing: MLOps Engineer-Reviewer

Figure 8-25. Review documentation for production model prior to monitoring

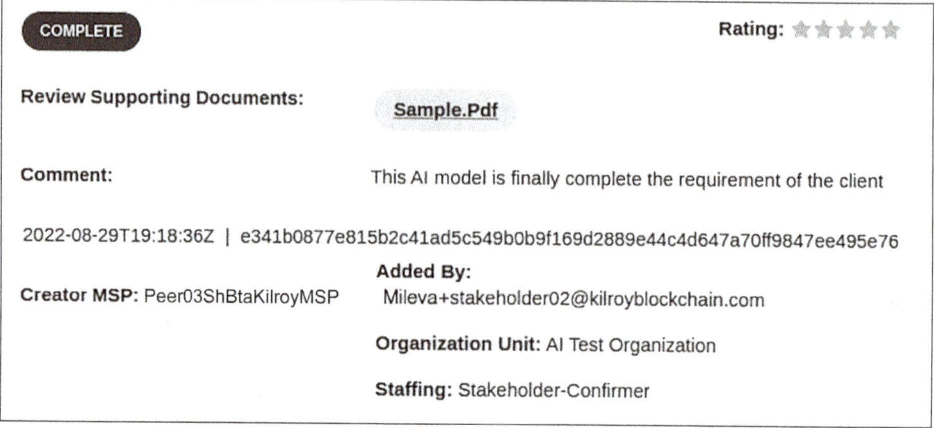

Figure 8-26. Stakeholder completing the AI model development process

Identifying Tampering

As you have noticed by now, blockchain hashes from the blockchain history section are compared with the real-time hash of the data from the bucket to detect any data that has undergone tampering since it was introduced into the BTA. If any model version data on the bucket is changed after the submission, the hashes on that data will be different. The authenticity of the data is proven from the hash comparison itself.

If the hashes are the same, the status is *Verified*. If even one single character changes in the data, the hashes will no longer compute to the same value and the status will be *Unverified*, as shown next to Test DataSets BC Hash in Figure 8-27. The hashes on the left are generated on blockchain after the model is submitted by the AI engineer, and the hashes on the right are from the Oracle Cloud bucket data. The Test DataSets are Unverified, meaning that the hashes do not match and the data has undergone tampering or corruption.

Type	Submitted Data Blockchain Hash	Bucket Data Blockchain Hash	Status
Log	9275e1a764a87d19b5a9be57a7b87e79af1a724b9dd20dc97054a9b92289febd	9275e1a764a87d19b5a9be57a7b87e79af1a724b9dd20dc97054a9b92289febd	Verified
Test	9a44cbbe04b208e212a21157b71b051ec14e9178d6134371f354287c00bfaa88	9275e1a764a87d19b5a9be57a7b87e79af1a724b9dd20dc9	Unverified
Train	1096f55547a3d7ad1931ee32cb25bf10f8cf41857610b6f64cedaec7c7e4f018	1096f55547a3d7ad1931ee32cb25bf10f8cf41857610b6f64cedaec7c7e4f018	Verified

Figure 8-27. An unverified hash

Reversing Your Blockchain Tethered Model

Although all the possibilities for reversing your model and whether or not reversing is feasible in production are beyond the scope of this book, here is some food for thought so you can consider ways you might plan to reverse problems in your models. Building an AI model with a poisoned data set leads to the model being highly biased. A fabricated data set with ill intentions leads to models being trained with high bias and false information. In any critical business needs, this will become very risky and may cause huge problems for the business, especially in terms of trust, reliability, and confidentiality.

To correct this problem, you need to be able to revert your production model to the model version that was working fine, called *reversing*. There are several ways of reversing or correcting a bad model. Your BTA gives you the foundational tools to form a disaster recovery plan for bad and misbehaving models, since it has all the tools to track and trace the provenance of the model and its dependencies.

Example Case Study: Reversing a Model

Let's say that ABC Bank Ltd. built a very "sophisticated" AI model that was supposed to classify whether a customer should be given a loan or not. The bank was heavily relying on the AI model to make the decision for them and spent a huge amount of money, time, and resources to build the model.

After a while, someone at the bank notices a certain pattern in the prediction of the AI model. After analyzing the reports for months, they notice that the AI model is gender biased. Loan requests from females are extremely likely to be rejected (based on the prediction from the AI model).

ABC Bank needs to eliminate the issue. But do they start over, or can they reverse the problem?

There could be many other types of cases where models are trained by biased data sets with the outcome of benefitting a certain group or discriminating against another group. Certainly that was not the intention of the system, and the stakeholders want to correct this bias going back to the AI training process and reverse the model.

To reverse the model, you would need to put on your detective hat and investigate to find the cause, or causes, of the issues. Your BTA gives you a rich audit trail so you can really dig into the reasons why the model is having a problem, tracing every part of the model back to its source.

Check and confirm the biases of the AI model by looking at your organization's real-world experience (in the example case study, it is repayment of actual loans made to women) and the predictions of the model (whether or not women will pay). If you see a discrepancy, then your model probably has a problem that you can find and fix by looking at how the model was trained. This will lead you down the path of investigating how these biases may have been introduced.

Checking the Training Data Sets

If the data set that was used to train the model was poisoned with ill intention by someone involved in building the model, then it is highly likely the model is wrong because of that poisoned data set. BTA can facilitate auditors by providing data sets of a previous version that gets verified by blockchain hashes as well. Check for patterns in output that may indicate that the model is no longer working properly.

Checking the Algorithms

Bad or sloppy actors can write bad algorithms that throw off your system, so make sure you know and verify your source (*https://oreil.ly/rcdrV*) for algorithms and libraries, and select wisely.

Retraining the Model

Once you identify the issues, retraining the model will generally not be a big problem because you are not retraining all of your models, only the model that has issues. You can use your BTA to create a new version and once again be able to track and trace its components.

Summary

Congratulations! You have learned how to create something brand new in AI by integrating blockchain as a tether to keep it under control. BTA adds blockchain to the MLOps process in your AI stack and helps you to interweave the history of models with the models themselves, to the point where the models will not function without leaving a tamper-evident audit trail.

As you journey ahead, remember that local and regional regulations around AI are rapidly changing, and you may quickly find that tools like the ones in this book are necessary to maintain compliance. Be aware of laws like the EU AI Act (*https://oreil.ly/s-VcZ*), which focuses on creating Responsible AI, that was finalized in December 2022. Like EU data privacy laws, the EU AI Act is expected to be far-reaching and impact most AI projects around the world.

The exercises in this book are designed to only get you started building transparent, traceable, accountable AI systems. Your challenge is to apply this technique to illuminate your own models, creating an accountable AI/ML supply chain.

Your work in building blockchain tethered AI will help people to manage the potential perils of AI while still realizing its vast potential.

Index

B

C

D

E

F

G

H

I

J

K

L

M

N

O

P

Q

R

S

U

V

W

About the Authors

Karen Kilroy is a lifelong technologist with heart, as well as a full-stack software engineer, speaker, and author living in Northwest Arkansas. This book is Karen's third publication for O'Reilly, following *Blockchain as a Service* (2019) and *AI and the Law* (2021). As CEO of Kilroy Blockchain (*https://kilroyblockchain.com*), Karen has invented several products, including FLO, CASEY, Kilroy Blockchain PaaS, CARNAK, and RILEY, an AI mobile app that won the IBM Watson Build award for North America in 2017. Karen and Lynn Riley were selected as recipients of a National Science Foundation research grant in 2018 and focused their studies on autonomous vehicles. Karen was selected as a 2022 recipient of the Life Works Here award by the Northwest Arkansas Council and is a four-time IBM Champion. Karen is also a professional dragon boat coach.

Lynn Riley, a graduate of MIT in chemical engineering, has worked at Motorola, Apple, and CORT Business Services and is Kilroy Blockchain's CIO. Lynn is instrumental to Kilroy Blockchain's AI and machine learning development and trained RILEY, Kilroy Blockchain's AI app that won the IBM Watson Build award for North America in 2017. Lynn specializes in blockchain and AI governance and helps guide Kilroy Blockchain's customers with application architecture in the design thinking stage of development. Lynn has been instrumental to the workflow design of Kilroy Blockchain's products and spent most of 2018 traveling with Karen Kilroy on a National Science Foundation research project focused on autonomous vehicles, which resulted in the CARNAK product. From 2019 to 2021, she was the Industry/Government Chairperson for the CMD-IT/ACM Richard Tapia Conference for Diversity in Computing. Lynn is also a tech reviewer for O'Reilly Media and resides in Austin, Texas.

A Certified IBM Foundation Blockchain Developer, **Deepak Bhatta** is an award-winning, hands-on technology leader with more than 15 years in open source software development. He has more than a decade of experience in developing ecommerce and mobile apps and also handles the customer, understands business requirements, and finally converts them into a solution. He was a presenter on blockchain at the RegTech MENA Conference in Dubai in April 2017 and the Conclave 2019 conference in Kathmandu, Nepal.

Colophon

The bird on the cover of *Blockchain Tethered AI* is the killdeer (*Charadrius vociferus*), so named for its doleful, penetrating call of "kil-deee" or "kil-deer." This large plover is typically found in the coastal wetlands, beaches, and open fields of North America and northernmost South America.

Though considered shorebirds, killdeer are not infrequently found far inland and thus may be associated less with water than many shorebirds. They share with other plovers several characteristic physical features, such as a large, round head, large eye, and short bill, though they are particularly slender, with long legs, wings, and tail.

When searching for food, killdeer have been observed to run a few steps and then pause, then run again, pecking at the ground whenever they spot a source of food—typically insects or, less frequently, seeds. Conversely, as prey to various birds and mammals, killdeer suffer heavy annual egg and hatchling losses due to predation and are known to use distraction behaviors, such as "false brooding" and "injury feigning," as a deterrence strategy. Direct, aggressive antipredator behaviors like "ungulate displays"—in which the birds rush from the nest toward the attacker with their feathers fluffed and wings extended—have been reported but are less common.

Due to their extensive range and large population, killdeer have been categorized by the IUCN as *of least concern*, despite some recent declines in population. Like all animals on O'Reilly covers, they are vitally important to our world.

The cover illustration is by Karen Montgomery, based on an antique line engraving from *A History of British Birds*. The cover fonts are Gilroy Semibold and Guardian Sans. The text font is Adobe Minion Pro; the heading font is Adobe Myriad Condensed; and the code font is Dalton Maag's Ubuntu Mono.

CPSIA information can be obtained
at www.ICGtesting.com
Printed in the USA
JSHW060121040323
38361JS00013B/62

9 781098 130480